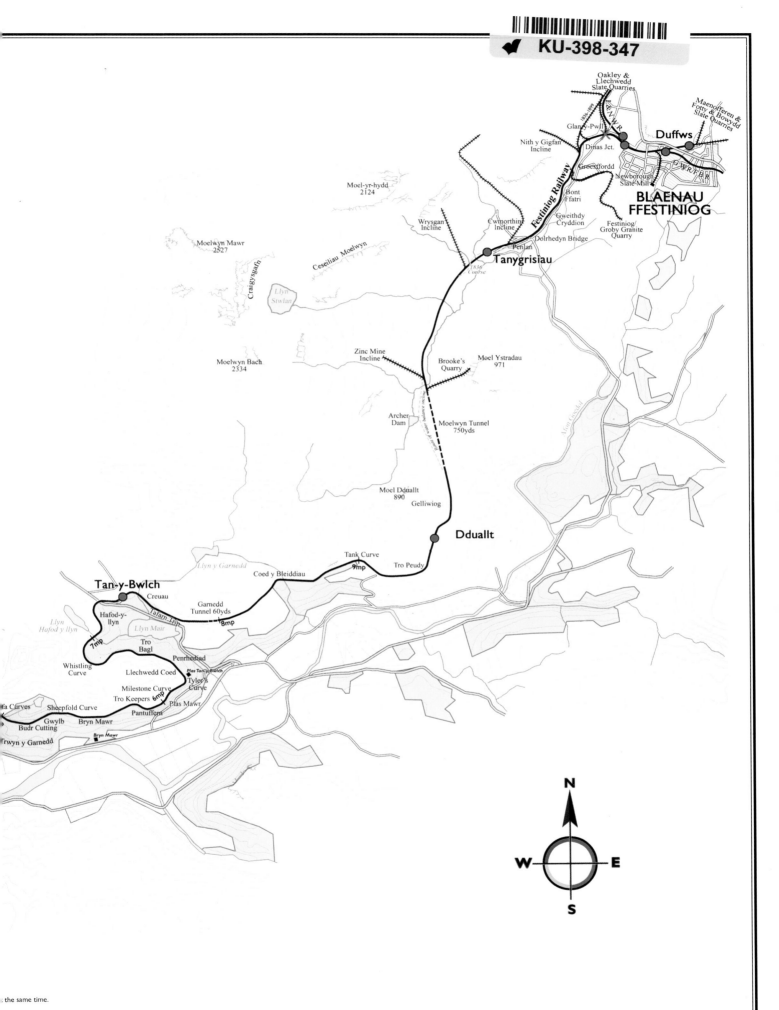

the same time.

History of the
RAILWAY
1832-1954

An Illustrated History of the

FESTINIOG RAILWAY 1832-1954

Peter Johnson

OPC

An imprint of
Ian Allan Publishing

First published 2007

ISBN (10) 0 86093 603 1
ISBN (13) 978 0 86093 603 9

Published by Oxford Publishing Co

an imprint of Ian Allan Publishing Ltd, Hersham, Surrey KT12 4RG.
Printed in England by Ian Allan Printing Ltd, Hersham, Surrey KT12
4RG.

Code: 0706/B2

Visit the Ian Allan Publishing website at www.ianallanpublishing.com

THE FFESTINIOG RAILWAY COMPANY
ESTABLISHED BY ACT OF PARLIAMENT
WILLIAM IV CAP. 48, 23RD MAY 1832

THE OLDEST
INDEPENDENT RAILWAY COMPANY
IN THE WORLD

ERECTED
23RD MAY 2007

'To the best of my abilities, I have taken great pains with it.'

James Spooner
30 April 1836

Front cover: **Wreathed in steam, *Livingston Thompson* leaves
Tan-y-bwlch for Blaenau Festiniog in the 1930s. The driver is
Tom Davies, a long-serving FR loco man.** *FR Archives*

Back cover, top: **Dolgaregddu, the Festiniog Railway's junction with
the Festiniog & Blaenau Railway, *c*1880. *Little Wonder*, the first
of the FR's iconic double Fairlie locomotives, is seen with a
passenger train bound for Porthmadoc whilst on the right, one of
the FBR's Manning, Wardle locomotives is shunting slate wagons.**
Original watercolour by Jonathan Clay

Back cover, bottom: **Plan of Porthmadoc station.**
Map by Gordon Rushton

Below left: **On 22 May 2007 a slate plaque was unveiled at
Tan-y-bwlch to commemorate the 175th anniversary of the
incorporation of the Festiniog Railway Company. The size and
shape reproduce those of the foundation stone laid by
W. G. Oakeley on 26 February 1833.** *Author*

Half title page: **So far as the tourists were concerned Bessie Jones
was a popular part of Tan-y-bwlch operations during the 1930s.
She does not appear to have been employed by the company, her
husband was, but appeared in Welsh dress as 'station mistress',
posing for photographs and serving refreshments at the station
house. Here, *Taliesin's* fireman looks on as she sells picture
postcards to passengers.** *Author's collection*

Title page: **In its final form, just a few days before the railway
closed, *Princess* shunts past the Minffordd weighbridge on 24 July
1946.** *B. B. Edmonds*

Below: **Merddin Emrys at Duffws with a train of first- and second-
generation quarrymen's stock; the first-generation vehicles were
fully open when built, *c*1876; *Little Wonder* is on the right.**
FR Archives

Contents

Introduction

The Festiniog Railway Company is an unusual company. It owns and operates a 2ft gauge railway (actually 1ft 11½in), built to serve Welsh slate quarries, which was the idea of an English slate quarry owner, yet was promoted by an Irishman who raised all of the company's original capital in Ireland. Established by statute in 1832 it is, at 175 years in 2007, possibly the oldest independent railway company in the world.

Some of the people who have been associated with the company often brought to it a touch of genius. These include James Spooner, who surveyed a 14-mile route with a continuous gradient that favoured the slate traffic; his son, Charles Easton Spooner, who refined the railway with the introduction of steam locomotives and a passenger service; and George England, whose sturdy tank engines transformed the railway. Henry Whatley Tyler was the government inspector who approved of the carriage of passengers and who saw in the railway a concept that could be used elsewhere, while Robert Francis Fairlie's articulated locomotives saved the company the expense and inconvenience of doubling the formation and came to symbolise the railway. Also, there was George Percival Spooner, Charles Easton's son, who fine-tuned the Fairlie concept and who put whimsy into brake van design.

Although he never knew the company, the contribution of William Alexander Madocks must be acknowledged, for his one-mile long embankment across the Glaslyn estuary made it feasible, as he conceived, to link the Festiniog slate quarries with the developing town and port of Portmadoc by a railway.

After a struggle to get established, the company turned out to be a real money-spinner, not too surprising, as it was in a monopoly position. In less than 40 years the original investment had doubled in value and the shareholders were receiving double-figure dividends. Financial success and the reports of the successful conversion from horse tramway to steam passenger railway brought the Festiniog Railway, and the people associated with it, great fame, and its influence spread internationally.

Success inevitably attracted competition. Encouraged by quarry proprietors who were never satisfied with the considerable reductions in rates that the railway had given them, there were, by 1883, two competing standard gauge railway routes into Blaenau Festiniog. In consequence, as soon as the monopoly was broken, when the London & North Western Railway commenced services in 1879, the company's revenues started a long decline that was to end with closure in 1946.

There were interruptions on the passage to closure. The government took control of the railway during the First World War and left the company in debt, a position from which it never recovered. After the war it was taken over by the Welsh Highland Railway's promoters, a move that saw the FR become a light railway and its trains working to Dinas, near Caernarfon. The takeover introduced new characters, amongst them Evan R. Davies and the light railways expert, Colonel Stephens, who left their mark on the railway. The decline in ordinary passengers during the 1920s was partially offset by an increase in tourism which, during the 1930s, subsidised the slate traffic.

By the end of the Second World War the railway was so badly run down that, as the company had no resources to revive it, closure was inevitable. Reopening could happen only with new management and a fresh start. That is what happened.

This book tells the Festiniog Railway's story from its origins to the change of control in 1954. A major source is the company board's minutes, and the story is told mainly from the company's perspective, providing an insight into its dealings with its employees, its quarry customers and other railway companies. The records at the House of Lords dating from 1836 and 1869 give first-hand insights into the FR's early days from, amongst others, James and Charles Easton Spooner, and Livingston Thompson.

It was while reading the background documents that I became aware that some aspects of the FR's story might be different to what had been previously understood. This was especially true in the case of the Welsh Highland Railway and its alleged effect on the FR. The view that the FR was 'dragged down' by the WHR probably originates from Robert Evans who, judging by his letters, did not like it. The documents I read suggest that the FR was fatally weakened before it was involved with the WHR.

The FR emerged from the First World War, and the period of government control, with an unauthorised overdraft with the preference share interest and maintenance in arrears. The 1923 Light Railway Order regularised the financial position and the company borrowed a total of £11,500 secured on debentures. Expenditure, capital and revenue, attributable to the WHR between 1923 and 1937 totalled around £7,000, a substantial part of it borrowed and not repaid.

Without the WHR the FR might not have become a light railway. It still would have struggled, having no resources for maintenance and no investment in the business, but would have paid its tolls, rents and the debenture interest for a little longer. The passenger service would still have been withdrawn in 1930 while the tourist traffic subsidised the slate traffic, although the extent might have been less. So, had the railway survived until the Second World War it would have suffered the same withdrawal of the tourist service and reduction of slate traffic with closure being equally unavoidable, as the world in which it had operated was, irrevocably, changed.

Only an outline of the history of the railway's locomotives and carriages is included here, together with a look at the activities of the railway's workshops at Boston Lodge, taken from the loco repair books. I anticipate that one day, someone else, having a sound understanding of things mechanical, will produce the in-depth history of the FR's locomotives and rolling stock.

I hope that by using these sources, and others referred to in the acknowledgements and bibliography, I have developed a fresh view of the FR's history, a view that seeks to explain why things happened, and their consequences. They have certainly allowed me to enlarge on the contributions made by some of the railway's lesser-known personalities.

While researching this book I have been able to handle documents produced by such luminaries as Henry Archer, James Spooner, Samuel Holland, Charles Spooner, Robert Fairlie and Henry Tyler. From the 20th century, there were documents by Frederick Vaughan, Holman Fred Stephens, members of the Davies family, and Robert Evans. In the parliamentary record it was possible to read the words spoken by the Spooners and Livingston Thompson. Taken together, they created a real sense of connection with the Festiniog Railway's past.

Acknowledgements

Whenever anyone starts to take an interest in the Festiniog Railway it isn't long before they hear the name Boyd. It was the same for me some 35 years ago. Over a period of 40 years, James I. C. Boyd researched and wrote more about Welsh narrow gauge railways, particularly the Festiniog Railway, than anyone else. His first book, *Narrow Gauge Rails to Portmadoc*, published in 1948, raised awareness of the railway at a crucial time in its history. Having his 1975 volumes on the FR to hand was a great assistance while writing this book.

Michael J. Lewis is the acknowledged expert on the FR's prehistory and I drew on his published work in Chapter 1.

Once again I am indebted to Adrian Gray, the Festiniog Railway Company's archivist, for his help and support during the gestation of this project; as always he gave access to the photograph collections at his disposal and imparted words of wisdom regarding the text. His deputy, Patricia Ward, kindly made available a draft of the catalogue that she is creating of the company's archives and produced some fascinating documents for me to make use of. Both she and her husband, Geoff, made insightful comments on the text.

The honourable Sir William Hepburn McAlpine Bt, 'Bill', supplied photocopies of his FR debenture certificates, the first of which was issued to his uncle, also William Hepburn McAlpine, in lieu of debt, that was never repaid, *c*1923.

Jim Hewett let me have a draft of his transcript of the Spooner letter book that is to be found in the National Archives at Kew. Tim Edmonds supplied the photographs taken by his father, Bernard Edmonds, on 24 July 1946, just a few days before the railway closed. The photograph of *Prince* and the Duffws bridge reconstruction was provided by Paul Molyneux-Berry.

Jonathan Clay produced the cover painting at very little notice and Gordon Rushton drew the endpaper map and other artwork with a little more forewarning. Colin Lea and Stuart L. Baker made contributions that I was unable to make use of.

The company's general manager, Paul Lewin, drew my attention to the significance of the year 2007 in the company's history.

I made use of the Ministry of Transport files deposited at the National Archives, and at the House of Lords Records Office, I examined the committee cross-examinations made in pursuit of the failed 1836 application and the successful 1869 application for additional powers.

The Board of Trade data was extracted from the material kept in the Transport History Collection at the University of Leicester Library, filling in the gaps with the aid of the Birmingham Reference Library.

Portmadoc Urban District Council records were seen at the Gwynedd Archives at Caernarfon, as was the 1833 letter from Henry Archer and other papers from the Newborough collection. The FR Company's surviving minute books and locomotive repair books are deposited at Caernarfon and I was able to make use of the microfilm copy that the company's late archivist, Michael Seymour, arranged when they were deposited there. The volume of minutes covering the period prior to 1869 was believed by Michael Seymour to be in the possession of a public museum but that body was unable to assist when I enquired about it.

Peter Jarvis is always good company and a generous host;

he loaned me some of the photocopies that he had made at the National Archives.

I am obliged and grateful to all those named for their assistance with this book, but none of them is responsible for any errors that it may contain.

Crown copyright is reserved in the Ordnance Survey mapping.

No apology is offered for reusing photographs that some readers will have seen before; some of them are just too good to set aside, and in any event, it is not possible to illustrate a book like this completely with unpublished images. Thanks to the internet, photographs have been obtained from as far away as Australia and the USA. The inclusion of a small number of sub-standard photographs has been determined by their historical interest. I have been collecting photographs for so long that I cannot remember where some of them came from, so I hope I have the attributions correct.

As the company celebrates its 175th anniversary just before this book is published I extend my thanks to the directors, its officers and servants (and it seems appropriate to use the Victorian expression), past and present, for the support of my various activities so readily given.

I would have liked to have shared this book with some late Festiniog friends: Michael Seymour, Rodney Weaver, Dan Wilson and Norman Gurley in particular. Also to Michael Harris and Handel Kardas, editors of *Railway World*, who both encouraged and facilitated my literary career.

Peter Johnson
Leicester
23 May 2007

Conventions

The Festiniog Railway Company was named thus in its acts of parliament. The spelling of Welsh place names was often inconsistent during the period covered by this book, eg Blaenau Festiniog is now known as Blaenau Ffestiniog and its predecessor, the village of Festiniog, as Llan Ffestiniog. Portmadoc is now known as Porthmadog. Carnarvon became Caernarvon during the 1930s and is now called Caernarfon.

An omission from a quoted document is indicated by an ellipsis (...) and an editorial insertion by the use of square brackets ([]). In order to avoid excessive use of [sic] in quoted documents, incorrect spellings have been amended and in some cases a modicum of punctuation introduced.

During the period covered,
£1 = 240d (pence) = 20s (shillings); 1s = 12d;
1 guinea = £1 1s.
1 ton = 20 hundredweight (cwt); 1cwt = 4 quarters (qtr);
1qtr = 2 stone (st); 1st = 14 pounds (lb); 1lb = 16 ounces (oz)

The value of money

Equivalent value of £1 in 2006

1830=£49.49	1840=£44.10	1850=£58.53	1860=£43.16
1870=£45.70	1880=£48.31	1890=£49.89	1900=£57.06
1905=£57.35	1910=£57.06	1915=£43.06	1920=£21.21
1925=£29.97	1930=£33.42	1935=£36.98	1940=£28.72
1945=£25.95	1950=£22.78		

Data extracted from the currency converter on the National Archives website: www.nationalarchives.gov.uk/currency/

1

Setting the scene – building the railway

1800-1836

On 30 January 1833, Henry Archer, writing from the Tan-y-bwlch Inn, informed Lord Newborough that on 14 February 'The company propose to commence to make the Festiniog Railway'. He went on to ask his lordship to lay, with Mr Oakeley, the first stone, adding that 'your lordship should thus countenance and mark your approbation of the undertaking'.

The Festiniog Railway (FR) was promoted to improve the transportation of slate between the developing quarries in the parish of Festiniog, above the area that became Blaenau Ffestiniog, 700ft above sea level and to the south-east of the Moelwyns, and the recently developed harbour at Port Madoc, on the Irish Sea in the north-east of Cardigan Bay, a distance of 10 miles as the crow flies, 12 miles by the present road network. Whilst the industrial revolution was undoubtedly fuelling the demand for slate and other minerals, the abolition of a duty on slate transported by sea in 1831 obviously encouraged the exploitation of slate in relatively inaccessible places like Festiniog, whence it could only be transported to industrial centres by this means.

The harbour was a consequence of William Alexander Madocks's construction of an embankment across the Traeth Mawr, the sandy mouth of the Afon Glaslyn, thus making a link between the counties of Merioneth, on the south side, and Carnarvon. The embankment, nearly a mile long and now known as the Cob, was completed in 1811; breached the following year, it was finally secured in 1814. Tramways were used during the embankment's construction and again during its repair. They were probably 3ft or 3ft 6in gauge, and although

some plateway rail from this period was uncovered when the Britannia Bridge was being rebuilt in 1996, it was not enough to establish the gauge.

Madocks, the MP for Boston, Lincolnshire, owned the Tan yr Allt estate on the Carnarvon shore and had developed the community of Tremadoc. He had built two other embankments by 1800, to protect and enlarge his property, so he was building on experience when he decided upon the Glaslyn scheme, sanctioned by Act of Parliament of 1807. In return for carrying out the construction at his own expense, Madocks was vested with the reclaimed lands, an area of some 3,000 acres reaching as far as Pont Aberglaslyn, a distance of about five miles. The act also enabled him to improve the existing mooring at Ynys Cyngor and required him to build roads, including one over the embankment, across the reclaimed lands. In recognition of the benefit to the public good, eliminating the risky foot crossing of the sands, he was permitted to charge tolls for their use. There were seven tollgates on the estate until 1842, but with the passage of time the roads, except that over the embankment, were taken over by the local authorities and the tolls ceased. Those who benefited from the embankment coincidentally, because their property was no longer subject to tidal flooding, were required to pay one fifth of the rental value of their land to Madocks annually!

The harbour, called Port Madoc, was an unexpected consequence of the sluices located at the Carnarvon end of the embankment to release the river waters. The preamble for an 1821 Act of Parliament described it 'by means of issuing a large body of inland waters through a main sluice, has excavated a

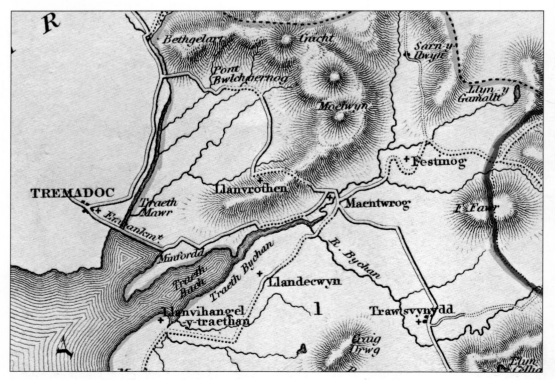

Left: **Location map, 1840.** *R. Creighton, Lewis' Topographical Dictionary, extract/ Author's collection*

Top right: **Pre-railway transport on the Afon Dwyryd; Maentwrog is on the centre right and Plas Tan-y-bwlch on the left.** *Newman & Co/ Author's collection*

Right: **Construction of Madocks's Glaslyn embankment, 1810.** *H. Billington/FR Archives*

Merionethshire

was transhipped into horse-drawn wagons for transporting to wharves on the Afon Dwyryd. Here it was transhipped into small boats for ferrying out to coastal craft, initially at Ynys Cyngor, an exposed mooring, but later at Port Madoc. So the slate was loaded and unloaded, with increased risk of damage, four times before it was 20 miles from the quarry. Just getting the slate to the sea nearly doubled the cost of its production. In 1832 the cost of exporting from Holland's quarry, as reported by Samuel Holland Junior in 1836, was:

For carriage along the roads to the wharf	7s 6d/ton
For carriage by the boats down the river	2s/ton
For wharf rent	about 3½d/ton
For repairs of roads	about 4½d/ton
For extra attendances at the port etc	about 1d/ton
	10s 3d
For breakage equal to 7½% or per ton	3s
	13s 3d

He added that slate could only be shipped during the spring tides (every other week) and then only if the weather was fine. According to Hughes (see bibliography) it would cost another £1 per ton to ship slate from Ynys Cyngor/Portmadoc to London.

It was the need to increase capacity and reduce costs that brought about the demand for a railway. There was not much precedent; as public railways, the Stockton & Darlington Railway opened in 1825 and the Liverpool & Manchester Railway was authorised in 1826. Acting privately, the coal owners of the English North East had built wagonways to export their coal. Closer to home, at Bethesda, Penrhyn slate had been exported by rail since 1798; at Llanberis, Dinorwic slate export by rail began in 1824. These were non-statutory lines built on private land. In contrast, the Nantlle Railway was a public line incorporated by Act of Parliament in 1825 and in 1828 opened as a horse-worked tramway to carry minerals, mainly slate, between Nantlle and Carnarvon.

Madocks first referred to the possibility of a railway in 1820. The problem was how to find a route that would be manageable in operation. For the first 100ft in altitude from the quarries the

commodious and well-sheltered harbour at a place extending from Garth Pen y Clogwyn to Ynys y Tywyn ... the said harbour is becoming a place of considerable trade, and increasing in resort for ships and vessels, merchants, and others trading to and from the same, and of great public utility...' By the act Madocks was empowered to erect such works as were necessary to improve the harbour and to provide facilities for its users. Interestingly, in the penultimate clause, it was enacted that if anyone made a railway from any part of the parish of Festiniog to the Merionethshire end of the embankment it would be lawful for them to use the railway existing upon it free of toll. The landowners subject to the betterment rental had, incidentally, decided that they were better off by conveying to Madocks one fifth of the affected holdings!

Commercial slate quarrying in the area had begun in the late 18th century. By the 1820s there were three quarries of substance, Diphwys, Lord's and Rhiwbryfdir. Growing demand, a product of the nascent industrial revolution, put pressures on the existing transport infrastructure. This entailed the use of pack animals to carry the finished slate to Congl y Wal, where it

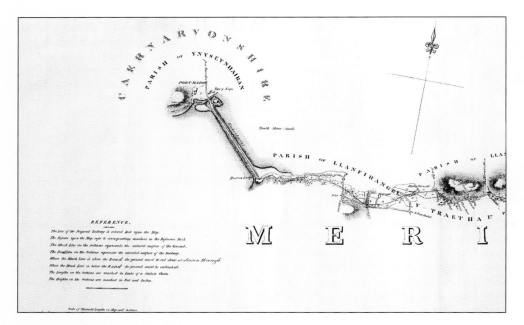

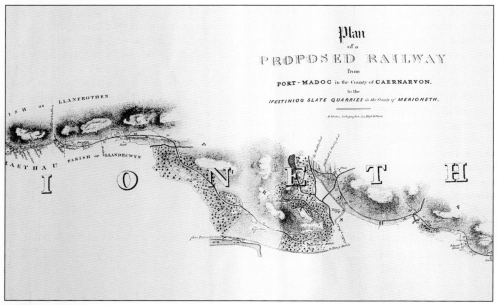

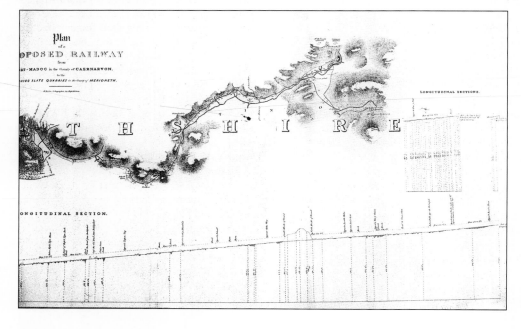

geography made the use of inclines almost inevitable. Given the date, it cannot be surprising that there was a strong Stephenson influence here, with an inclination to transfer the north eastern wagonway technology to Wales. Options considered varied according to whether more height was to be lost near to the quarries or further away.

One particular scheme is of interest, although at first sight appearing irrelevant to the Festiniog story, because it was for a route up the Croesor valley. In 1825, a bill for the proposed Moelwyn & Port Madoc Railway (MPMR) was deposited in Parliament. Promoted by the Royal Cambrian Company, a concern sponsored by Baron Nathan Meyer Rothschild and wishing to exploit slate deposits on the north west slopes of the Moelwyns, the railway, described by Michael Lewis (see bibliography) as 'an amazing essay in straight lines', took an almost straight and level route from Port Madoc for four miles before launching up the mountains with an incline that divided into four branches, two of them also inclines, that terminated over 2,000ft above sea level. The surveyor was James Spooner.

During the horse-trading that went on with the Festiniog quarry owners following the bill's deposit, they were concerned that the MPMR's access to the harbour would keep them out of it, so it was proposed to extend the MPMR to Festiniog. This proposal was without merit, and therefore perhaps not meant sincerely, as it would have involved hauling the Festiniog output up 1,200ft on one side of the Moelwyns before letting it down 1,900ft on the other side, an operation that would have been both time consuming and expensive. In 1826, the bill was lost following objections and the Royal Cambrian Company faded from the scene. The slate trade went into depression and it was not until 1829 that there was more talk about a railway to export the slate.

It was in December 1829 that Samuel Holland Junior, who was quarrying slate at Rhiwbryfdir on land leased from William Gryffydd Oakeley, first became acquainted with Henry Archer. They met at Penygroes while Holland was waiting for a Nantlle Railway tram to travel to his bank in Carnarvon; from the matter-of-fact way that Holland described this encounter, the Nantlle Railway was running a passenger service that it had no powers for! Archer was an Irishman of means but no profession or occupation, living in Penygroes. On one occasion he told Holland that he was considering taking an operating lease on the Nantlle Railway. Holland, by his own account, told Archer that he would be better served by taking on a scheme to build a railway between the Festiniog quarries and Port Madoc.

Archer visited Holland on 31 December 1829 and over several days was shown over the ground by him. When Archer raised the question of a survey, Holland recommended James Spooner. The latter was initially reluctant to take on the task but Holland encouraged him. In his memoirs, written in later years, Holland claimed that he further suggested that one of Robert Stephenson's assistants, then at work, he said, on the Chester & Holyhead Railway, might be available to assist. Michael Lewis however, points out that this is likely an error, as that railway was not completed until 1849, and he really meant Thomas Telford who had, at that time, nearly completed the Chester and Holyhead road. Calling himself a roadmaker, Thomas Pritchard had the skills required to build and to organise labour, complementing Spooner's skill as a surveyor. As a local man he would be able to communicate with the labour force in a way that the monoglot Spooner could not. In 1830, Spooner, with two of his sons, set out to survey the route for what became the Festiniog Railway.

The route was quite unlike Spooner's 1825 proposal for the Croesor valley, having an even gradient from the 600ft contour as far as Boston Lodge, the point where it was turned on to the Traeth Mawr embankment. At the inland end it bifurcated at Glan y Pwll, with a branch to Rhiwbryfdir targeting the output of Holland's and the Welsh Slate Company's quarries, and a branch to Duffws, for Lord Newborough's quarry. To make use of the railway the quarries would have to provide their own connections to it.

Archer, meanwhile, sought and obtained support from investors in Dublin who committed to take shares to the value of the £24,185 10s the line was estimated to cost. Archer himself subscribed £8,000. At a public meeting held in [Llan] Ffestiniog on 23 March 1831 a petition against the proposal was organised, signed by farmers, who carted the slate, Dwyryd boatmen and landowners. The Welsh Slate Company, which leased Oakeley land that Holland and other quarry owners needed to cross to access the railway, also objected. Support came from other landowners, ship owners and 'masters of vessels'. A bill presented to Parliament failed on a technicality, in that it did not allow for the succession of any parties that made agreements with the proposed railway company.

Table 1

Estimate of Expense of Railway from Port Madoc in the County of Caernarvon to the Rhiwbryfdir and Dyffws Slate Quarries in the County of Merioneth.

Excavating, embanking, forming and fencing	£14,275 9s 9d
Culverts and bridges on flats	£337 2s 0d
Rails, blocks, chairs and laying and bedding the same	£8,400 0s 0d
Purchase of land	£1,172 18s 3d
Total	£24,185 10s 0d
	James Spooner Engineer

A second attempt on Parliament, in June 1831, failed to pass standing orders. There were no problems with, or objections to, the third application, submitted later in 1831, and it gained royal assent on 23 May 1832.

Deposited in accordance with parliamentary standing orders in February 1832 were the books of reference, in this instance two documents of three and four sheets respectively, the first listing the owners of the 35 properties required for or affected by the railway, and two roads crossed by it, the second listing the 50 occupiers. Sir Joseph Huddart was abroad but had left instructions that he agreed to his land, near Boston Lodge and near Minffordd, the latter now occupied by the permanent way yard, being taken, provided it was on the same alignment as that surveyed for a previous scheme, in 1824/5, by William Alexander Provis; the Huddart family would have a long association with the railway.

Evan Griffith, who owned a garden at Penrhyn, would not give written approval but indicated that he did not object to the railway. A Mrs Jones, also of Penrhyn, had said that she supported it except that her attorney had told her not to! David Williams, the owner of a field below what became Penrhyn level crossing, was recorded as saying only 'dim byd' ('nothing'). Oakeley was agreeable 'provided certain conditions are complied with to the satisfaction of my solicitor'. Several owners, and more occupiers in the second list, were unable to write their names, while some of the occupiers would only follow the example or instruction of their landlords.

The act, 'for making and maintaining a railway or tramroad or railways or tramroads from a certain quay at Portmadock, in the parish of Ynyscynhaiarn in the county of Carnarvon, to certain slate quarries called Rhiwbryfdir and Duffws, in the parish of Festiniog in the county of Merioneth' comprised 152 clauses and a schedule of property needed for the railway. Principal amongst the clauses was that incorporating the company to 'be known ... by the name and style of "The Festiniog Railway Company".' As the named proprietors had contracted to provide all the capital required in February 1831, construction could start as soon as the act received the royal assent.

The company was empowered to make a railway, to be called 'The Festiniog Railway' and to be passable for wagons and other carriages, 'from on or near a certain shipping quay at Portmadock, commencing at the north-western end of the sluice bridge there ... and passing thence to the south-west end of a certain embankment called Traeth Mawr Embankment, and over and along said embankment, and also extending to or passing through or into the several parishes ... to and terminating at or near to a certain slate quarry or slate quarries called Rhiw-bryfder and Duffws slate quarries ... and also complete and maintain inclined planes ... as may appear ... to be necessary, and to make wharfs ... provided that nothing herein contained shall authorise or empower the said company to make the said railway ... within the distance of eighty-two yards from the nearest point of Plas Tan-y-bwlch ...' There were further clauses to protect Oakeley's interests, notably the requirement to build a stone-and-mortar wall with copings at least 4ft 6in above the rails, on either side of the railway where it passed through his property. Oakeley was to designate the location where 500yd of the walls was to be at least 10ft high!

Other aspects covered by the act included the limits of deviation, the rates to be charged, positioning of milestones, and tolls payable to the Tremadoc Estate and the Bankes estate at Dduallt. The only reference to gauge related to the embankment, where it was not to exceed 3ft, implying that that was the gauge of Madocks's Tramroad. The quarry proprietors, provided they were paying for their slate to be conveyed to the port along the railway, were to be allowed to pass to and from their quarries on the railway without payment. This particular facility appeared to be overlooked in the early years but was to cause problems some 40 years later.

Administratively, Archer was appointed 'the director for managing the affairs of the company'; directors, including Archer, were to be elected annually and any existing director could be re-elected but the act provided no mechanism for their initial appointments. No person holding any office or employment or having any interest in any contract with the company could qualify as a director and neither could a director take any position of profit or enter into any contract with the company. A clerk and treasurer, not to be the same person, were to be appointed.

The capital was to be divided into £25 shares, each having one vote. The company was also permitted to borrow up to £10,000 by mortgage.

Reflecting the Irish connection, the company's office was established at 41 Dame Street in Dublin. Although the company's name was specified as 'Festiniog', the Welsh form is Ffestiniog; it could well be that the two forms were considered to be interchangeable; a notice published in the *North Wales*

Chronicle dated 20 August 1833, calling a general meeting in Dublin on 22 August was headed 'Ffestiniog Railway' and referred to the 'Ffestiniog Railway Company'; there is no way of telling if this was due to the company secretary, J. Greenwood Pim, or the newspaper's compositor. The company always used the anglicised version subsequently.

In newspaper reports of the act being passed Archer was given full credit for it. He had, after all, raised the capital and secured the powers, but his efforts would soon be overshadowed by others. It was 26 February 1833, not 14 February as Archer told Newborough, before construction started. Archer's entreaties to Newborough had no effect, for he did not participate in the stone-laying ceremony and Oakeley performed it on his own. A stone laid near the site of the present Tan-y-bwlch station marked the location and Archer presented Oakeley with a suitably engraved silver trowel. Afterwards, the guests were treated to champagne and pineapples at Plas Tan-y-bwlch, and at the Tan-y-bwlch Inn an ox was roasted and much beer served.

James Smith, first of Bangor, then of Carnarvon, contracted to build the railway for £6,972. Working under Spooner's direction, he was to build the formation, obtain stone blocks for sleepers and lay the track. Rail, chairs and rolling stock and payment of the engineer and foreman were the responsibility of the company. Smith, at 23 years old, had only previous experience as a road builder; he had built the lower road on the embankment and other roads in North Wales. It soon became apparent that he

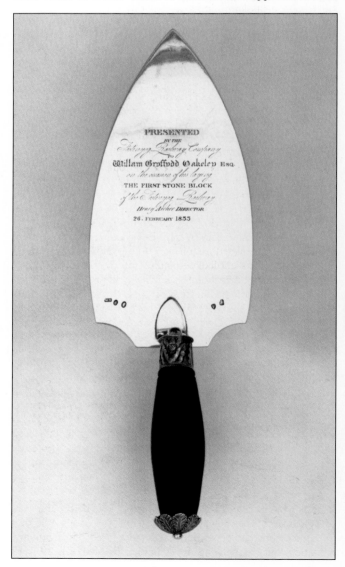

The silver trowel presented to William Gryffydd Oakeley by Henry Archer to record Oakeley's part in laying the first stone of the Festiniog Railway on 26 February 1833. Attesting to the railway's Irish connections, it has a Dublin hallmark. *Christie's/Author's collection*

had underpriced the contract and in April 1834 there was a disagreement over payment and he was discharged, subsequently being made bankrupt. His claim against the company for damages, although he was awarded less than £1, was settled only after his death in 1837.

The company decided to complete the work using direct labour, still under Spooner's direction. Although the route was substantially complete, Smith had claimed seven-eighths, the company three-quarters, much of Smith's work was redone. Within the company there was a difference over the proposed tunnel, with Spooner pushing for it to be built despite the expense of construction, estimated at £5,000, whilst Archer pressed for a pair of inclines as a cheaper alternative, perhaps saving £2,000 in capital. Spooner obviously knew that this was false economy as it would put the company to the expense of hauling loaded trains against the gradient, at a cost of £200 per annum, and could prove a bottleneck as business developed. Archer got his way, leading Spooner to submit his resignation, but the company would not accept it.

Robert Stephenson, the son of George, advised on the inclines during 1834. Spooner and Stephenson were acquainted at the time the railway gained its act and Stephenson had examined the FR's route before construction had started. Coming from a background of wagonways and railways with inclines, it can be no surprise that he was in favour of the FR's incline, saying in 1836 that a tunnel could only be justified if the traffic was enormously great; he considered the FR's expected traffic to be limited. The cost of working the inclines would be less than the interest due on the capital cost of a tunnel in his opinion.

To work the inclines Stephenson proposed a waterwheel, fed by a reservoir created by damming the Ystradau stream, to haul loaded wagons up on their downhill journey. The incline on the Portmadoc side would be self-acting, with loaded wagons going down hauling up the empties and any back traffic. He thought that for every 11 tons of slate descending, the railway ought to be able to pass seven to eight tons of coal up the line; if the inclines were well regulated they could handle 1,000 tons a day.

Archer employed Ellis Owen, a road builder of Harlech, to complete the inclines which Smith had started but Spooner would have nothing to do with them. Owen had been an engineer and surveyor since 1831 and had not previously undertaken railway work. There were problems with the work on the inclines, the reservoir dam being damaged by flooding before it was completed, requiring it to be rebuilt. Spooner said that as built it was not likely to stand and that as rebuilt it was like two dams and incorporated a spillway to prevent a reoccurrence of the flooding. Questioning of Owen in Parliament in 1836 implied that the wheel was set too low to allow the wagons to pass underneath. Owen said that he had left before the railway was completed and avoided the question by saying that he had not seen the inclines in use.

Of the quarry proprietors, only Holland was willing to commit to using the railway in advance of its completion. On 27 August 1834 Holland and the railway company had entered into an agreement that if the railway company made proper inclines to connect with his quarry, he would send his output by rail. He also agreed to repay the cost of the inclines within two years of them being brought into use. The railway company would be paid 6s per ton, an amount that would be rebated if the railway contracted to carry any other quarry's slate for a lesser amount within five years.

On Wednesday, 20 April 1836, a few weeks before the act's four-year limit, the railway was opened. This was also the first time the incline had been tried, the results surely tempering any jubilation that the opening might have generated. On 29 April

Old rail laid on stone blocks, discovered at Boston Lodge in 1956.
G. E. Baddeley/Author's collection

Spooner told the parliamentary committee that a single wagon containing a ton and a half of slate had been hauled up in four minutes and that two wagons had taken the same amount of time. A rake of three wagons, however, had nearly reached the top at the same velocity when an iron band on the drum broke! The strap, Spooner explained, 'was not half an inch in thickness and made of bad iron', its fixing was always likely to fail, he felt, and he had had it replaced by a copper block. He could not condemn the machinery, he said, because 'all machines upon the first trial are liable to accidents' and he was satisfied that the incline could cope with five wagons although he had not seen it since 20 April. He did not comment, and was not asked to, on the allegation that wagons could not pass under the drum.

George Homfray, the Welsh Slate Company's agent, examined by the same committee, had also been present at the incline on 20 April. He was standing on the framework of the waterwheel when it started to shake before the strap broke and had the strap not broken something else would have given way he felt. He thought that it was a complete failure; there would not be sufficient water for it in summer in any event.

Homfray went on to say that the Welsh Slate Company, together with Edwin Shelton and John Whitehead Greaves, was proposing to build its own railway to Portmadoc using George Overton's 1824 route down the Dwyryd valley. This would have followed the later Cambrian route through the defile at Minffordd and then the FR route to the embankment.

Archer might have proved his worth in raising the capital and getting the bill through Parliament but he caused more upset and additional expense during the construction. He appeared willing to accept the poorest quality of work on the capital account even if it led to greater expense on the revenue account putting things right in the future.

He had fallen out with Oakeley over the walls through the Plas Tan-y-bwlch estate and that led to problems in connecting the railway to the quarries. The act contained no provision for the connections as they were to be provided by agreement. In 1833, Archer had obtained Oakeley's approval to build a line to Holland's Rhiwbryfdir quarry across land leased to the Welsh Slate Company but lost it in the dispute over the walls. Owen and Owen Humphrey Owen were contracted to build the line

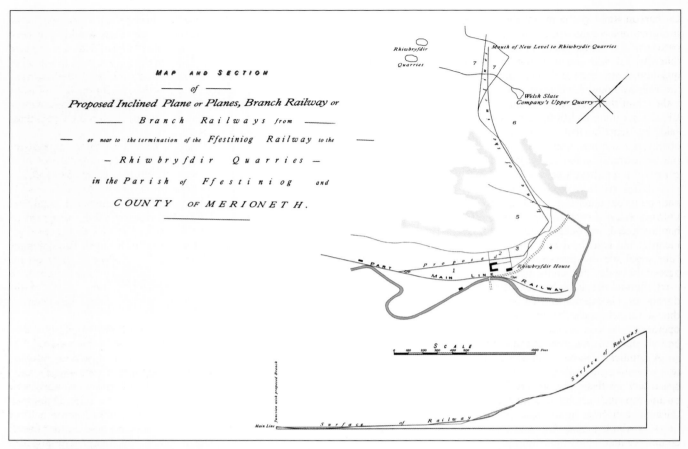

The plan of the railway proposed to connect the FR to Holland's Rhiwbryfdir quarry in 1836. *HLRO/Redrawn by Gordon Rushton*

and started on 20 May 1834, whereupon the Welsh Slate Company stopped the work the next day and obtained an injunction asserting that the FR had no authority to build. Holland claimed that he had a right of way across the land and that he did not need the WSC's consent. The pleas submitted to the Chancery Court by both sides in 1834 and 1835 cover ten very large pieces of vellum.

Failing to have the Welsh Slate Company's injunction overturned, the FR submitted a bill to Parliament in 1836. It sought powers for inclines to serve Holland's quarry and authority to raise further capital. The connection proposed had one 950ft-long incline, with a gradient of 1 in 3, and one 55ft in length graded at 1 in 5, its estimated cost was £1,500. The land needed was mostly mountainous, some was meadow, the route passing over an untried slate vein. The parliamentary committee hearing the objections proposed that the matter be put to arbitration but the Welsh Slate Company refused. Questioning was quite wide-ranging and seemed to be more concerned with the railway already built rather than the merits of the proposals.

The railway's iron rails were laid at 2ft 1in between the centres, Spooner told the committee. The choice of gauge, now defined as 1ft 11½in between the rails' inner edges, has never been satisfactorily explained. Obviously, the narrower the gauge the cheaper the cost of construction, but the closest precedent as a public carrier of slate from quarries to port, the Nantlle Railway, was 3ft 6in gauge, with not all of its connecting quarries feeling obliged to use the same gauge internally. Locally, the embankment tramway was, as stated earlier, either 3ft or 3ft 6in gauge.

In Festiniog, Lord's (Bowydd) quarry had had a rail system from 1825, the first in the area, but that was 2ft 2in gauge, and as the quarry did not have direct connection to the FR until 1854

it was unlikely to have influenced events in the 1830s. A little further away, the first quarry railways at Bethesda, in 1798/1800, were around 2ft gauge, as was the first railway at Dinorwic in 1824. Both 2ft and 3ft/3ft 6in gauge were suitable for haulage by animals, while the narrower had the advantage of being able to penetrate confined areas within the quarries. Wagons of 2ft gauge, or thereabouts, capacity about 2 tons, were certainly easier to load than larger vehicles and the 3 ton capacity wagons introduced by the FR in later years were not at all liked by the loaders. They also caused problems in restricted places.

The track specification called for the materials to be like those of the Nantlle Railway: iron rails fixed with iron chairs on to stone-block sleepers. Some of the fishbellied 'T'-section rail was supplied in 18ft lengths by the Dowlais Iron Works in South Wales. The Carnarvon ironfounder Thomas Jones, responsible for the chairs, set up a foundry in Portmadoc to produce them. This venture was continued by his son afterwards and became the Glaslyn Foundry.

Samuel Homfray said that the rails were too light, and that they should have been 25lb per yard, but were only 16lb. He thought that there should be turnouts or pass-bys at quarter-mile intervals, and understood that preparations were in hand for nine more. Homfray had an engineering background; he was related to South Wales ironfounders, although his qualifications were not given. Spooner had specified heavier rail but had been overruled by Archer, the latter having Stephenson's support.

George Bush, an engineer of four years' experience, told the committee that he did not think that the railway had been well constructed. He also said that the rails were too light, adding that the stone sleepers were too small. In cross-examination he supported Homfray's call for turnouts at quarter-mile intervals, rather than the three that had been built. He said that the

Carnarvon Railway (he meant the Nantlle), had such frequent turnouts, but admitted that that railway used rails of the same pattern and weight as those on the FR. He was pushed to accept that the FR was practical for slate traffic, being asked the question three times and agreeing each time! He thought that the railway could have been well constructed in 15 months, rather than the four years it had taken. It would take another £1,000 per mile, £13,000, he claimed, to make it efficient. He said, incidentally, that the gauge was 2ft, an indication that observers were not always precise with their answers, or that that measurement was convenient shorthand from a very early period of the railway's history.

John Hurpeth Rastrick, an engineer of some standing, who had built or otherwise been involved with several notable railways and had been a judge at the Rainhill Trials, said that he had inspected the route between Portmadoc and the foot of the inclines. He added: 'it appears to me to be made sufficiently substantial for the purposes for which it was intended'. He agreed that a decision on the preference of an inclined plane vis-à-vis a tunnel should be one for the engineer to make and would depend on his experience. Under cross-examination he agreed that a tunnel would be the easier option so far as railway operation was concerned, but that the decision 'must depend entirely upon the quantity of traffic they have...'

A significant feature of construction was the use of dry stone wall embankments, where two (usually) parallel walls had the space between them filled with rubble and earth, the track resting on the top; they are 8ft wide at the top with the walls inclined towards each other at an angle of 1 in 6. The largest of these, known as the Big Quay, Cei Mawr, is 62ft high. Spooner told the committee that the embankments could not be made in any other efficient way. A tipped embankment, being wider, would have required more land so would have been more expensive from that perspective. Given that much of the route was cut through rock, obtaining the greater amount of material needed for tipped embankments would also have increased costs. Lord Palmerston, the major shareholder in the Welsh Slate Company, was reported to be critical of the likelihood of the fill to subside, to which Spooner responded: 'They must sink, and will for some time.' Some of them were still sinking over 100 years later.

By the time the railway was ready for opening Holland's cost of road haulage had been reduced by 1s per ton, most likely the hauliers' response to the threatened railway competition. Homfray told the committee that although his carriage was 6s 6d plus 2s boatage per ton he was negotiating to reduce it to 5s 6d and 1s 6d. A new road to be built from Duffws, by Shelton

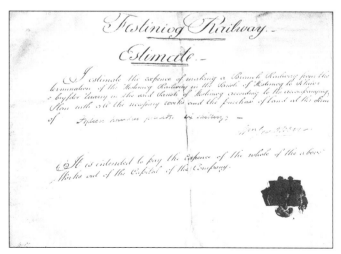

The estimate for the 1836 extension. *HLRO*

and Greaves, would reduce the cartage to 4s or 4s 6d he thought. His wharfage and other incidentals would have been much the same as Holland's and should be added to his figures to obtain a comparable rate. During the previous year a total of 180,000 tons of slate had been produced by all the quarries, with back carriage being a mere 500 tons. On the face of it the FR should have had no difficulty in attracting business with a rate of 6s per ton *vice* Holland's 12s 3d, or even the Welsh Slate Company's hoped-for 10s 9d.

When matters touched on the company's financial position, Spooner was questioned. He said it owed between £20 and £50 for damage and that there were outstanding claims for land, less than £200, and that there was money available to pay for it, and he was waiting for the conveyances to be completed. A bill had just been received for £264, otherwise everything was paid up to date and that had been the position for several months. Was Spooner being economical with the truth here? The company had spent its capital and was nearly £8,000 overspent on the construction account. Where did this money come from if all the bills had been paid? It was not until July 1836 that the company's financial position was eased by using the powers to borrow £10,000 on mortgage from Huddart.

Spooner also agreed that he concurred with Stephenson over 'the eligibility of this inclination as a mode of conveyance'. His concern not to get into a dispute with Stephenson was apparent, Spooner saying not only that he now agreed with him over the incline but also about the weight of the rails – as both were replaced within 10 years his first instincts were obviously correct.

Spooner was recalled and interrogated about a plan deposited in Parliament in 1832 – this copy does not survive. It indicated where the tunnel was to go by symbols but Spooner said he had scratched out the word 'tunnel' on Archer's instruction. He thought that by taking this action the railway had the option of building either a tunnel or inclines. He could not recall whether he had made the alteration before or after the plan had been deposited. Asked 'Is it a good railway?' he replied: 'To the best of my abilities, I have taken great pains with it.'

The bill was lost and Holland, the only quarry owner at all interested in the railway, was left to cart his slate to the railway at Dinas.

After the hiatus with the Moelwyn incline, services were resumed on 25 April. It was to be November before Stephenson's recommendations were completed; he was paid £21 for his services, although it is not clear if this payment was in respect of his 1834 activities, or included an element for them. In the end the inclines had cost nearly the same as Spooner's estimate for the tunnel.

Unusually, the railway supplied the wagons, and apart from the later gunpowder vans, the FR was not used by any private-owner wagons. This might have been a means of encouraging the quarry proprietors to use the railway, in the same way that the railway was to contribute to the cost of inclines, or perhaps it was a device to ensure that the vehicles were made and maintained to the railway's standards.

For those who had objected, things turned out better than expected. According to Williams (see bibliography) the farmers, who had operated the carts, made more money by paying more attention to their farms, and the boatmen had work unloading slates from wagons and reloading them onto ships.

Within the company, the shareholders had taken control in 1835 and appointed directors, including Huddart, Livingston Thompson, Francis Mayne and Edward Carreg, reducing Archer's influence. In 1869, Thompson was to say of Archer: '... we considered him partly to have mismanaged the company and we displaced him ...'

2

From horses and slate to steam locomotives and passengers

1836-1868

As built, the Festiniog Railway was very basic, having nothing more than a route with a line of rails and the inclines. At Portmadoc the terminus was by the public wharf, the line thence describing an arc across Ynys y Towyn green. Inland there were two termini, at Dinas and Duffws, only the former in use initially, whilst Holland was the only customer. The ruling gradient was 1 in 79 and the sharpest curve less than two chains radius. The company now had to learn how to make it work and how to make it pay, to turn it into a business. James Spooner was appointed its manager on a part-time basis, continuing his surveying practice independently of the railway. Despite the Act of Parliament, officialdom took no interest in the line because it was intended only for freight.

Holland's description of the events of 20 April 1836, written many years after the event, gives an insight into early railway operating: '... we all came down without horses, the inclination being sufficient to enable us to do so ... over the embankment we were drawn by horses – until reaching the embankment the horses rode at the tail of the train, in boxes made purposely, feeding all the way.' Those horses must have been sturdy creatures if they really faced up to that experience with such equanimity.

The use of gravity on early railways was not uncommon but on the FR it was developed to a fine art. In the early days, with only one quarry using the line, loaded trains of six to eight wagons ran at speeds of not more than 10mph. They did not run non-stop, having a mandatory ten-minute stop at the inclines, Hafod y Llyn and Rhiw Goch, to cross the empties. Boston Lodge was the terminus, where the wagons were weighed and sorted for delivery to the harbourside wharves, being hauled thence by horses. Horses hauled the empty wagons back to the quarries, being changed at the stations and riding back down in dandy wagons as described by Holland. There were stables at Cae Ednyfed, near the later Minffordd station.

The earliest extant timetable dates from 1856, post-dating completion of the tunnel, although earlier services probably would not have been much different. There were six trains each day and some were stabled overnight en route. The time allowed between sections was 18 minutes for the loaded trains, while the empties took about 40 minutes.

The weighbridge was located at the site of the later Boston Lodge halt and a second weighing table was installed in 1857 when Spooner issued instructions that the brake wagons should be spread out through the trains. This building is still there, attached to the stone loco shed. The railway adapted the stable built under Madocks's regime at Boston Lodge for occupation by the 'weighmaster and constable', and took over the wagon works. A yard was cleared to provide storage facilities.

The original slate wagons had wooden frames that were carried on four wheels, the axles running in plain iron bearings, with 100 ordered to equip the railway when it opened. They weighed just over half a ton and had a capacity of two tons. Initially the company used labour employed on a daily basis but it soon found that it was cheaper to put the work out to contract. The tender was readvertised in November 1857, when Spooner called for 'tenders for haulage of carriages of slates, slabs and minerals from their termini at Rhiwbryfdir and stations on other parts of the line to the wharfs at Portmadoc'. The contract was to start on 1 January 1858.

Perhaps feeling that his contribution was being ignored, Henry Archer commenced a dispute with the company concerning his remuneration and expenses as manager. He had been involved with the promotion of a railway to Porthdinllaen

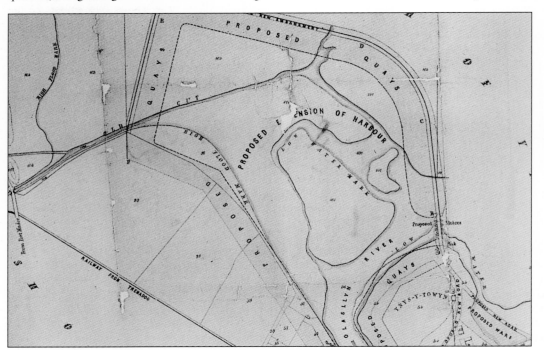

Left: **Enlargement proposals for Portmadoc harbour in 1845.** *HLRO*

Top right: **After being weighed at Boston Lodge wagons loaded with slate are about to be hauled across the embankment, c1849.** *Elton Collection/ Ironbridge Gorge Museum Trust*

since at least 1835, an activity that must have detracted from the effort needed to complete the FR and which must have contributed to the shareholders' antipathy towards him. He started selling his shares, an advertisement placed in the *Carnarvon & Denbigh Herald* in 1839 for a holding of £4,000 being attributed to him, and he soon had only a token holding. In 1848, he invented a postage stamp perforating machine, selling the rights for it to the General Post Office.

There were no objections when the company returned to Parliament in 1838, seeking powers to raise further capital, a short act of six clauses gaining royal assent on 27 July. The act empowered the company to raise a further £12,000 in £25 shares and up to £4,000 by mortgage. The company was not permitted to borrow on mortgage, however, until all of the £12,000 had been subscribed and half of it had been paid up. Alternatively it could, after the £12,000 had been subscribed, issue more shares to a maximum of £16,000 instead of borrowing.

Despite its lack of interest and recalcitrance during the construction stage, the Welsh Slate Company came to see that the FR could be of use to it and made an agreement with the railway that Palmerston signed on 14 December 1837; the FR contributed £151 4s 1d to the cost of the incline. It might well be an indication of Archer's reduced involvement with the FR that it was also possible to connect Holland's quarry to the railway during 1839, when the FR paid £642 1s 3d. Oakeley had died in 1835 and his widow, Louise Jane, accepted £500 from the company to withdraw the objection. She also agreed not to press for the 10ft high walls through the Plas Tan-y-bwlch estate. It is probably no coincidence that £500 was the penalty specified by the act for failure to comply with the clause regarding the walls.

Construction of the tunnel to replace the inclines was started in 1839. At 730yd long, it was opened in the summer of 1842. With the approaches it cost £7,600.

Rail replacement started from 1842, with the introduction of a parallel 'T'-section rail, still weighing 16lb per yard. From 1846 heavier rail, weighing 30lb per yard, was used in 21ft lengths and was held in iron chairs by iron keys. The chairs were fixed to pre-drilled granite block or slate slab sleepers by iron pins, oak pegs holding them in place. The early rail was not fishplated, being butted together in special joint chairs. Ballast was obtained from ships arriving to load at Portmadoc harbour, so came from a wide range of, usually, Continental sources. The surplus was dumped near the harbour to form Cei Ballast (Ballast Island).

By the early part of 1844 the railway had grown sufficiently and, more importantly, was making enough profit, for the directors to decide to pay a dividend for the second half of 1843. At 3½%, the ordinary shareholders received a total of £1,056 9s 10d from the business.

Facilities at Boston Lodge were increased in 1847 when a foundry was established there. A saw mill was set up in 1855. A stationary steam engine was advertised for sale in August 1857, Spooner describing it as being 11ft 11in long overall, with a vertical cylinder 18in diameter x 2ft stroke and a boiler 4ft 6in diameter and 6ft long. It was complete except for steam piping, crank and flywheel. He wanted £125 for it and would deliver it to a ship at Portmadoc, but it took a while to sell, for those who expressed an interest found the transport costs too high.

The slate business expanded gradually. Newborough's Bowydd and Greaves's Llechwedd quarries were connected to the FR in 1854, via Duffws and Dinas respectively. On 23 August 1853 the FR had entered into a covenant with Greaves that it would carry his slate for 3s 3d per ton, 'the whole distance' or pro rata for less. Maenofferen shipped slate via the FR most years from 1857, probably using Bowydd's incline at first. Duffws Casson also connected via Bowydd from 1860. Near Tanygrisiau, Wrysgan was connected in 1850, Moelwyn in 1860, and Cwmorthin in the early 1860s.

A little further away, to the east, the Festiniog Slate Quarry Ltd (FSQ), operators of the Rhiwbach slate quarry, wished to make a connection with the FR and proposed a railway between their quarry and Duffws. Designed by Charles Easton Spooner and built by agreement with the relevant landowners, the 3¼ mile-long line, known as the Rhiwbach Tramway, was completed in March 1863. It had four inclines, one to lift slate out of the quarry and three to lower it down 950ft to Duffws. Had things gone a little differently the tramway might have been a part of the FR, for a bill deposited in Parliament in December 1853 had sought powers to 'authorise the construction of a new line of railway from Duffws to the Machno slate quarries'.

Bowydd and Maenofferen made use of the Rhiwbach inclines at Duffws and several other quarries, including Cwt y Bugail, Blaen y Cwm and Bwlch Slaters, made use of the tramway, although charges for its use were considered to be high. It is likely that at times, FSQ made more from the tramway than they did from quarrying.

The availability of the railway played a large part in the

development of the slate trade and to both must be attributed the increase in the local community. In 1821, the population of Festiniog parish was 1,168 persons, a figure that had all but tripled by 1841. It doubled again by 1871, to 8,062. The hamlets of Tan y Manod, Congl y Wal, Four Crosses, Rhiwbryfdir and Tanygrisiau, all in Festiniog parish, became villages. As they grew and became conjoined, the area became known as Blaenau Festiniog.

Portmadoc also grew after the arrival of the railway, with shipbuilding developing on the back of the export trade. It had a population of 2,347 in 1851 and 5,506 in 1881 and, just as the railway declined after the opening of the competitive routes out of Blaenau Festiniog, so Portmadoc's population fell, too, to 5,097 in 1891 and 4,445 in 1911.

On the railway, a programme of improvements was put in place, the need for which must have arisen from experience gained with the gravity trains. Financed from revenue, they included widening the formation in cuttings, which suggests that Archer's influence during construction had limited the quantity of rock removed to an amount that proved impractical in use. At Rhiw Goch and Tanygrisiau there were deviations, which must have been when the horse-turning area was built at the former; the land needed at Tanygrisiau was valued at £10. A deviation at Garnedd included the short tunnel, 60yd long, costing £221 18s 9d. At less than £4 per yard, Garnedd is a model of efficiency and must have been relatively easy to build; the long tunnel, cut through syenite, a hard granite, cost more than £10 per yard. The crossing keeper's cottage at Minffordd was built in 1856/7.

The road at Tan-y-bwlch was diverted and bridged with a handsome cast-iron structure. According to C. E. Spooner's submission to Parliament in 1869 (Appendix 1) the latter was carried out in 1851 but the date on the bridge itself is 1854. The lettering on the bridge, 'Boston Lodge Foundry 1854', appears to be fixed by screws and may not be part of the castings. There has to be some doubt that the foundry ever had the capacity to make such large pours, especially at such an early date.

James Spooner died on 19 August 1856. In addition to being manager, he had been secretary or clerk since 1844 and engineer since 1847. There is a stained-glass memorial window to him in St John's church in Portmadoc. His son, Charles Easton Spooner, who had been treasurer since 1847, resigned that post and succeeded as clerk and engineer.

Increasing traffic had brought with it an increase in train lengths of up to 30 wagons, but with only three passing places the service could not otherwise be increased. Up to 16 horses, four per section, were needed to haul the empty wagons back to the quarries, increasing costs. The railway was becoming constipated by its own success and operating methods.

In 1860 the board, particularly concerned about the cost of the existing operation, decided to take action, instructing Spooner to investigate the availability and practicality of steam locomotives. As a long-standing customer, Holland used his influence to persuade the board that his nephew, Charles Menzies Holland, should be involved in the design and acquisition of any locomotives obtained and Spooner was so instructed. They were instructed to look at the locomotives in use at the 2ft 7½in gauge Neath Abbey Ironworks in South Wales.

Above: **The Tan-y-bwlch roadbridge, which Charles Spooner said was built in 1851.** *R. Piercy/Author's collection*

Right: **Two horses haul ten empty wagons across the embankment.** *Newman & Co/Author's collection*

The specification put to the board in 1862 called for a locomotive weighing not more than five tons, having a low centre of gravity and capable of running uphill at 8mph and downhill at 10mph. Downhill running would be without a load as the railway intended to continue with the gravity trains. The locomotive weight was subsequently allowed to be eight tons. An invitation to tender for the construction of three locomotives of Holland's design, placed in *The Engineer*, attracted 29 responses.

Being based in London, the younger Holland was familiar with the locomotive works of George England at Hatcham. Having locomotives built there would allow him to supervise their construction but England had not responded to the advertisement. That did not deter Holland and Spooner from contacting England, though, and in February 1863 he agreed to 'make three small locomotive engines' to Holland's design, 'subject to any alterations that will be necessary' for £900 each. The third locomotive was not to be delivered until the first two had been tried in traffic and was to incorporate any modifications found necessary.

Having secured the contract England then succeeded in persuading Holland that his proposal was inadequate, coming up with a design for a four-coupled tank engine with an auxiliary coal tender. As a successful locomotive builder, England was probably more concerned with making the locomotives comply with his existing construction techniques than in developing untried features. He was also successful in negotiating a £100 price increase for the tender, to make it £1,000 each for the first two locomotives, £800 for the third. Delivery of the first two was to be 1 June 1863 but in the event it was July before they reached Portmadoc, being transported by sea to Carnarvon and thence by road.

These two locomotives were named *The Princess* and *Mountaineer* and the former was the first to be steamed, on 4 August. As might be expected with new technology, there was a period of trial and tribulation before the locomotives were

working reliably; in particular they were found to lack adhesive weight and adequate water capacity. They were also delivered without boiler domes, at Holland's insistence and against England's advice, which caused them to prime. They were modified and the later locos had domed boilers from the start.

It was October before Spooner was confident enough to invite guests to join him for a steam-hauled journey up the line and a celebratory dinner in Portmadoc. The event took place on 23 October, two trains running at speeds of 10-12mph, it was reported, and with Holland and England driving the locomotives. Approximately 100 passengers rode on each train. Two contemporary reports describe the passengers as riding in carriages but most of them must have been riding in wagons for at this time the railway only had two 'carriages', the details of which are unknown. Their existence is known only from valuations included with accounts, and so the possibility of them being road vehicles cannot be ruled out. In which case, all passengers would have been travelling in wagons.

Probably as a result of the problems arising from the commissioning of *The Princess* and *Mountaineer*, England's order was increased to four locomotives. It is easy to envisage that England successfully claimed such problems arose from complying with Holland's requirements and that he was discouraged from charging for remedial work by an offer to buy a fourth locomotive. *The Prince* was built later in 1863 and delivered in 1864 and *Palmerston* (the name obviously a desire

Right: **George England's works at Hatcham, south London, photographed in 1965.** *D. H. Wilson/Author's collection*

Below: **The Princess was the first locomotive to be steamed on the FR. Seen at the original Portmadoc station *c*1871, the train consists of an Ashbury and four Brown, Marshalls carriages and one of the first four-wheeled brake vans.** *John Owen/FR Archives*

to keep on good terms with a distinguished customer) was built and delivered in 1864. These two cost £975 7s 6d each. What does seem remarkable is how quickly these locomotives were built, especially the first two, considering that they were to a new design and the machinery available was not that sophisticated. It would be difficult, if not impossible, to meet such a deadline in the 21st century.

The FR of course, was a horse tramway, and track that was suitable for wagons with a loaded weight of less than two tons per axle would not cope too well with a relatively primitive steam locomotive of more than twice that weight. Spooner, in 1869, said that it cost £12,844 8s 5d to convert the FR to being a locomotive railway and that this figure included the 'cost of rolling stock for passenger and goods traffic'. It would have included the cost of the buildings and maintenance facilities needed, too, and probably also the cost of rerailing with double-headed rail which started in 1868.

It appears that there was not a conscious decision to adapt the railway both for locomotives *and* for passengers, otherwise carriages might have been ordered for delivery to coincide with the arrival of the locomotives. As it was, it was only when the first steam locomotives were due to arrive that Spooner began correspondence with Brown, Marshalls & Co of Birmingham concerning an order for passenger rolling stock. Eight bodies for four-wheeled carriages were ordered at a total cost of £713 14s plus £48 18s for transport. The railway was to supply the running gear and they were delivered by February 1864.

The railway was taking a huge leap into the unknown with this move to carry passengers. Arising from the confusion that followed the adoption of both the standard (4ft 8½in) and broad (7ft 0¼in) gauge elsewhere in the UK, the Gauge of Railways Act of 1846 had forbidden the construction of passenger railways with other than standard gauge, except in Ireland, where 5ft 3in gauge was the norm. However, the act had made no mention of existing non-passenger railways being adapted to become passenger lines. So, whilst the FR's move to carry passengers was not expressly prohibited, it was not exactly approved either. The board could have had no idea what the legal consequences, if any, might be. The FR was already in a legal limbo over its use of steam locomotives; now it was taking a chance on the introduction of a passenger service.

Perhaps the commissioning of the carriages was subject to some trial and error, for it was not until 20 June 1864 that Spooner wrote to the 'Lords of the committee of Her Majesty's Privy Council for Trade and Foreign Plantations' that 'As secretary and on behalf of the Festiniog Railway Company, established pursuant to act of parliament of the 2 George [error for William] the 4 C48, I hereby give notice that it is intended to open the said railway which is situate in the parishes of Festiniog, Llanfrothen, Llandecwyn, Llanfihangel y Treathau and Ynyscynhaiarn in the counties of Merioneth and Carnarvon for the public conveyance of passengers, as speedily as possible, and that the said railway will be sufficiently complete for the conveyance of passengers and ready for inspection the 26 of July 1864.'

Spooner obviously thought that the application needed some amplification, for he wrote again on 30 July, saying: 'This railway as a steam locomotive line being a novel one of the present day, it appears necessary to make some few remarks thereon to prevent prejudices that might naturally arise as to the safety of steam application on so small a gauge as two feet as well as to the safety of running over curves of unusually short radii.

'An act of parliament was obtained for the construction of this line in the year 1832 at which time the population of the district was very limited, and the little business carried on was chiefly in the neighbourhood of the quarries. Since then the

Captain Henry Whatley Tyler, RE. *FR Archives*

produce of the slate quarries has considerably increased, and the shipping port has become a town of much importance. The railway runs through a wild and beautiful country a distance of 13 miles with a continuous descent from the quarries to the port, the difference of level between the one terminus and the other is 700ft and average grade 1 in 92.

'The line in consequence of the traffic formerly being very limited was made economically to meet the necessities of the time. As the traffic increased the company improved the line from time to time, easing many of the curves, and laying out large sums on deviations and improvements of permanent way. Upon which being done it was contemplated by the late manager to use steam locomotive engines, and engineers were consulted as to the practicality and utility of such a power. The result of enquiries made being discouraging, the project at that time was abandoned. However from the continued advance of the slate traffic and increasing trade of the neighbourhood it was considered most desirable by the company to use steam power on the line in place of horse power heretofore adopted and steps were taken for constructing suitable engines. The result is that the locomotives are made and have worked the traffic for the last eleven months with the greatest possible satisfaction. Two engines during that time having run over a distance of 36,300 miles without an instance of running off the line.

'The locomotives are made to the same centre of gravity as those on the Great Western Railway. Also in the passenger carriages made and trucks used on the line, the gravity is brought as low as possible with proportionate distance between centre of wheels and the outer rail is raised around the curves, hence the perfect safety of traversing the line. The speed is limited to low rates viz 10 miles an hour; notwithstanding experiments have been made at the rate of 24 miles an hour throughout the entire length of the line with safety.

'The necessity of carrying passengers between the source of traffic and the place of export, has become an object of necessity to the company and much importance to the public, they have therefore prepared their line for that purpose, and are waiting the sanction of the Board of Trade.'

The letter is quoted in full as an early example of Spooner's hyperbole. Their lordships were clearly in no mood to be rushed, however, for it was not until 13 October that they instructed Captain Henry Whatley Tyler, formerly of the Royal Engineers, to inspect the railway. He had joined the inspectorate in 1853 and was chief inspecting officer from 1871 until 1877. Writing from the Oakeley Arms at Tan-y-bwlch, on 27 October 1864, he reported that:

- The average gradient between Dinas and Boston Lodge was 1 in 92 for the 12¼ miles and that the steepest gradient on the portion now proposed to be used for passengers between Dinas and Portmadoc was 1 in 79.82.
- The maximum speed was 10mph and not more than 6mph on the sharpest curves. He had ridden at speeds of more than 30mph and had assessed the riding qualities of locomotives, tenders, passenger carriages, brake vans and slate trucks.
- The permanent way was laid with 30lb rails in 16ft and 21ft lengths; cast-iron chairs weighed 6lb except at joints where they weighed 13lb. Sleepers were larch, 4ft 6in long, averaging 9 x 4½in in section, laid at 2ft intervals and under joints they were 10 x 5in in section and laid at 18in intervals. Wooden keys secured the rails to the chairs and wrought-iron spikes the chairs to the sleepers. Some spikes were missing and the drainage and packing was poor.
- The space between the carriage windows and bridge abutments was only 9in and that there was insufficient space between the sides of the carriages and the 'stone walls or other works at the side of the railway over the greater part of it'; he recommended barring the carriage windows, 'which is in progress', and keeping the doors locked on both sides of the carriages while the trains were in motion.
- Trains were hauled up by locomotives but 'are allowed to descend by the force of gravity for 12¼ miles to within three quarters of a mile of Portmadoc'. It was proposed, by the railway, to allow the loaded slate trains to descend in front of the carriages with the locomotive following behind and to attach the carriages behind the empty slate or good wagons for the uphill journey.
- Most of the line was enclosed by stone walls, with timber and wire fencing either erected or being erected in other places where needed. When the fencing was completed, gates that had been placed across the railway to control animal movements would be removed.
- Bridges and culverts were constructed of masonry, timber, cast iron or slate beams; the largest span was 19ft, while the largest span using slate beams was 8ft.
- The long tunnel was in want of improved drainage.
- The long tunnel should be operated by a telegraph, the existing bells being subject to misunderstanding as well as not being reliable.
- There were three crossings of public roads, two of them parish roads and one a turnpike road. He pointed out that according to the act, turnpike roads could not be crossed on the level but that the latter had only become a turnpike road in the previous year. Full gates were required at one, unspecified, crossing.

The land required from Sir John Bankes for the long tunnel, extracted from the indenture dated 30 September 1839.
National Archives

- The branch line to Duffws was 61 chains long, its steepest gradient was 1 in 68 and the sharpest curve three chains. It crossed the parish road on the level. The company did not propose to open it for passenger traffic at the same time as the rest of the railway, although it was making improvements with that objective in mind. The junction should be signalled.
- The engines and tenders were in need of safety guards to clear obstructions from the line. Stability would be improved if the engines had trailing wheels to support the weight overhanging at the rear. Because the carriages were intended to run separately from the locomotives they should also be equipped with safety guards.
- Although the carriages ran easily and steadily around the curves, the company might benefit, as trains became heavier, by adopting 'longer carriages on eight wheels with what are called 'bogie frames', similar but on a smaller scale to those which are in use in America and on lines with sharp curves in parts of Germany and Switzerland'.
- The Cwmorthin quarry incline ran down directly towards the railway and to within a short distance of it and there would be substantial danger to the trains if wagons or trucks were permitted to be worked on this incline while trains were passing. There was no space for placing any obstruction between the incline and the railway that would be adequate for protection against runaway trucks and he recommended that a telegraph be established between the top and the bottom of the quarry incline, with distant signals on the railway. An FR signalman would thus be able to prevent trains from passing when the quarry incline was being worked.
- The adoption of locomotives upon 'this little line' was very

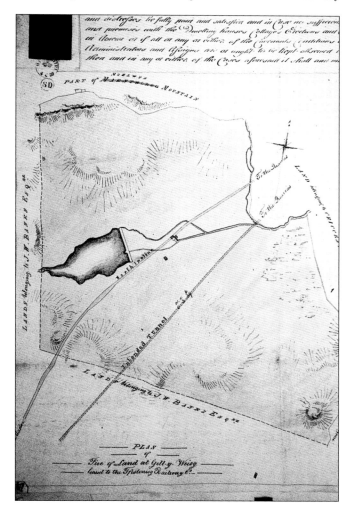

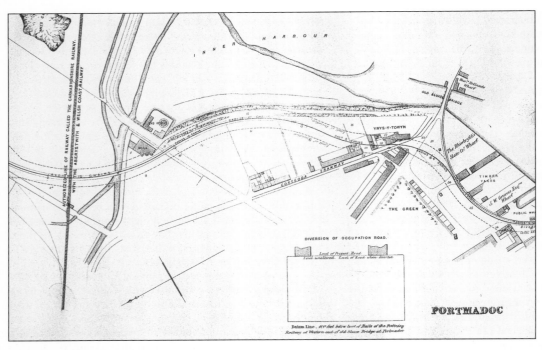

PORTMADOC

important. The cheapness with which such a line could be constructed, the quantity of work that could be economically performed upon it, and the safety with which the trains ran over it made it an example that would be followed elsewhere in Britain, India, and in the Colonies, where it was desirable to form cheap lines for small traffic, or as a commencement in developing the resources of a new country.

● Passengers had already been carried upon it without payment for some months, and considering the slow speed at which the traffic was worked, he did not think it necessary that all the improvements that he suggested should be completed before sanction was given for opening for passengers with payment, but he thought that the following improvements should be completed before that sanction was given:

1 Better approaches to and accommodation for passengers at the stations
2 The tunnel telegraph
3 The means of protection above referred to at the Cwmorthin quarry incline
4 Safety guards for the engines, tenders and brake vans
5 Stop blocks at the lower end of the different sidings
6 The level crossing gates to close across the rails
7 All signals not seen by the signalman working there to be provided with return signals.
8 All missing spikes to be inserted in the permanent way

● Pending the completion of these requirements it was his duty to report (under the terms of the act) that the line could not, by reason of the incompleteness of the works, be opened without danger to the public using it.

● He had recommended that the train staff and ticket system be adopted for securing the safety of the traffic on the single line, and had made suggestions for improvements to the company's printed book of rules which had been handed to him.

Tyler said nothing about the stations apart from requiring them to be improved. The railway leased a strip of land at the town end of the embankment from the Tremadoc Estate for its Portmadoc passenger terminus, where a wooden building was erected. At some unknown date (it was there by 1869), a weighbridge was established at the station throat, which was probably for weighing the back traffic.

Clearly, Tyler was the right man to inspect the FR. Taking account of his perception that the lessons learned on the FR, with regard to the benefits arising from the cheapness of its construction, could be applied elsewhere, this report is probably the most significant document to be produced in regard to furthering the cause of narrow gauge railways. Both Tyler and Spooner started to sell the narrow gauge concept, with the FR as an exemplar, as a system that could be used elsewhere. It was from this moment that the FR came to be more widely known to the outside world.

Tyler's requirement for the locking of carriage doors has remained a feature of the railway's operations ever since and only the demands of modern safety requirements have brought about the permanent removal of bars from carriage windows. Although the engines never received trailing wheels, it was not too long before the idea of bogie carriages was taken up. It must be considered rather strange that Tyler made no comment about brakes on passenger trains, especially as he describes the company's practice of running them downhill by gravity! However, he did call for safety guards to be fitted to brake vans – these must be the three 'luggage vans' first appearing in a Boston Lodge stock list in June 1865. Little is known about these four-wheeled, timber-bodied, vehicles although they do appear in early photographs. Probably built at Boston Lodge, they had an external platform with a brake wheel for the guard at the downhill end.

On 1 November, the Board of Trade gave the company formal notification that its opening must be delayed for one month. Spooner gave notice on 26 November that the line would be ready on 13 December, but Tyler was not available to make a follow-up inspection. Following a reminder, the Board of Trade informed the company that although Tyler was unavailable to re-inspect the line, he had recommended that the railway be allowed to open on 1 January and added he recommended that the 'train staff system' be adopted for working the traffic.

The official opening that took place on 5 January 1865 was marred by the death of John Roberts, an engine cleaner who jumped off a loco at Boston Lodge, tripped and was hit by both the tender and the following carriage. A report of the incident in the *Carnarvon & Denbigh Herald* blamed Roberts's recklessness. Spooner's note for the chairman's use at the August 1866 annual meeting added that Roberts left a widow and six children and had been in the company's employ for four years. Notwithstanding this unfortunate event, the railway continued in operation for the rest of the day, the local population enjoying the privilege of free rides. Two hundred invitations had been issued to the area's 'great and good' to experience the new mode of transport and partake of a celebratory dinner at the town hall.

Tyler visited again on 6 March 1865, reporting that his recommendations of the previous year had been attended to. He also commented that the fencing was much improved; gates had been added at level crossings, and removed elsewhere; the trackwork at points had been improved, additional sleepers installed with more to be added when the weather permitted; safety guards had been added to locomotives, tenders and brake vans; station and signal arrangements had been improved; a telegraph had been installed at the long tunnel; train staffs were in use, and the speed limit of 10-12mph appeared to be being adhered to. He went on to recommend that the train staffs should be painted to distinguish the two sections and recommended that further protection should be installed at the foot of the Cwmorthin incline. Finally, he reported that the company proposed to install a bell in the tunnel in the first instance, and if that was not satisfactory then a telegraph 'which would be the most efficient means of protection if worked properly' would have to be installed.

Tyler's reference to two sections for the train staff draws attention to the method of working introduced during 1863, where all trains were crossed at Hafod y Llyn. There were six return workings per day, each taking 1 hour 50 minutes for a single journey. There were stations at Portmadoc, Penrhyn, Hafod y Llyn, Tanygrisiau and Rhiw (Dinas). In his paper, read to the Inventors' Institute in 1865, Spooner said: 'At the present time they work the traffic with these engines and two spare ones... ', that is, the service was worked with just two locomotives, perhaps with one of them out-stationed at Dinas. Reliability would have been dependent on regularly achieving a ten-minute turn-round at termini, as well as the consistency of the locomotives, and at this distance in time it would seem to have been asking rather a lot of them. In 1864, stops were introduced at Rhiw Goch and Dduallt, each of three minutes, without an increase in running times.

Also in 1864, Brown, Marshalls & Co supplied signalling equipment: on 9 April '2 disc signals with bells and lamps complete' and '2 lamps and sockets for tunnel to show red, white and green' and on 25 July, '7 semaphore signals and lamps complete' and '16 disc signals and lamps complete'. Presumably the disc signals with bells of the first order were also for the tunnel. The semaphores were located in the centre of each station and had two arms, one for each direction, and gave three aspects: clear, caution and stop. The 3ft diameter discs were located at each end of a station and acted as distant signals for approaching trains, but some were used as repeaters where sighting was restricted.

Arising from the introduction of the passenger service was a claim from the Tremadoc Estate for tolls payable in respect of the passengers carried over the embankment. The railway, of course, had no statutory powers to carry passengers and the estate appeared to have no powers to charge tolls for them. The FR refused the claim, the dispute rumbling on for several years. In summer it was also found necessary to arrange for firewatchers in the woodland through which the railway ran, particularly in the Oakeley estate.

So, over a period of five years, the FR was transformed from being a gravity railway carrying only goods to being a steam railway operating a public passenger service. Experience showed that the first four locomotives could not cope with the increasing traffic so two more were obtained from George England in 1867. They were slightly larger all-round and had saddle tanks instead of side tanks. Named *Welsh Pony* and *Little Giant*, it is likely that they would have been allocated to the main line while the original locomotives were put to shunting. The introduction of the passenger service was so successful that in 1868 six more carriage bodies were ordered, this time from the Ashbury Railway Carriage & Iron Company in Manchester. The running gear for these four-wheeled vehicles was manufactured by the railway.

A primitive quarrymen's service was started in 1867, primitive in two senses: the timetable and the accommodation. Most of the quarrymen travelled to work on Monday morning and lived in barracks located at the quarry until they returned home at Saturday midday. There was obviously not much scope for revenue from the FR perspective and in December 1866 Spooner asked the Board of Trade for approval to carry the quarrymen in the slate wagons, submitting a printed copy of the 1863 agreement with the proprietors, (p24) in justification for his request. On 22 December 1866 he was advised that, having consulted Tyler, the Board of Trade was of the 'opinion that all passengers, labourers or others, ought to be conveyed upon the railway only in properly constructed passenger carriages'. Some small, primitive carriages were made for the purpose; constructed of timber and completely open, they were as close to being wagons as it was possible to get without breaching the Board of Trade's requirements. The fare was 6d for a single journey, any station to any station. The vehicles were given roofs from 1873, but remained without doors or windows until the late 1880s.

Since the first dividend of 3½%, for the six months ended 31 December 1843, had been paid the company had been enormously successful in commercial terms. From 1845 it had paid dividends of 4% twice a year and in 1853 had paid a total of 10% and only in 1864 and 1865 did it pay less, representing an average of 5.35% between 1832 and 1868. It must come as no surprise that some of the railway's customers were complaining that, despite the significant reduction in carriage rates the FR had already brought them, its charges were too high and that the money being paid in dividends should be allocated to the reduction of rates, and that there were others who were interested in tapping into its market.

The Festiniog & Blaenau Railway (FBR) might have seemed insignificant. It was a 3½ mile-long 2ft gauge line from a junction with the FR at Dolgarregddu, near Duffws, to the village of Ffestiniog, serving the Craig Ddu and Manod slate quarries at Tan y Manod. The quarrymen were also anticipated as a source of traffic. The railway company was registered in 1862 under that year's Limited Liability Act and there was no Act of Parliament, the land needed being given to the railway, its route carefully planned so that, although it was quite curvaceous, it might be converted to standard gauge at a later date. A prospectus issued in 1866 offered the possibility of attracting tourist traffic from as far away as Betws y Coed, via a proposed new turnpike road, and that locally it would serve as a link in the journey to Portmadoc for inhabitants of Trawsfynydd and parts of Maentwrog. It was effectively an extension of the FR and if circumstances had been different, it might have been promoted by the FR. As it was, it was promoted by the FR's critics, including its largest user, Samuel Holland.

Construction was overseen by Charles Menzies Holland, who at the same time was involved with the design and manufacture of the FR's steam locomotives. Holland notified

The first trains on the Festiniog & Blaenau Railway were worked by Festiniog Railway locomotives; thereafter it seems to have been a regular occurrence. *The Princess* was photographed at the FBR's Dolgarreddu terminus. The loco has a different chimney and a new tender. The worksplate reads 'G. England & Co Engineers London'. *FR Archives*

the Board of Trade that the line would be ready for inspection from 25 April 1868. Tyler made his inspection and submitted his report on 26 May. He required a facing point and a semaphore signal at the Blaenau terminus to be removed, the point to be kept locked until the work was done, and the viaduct at Tan y Manod to be strengthened, extracting a written legal undertaking to have the work done from FBR chairman John Casson, before he left. The line was opened on 29 May but approval was not given until 5 June. The FR worked the FBR's trains until its own steam locomotives, ordered from Manning, Wardle, were delivered in August 1868.

Developments at the Portmadoc end of the FR arguably had less impact but should not be overlooked. The Aberystwyth & Welsh Coast Railway (AWCR), then engaged on building its line along the coast, submitted an application for powers to build a branch to Ffestiniog in 1862. At a meeting with the quarry proprietors and agents concerning the proposal, held in Tremadoc on 14 August 1863, company chairman Charles Gaussen, explained the difficulties the FR had dealt with since its act had been obtained. The company had done its best to meet the proprietors in 'a liberal spirit' and had reduced the rate from the authorised 6s 6d per ton per mile to less than 3d. He offered a new agreement, superseding all previous ones and including new rates. Three agents objected, saying they would have to consult their companies.

The company sought a commitment of 14 years or the unexpired portion of any leases held from Oakeley. Tolls for back carriage were set out, the same as those offered by the AWCR in its 1861 act, and rates for parcels were also defined. The company undertook to haul all traffic using locomotives, notwithstanding its continued use of gravity for down trains. Failure to supply sufficient wagons within 30 daylight hours of their being requested in writing would result in a penalty of 1d per hour per wagon not supplied being paid. The company undertook to complete delivery from the foot of the relevant lowest incline to the 'lower terminus' within 18 daylight hours

or would allow 1d per ton compensation. It would not accept responsibility for 'ordinary' breakages but would accept responsibility for 'extraordinary' breakages caused by 'the upsetting, breaking down or concussion of wagons or carriages or from any other accident or occurrence arising from any default on the part of the company ...'

The railway would accept not less than 15 tons from any quarry on any day, a waybill to be handed to the railway's traffic clerk, traffic officer or left at the railway's office at the 'upper terminus'. The total volume of slate carried in each calendar year would be used to set the rate for the following year. There was a sliding scale of rates (Table 2), reducing to 2s 6d per ton when the combined volume carried exceeded 110,000 tons. The proprietors, called freighters in the agreement, were to load and unload wagons. The agreement included an undertaking to carry 'all the workmen and labourers of the freighters', when permitted, at a rate not exceeding ¼d per mile provided that 'the company shall not be obliged to carry such workmen and labourers at the rate aforesaid otherwise than in slate wagons and trucks'! The agreement also required the proprietors to undertake not to send their output 'in any other mode than along the entire length of the said railway or to some point beyond the third milestone nearest the lowest terminus'. The proprietors offered, although they were not bound, to support the FR against any competing line. The ACWR bill passed through the House of Commons but was rejected by the Lords; John Whitehead Greaves was one of the FR representatives opposing the bill in parliament. Only the Welsh Slate Company refused the agreement.

Table 2

Sliding scale of rates

Up to 70,000 tons	3s 3d
Exceeding 70,000 tons, up to 82,000 tons	3s
Exceeding 82,000 tons, up to 90,000 tons	2s 9d
Exceeding 90,000 tons, up to 110,000 tons	2s 7½d
Exceeding 110,000 tons	2s 6d

Not rejected, however, was the AWCR's 1865 bill, which included powers to acquire and enlarge the inner harbour at Portmadoc and to replace the existing stone (Britannia) bridge and replace it with a swing or draw-bridge. The FR's property in the locality was protected by the act and the new bridge was to be constructed in such a way that the FR could cross it. Considering that the bridge and basin were the property of the Tremadoc Estate it is surprising that the act contains no provision for the Estate's protection. Whilst the harbour and bridge works were not carried out, the land for the siding that would have served the harbour was acquired and continues to show on large-scale mapping.

Portmadoc became the terminus of another 2ft gauge mineral line from 1864, this serving the Croesor valley. Whilst the Ffestiniog slate quarries were expanding as a consequence of the existence of the FR improving access to markets, the Croesor slate quarry owners were also seeking to serve an expanding market and needed to improve the transportation of their product and to reduce their costs. In the upper Croesor valley there were quarries quite close to the FR-served Cwmorthin quarry. Exporting via Cwmorthin could not, as suggested when the FR was being promoted, be considered seriously as it would have required all outgoing slate to be lifted, at some expense, before it could be lowered to the FR.

Construction of an independent route, the Croesor Tramway, was started in 1863 and completed in 1864. It was about three miles long and almost level, and like the FBR, it was built without parliamentary powers and by agreement with the landowners. There was a family connection with the 1825 route, in so far as the 1863 route was surveyed by Charles Easton Spooner. Part of this utilised Madocks's 1800 embankment and at Portmadoc it connected to the FR near the wood yard on Ynys y Towyn green. Within the valley, quarries made their own connections to the tramway, using inclines to do so. In 1865 the Croesor & Port Madoc Railway Act regularised the tramway's position and authorised an extension to Borth y Gest. In failing to make provision for working the crossing of the Aberystwyth & Welsh Coast Railway's route to Portmadoc and Pwllheli, as approved in 1860, a legal problem was created that only came to light in the 1920s.

The AWCR had been absorbed into the Cambrian Railways in 1865, on the same day that its 1865 act was approved, giving it powers in Portmadoc, as previously mentioned. The line was opened to Portmadoc in October 1867, passing under the FR at Minffordd and, by making use of the Croesor Tramway, providing an opportunity to exchange traffic at Portmadoc.

During the five years to 1868 the FR experienced a considerable growth in business (Table 3). As this can only be partially due to the introduction of the passenger service the remainder must be attributed to the increase in capacity made possible by the locomotives. The substantial increase in slate traffic was not matched by a pro rata increase in revenue and some crude arithmetic shows that from 1866 the railway was carrying seven tons of slate per £1 earned – previously it had carried just over six tons per £1 earned – the result of the 1863 agreement coming into effect as the volume increased.

An indication of the attitude that the shareholders had towards the company, and some insight into the way the company was operated, may be had from the report of the annual general meeting held on 28 August 1868. Needham Shelton's and John Graves Livingston's proposal for a 6% dividend was countered by Andrew Durham and John Whitehead Greaves proposing that it should be 5%; the latter was lost. Durham and George Augustus Huddart proposed that Spooner's salary be increased to £300 per annum free of income tax. Durham went on to propose 'that the thanks of the company be given to Mr Spooner, for the zeal and diligence given by him towards the interests of the company'. There were no objections to Shelton and Greaves's proposal that Livingston Thompson and Huddart each be paid £100, plus travelling and hotel expenses, to attend once a month to the company's business during the ensuing year. None of the directors had been paid fees, apart from five guineas a year for expenses and it seems that previously they had had to wait a while before they received these.

Despite the increased capacity the FR was still not able to keep up with demand, something that probably had much to do with the limitations of the locomotives, the timetable and the method of working. Even if the locomotives were capable of hauling more than the 30 empty wagons up hill during the last of the horse days, their ability to do so must have been constrained by the limitations placed upon the service by crossing at the restricted site at Hafod y Llyn. In 1869, Livingston Thompson told a parliamentary committee that the railway ran long trains of 500(!) wagons that could cross only at one place and then while a short train was in the 'turnout' (loop). One of the problems was the failure of the quarry proprietors to have the wagons unloaded and returned to use quickly, but they would always complain that the railway was keeping them short of wagons.

It had not gone unnoticed that the FR was making considerable profits out of its monopoly on the transport of Festiniog slate. From 1879 onwards however, the railway was to face great competition in its own specialist market. During the autumn of 1868 the company decided to increase capacity by the radical measure of doubling the track, for which it needed additional parliamentary powers. It also learned about the unusual form of double-bogie, double-boiler steam locomotive patented by Robert Francis Fairlie.

Table 3

Slate and other traffic

Year ending (30 June)	Slates carried Tons cwt	Receipts	Goods carried Tons cwt qtrs	Receipts	Receipts from passengers	Compensation for goods
1863	64,092 17	£10,375	8,347	£417 6 10		
1864	70,467	£11,367 13 9	7,283 5 1	£1,206 2 3		
1865	73,439 10	£11,682 7 7	9,860	£1,486	£973 0 8*	
1866	76,919 3	£11,011 0 7	11,479	£1,784	£2,142 10 6	£15
1867	93,773	£13,397 10	13,790	£2,429 9 3	£2,666 17 2	£10
1868	112,051 19	£15,798 18 7	14,693 11 2	£2,676 4 6	£3,380 17 6	£21

* This amount includes the receipts from 6 January to 30 June 1865
Submitted to Parliament, 6 July 1869

THE QUARRIES

Top: **Votty & Bowydd quarry, 1947.**
J. Valentine/Author's collection

Above: **A view over Blaenau Festiniog with Duffws in the centre in 1957. The incline serves the Votty & Bowydd quarry; the Votty mill is on the right and the bridge over the incline carries the Votty rubbish tramway.**
J. Valentine/Author's collection

Right: **The Rhiwbach Tramway near Cwt y Bugail quarry, c1950.**
Brian Hilton/Author's collection

Above left: **The Welsh Slate Company viaduct as constructed, and before the LNWR line was built. The hamlet of Dinas is visible between the piers,** *c*1870s. *Author's collection*

Above: **A view underground at Llechwedd, where the slate has been worked through to the surface.** *J. C. Burrow/Author's collection*

Left: **The Festiniog Granite Company's branch line is very prominent in this view of Tanygrisiau, 1910.** *Commercial postcard/ Author's collection*

3

The 1869 Act - springboard for expansion

During the 1860s, the FR had made a transformation from being a relatively primitive line worked by gravity and horses. It had introduced steam locomotives and had started a passenger service. In doing so it had gained the support of the Board of Trade's inspector, Captain Henry Tyler, a visionary, in this context certainly, who saw in the FR an application that could be useful elsewhere. There were, however, problems with the infrastructure and the railway's operating procedures that needed to be addressed.

The company devised a scheme to double the track, to make a junction with the Cambrian Railways at Minffordd for the transhipment of slate, and to install a junction line at Glan y Pwll, so that uphill trains could serve both Dinas and Duffws without reversing down the main line, and had applied to Parliament for powers for these and other purposes. With an estimated cost of £65,049 for the works (Appendix 3) the company obviously envisaged continuous growth.

The application came before Parliament in April and July 1869. The questioning, some of it quite hard, allowed the railway's representatives, unwittingly or otherwise, to paint a portrait of the FR as a horse-worked gravity line and how it was coping with rapid expansion in the 1860s. As some of the witnesses, particularly Livingston Thompson and Charles Easton Spooner, appeared at both sessions and covered the same ground, their contributions in the following summary of highlights have been merged. Emphasis, *italics*, indicates pointing at a map.

The first witness was no less than Captain Tyler, obviously chosen as a figurehead. His evidence was brief and not altogether constructive. He thought that if the company wanted to spend money on doubling the line it should do so and that it would be in the public interest for it to be done. When asked: 'But if they can carry on their traffic conveniently over a single line, what is the use of the double line?' He answered simply: 'That is the question'!

Thompson described how the requirement for wagons had gone up as the number of quarry inclines had increased, only a third of the stock would be needed otherwise, and the non-agreement rate had been increased from 3s 3d per ton to 4s to cover the extra cost. Some of the trains were over a quarter of a mile long, 100 or as many as 150 wagons. The atmosphere got a little heated when the questioning came on to the subject of rates for agreement and non-agreement quarries:

Q What did you charge them for carrying slate down in the year 1863?

A I think it was 3s 3d.

Q Lately you have raised that, I believe, to 4s.

A Yes, but they have a large number of inclines. I was a party to it. I found great fault with the rails that were laid down. They were so narrow that they were cutting our wheels to pieces.

Q You admit the fact?

A Yes.

Q That is against 2s 6d per ton charged to the other owners?

A Yes. Only we were bound by agreement there.

Q That there is a differential rate in favour of the companies under agreement with you of 1s 6d per ton.

A Certainly.

Q There is another company under agreement with you, the Rhiwbach?

A Yes, that is the Festiniog Slate Company.

Q Do you not carry their slates down at 2s 1¼d all the distance?

A We charge them 3s 3d all the distance. They work all *that* and we take them into our possession *here* and run them down to the point *here* for 3s 3d, and we are in dispute with them as to the delivery below.

Q (by a lord) That is the most distance traffic that you have?

A Yes.

Q That is to say you charge them 2s 1¼d for the entire distance?

A No. We charge them 3s 3d for the entire distance.

Q We will take it now that Rhiwbach is the furthest of all from you.

A Granted.

Q From the quarry until you come down to the terminus of your line it is nearly all incline, is it not?

A No.

Q A great portion?

A No. When I was over the road about the year 1861, I think it was, a good part of it was nearly on the level. There is a very steep incline up *here* 13ft I think, then it runs forward, there is a pool and then there is a drop down at the other side.

Q There are six inclines altogether, are there not?

A I cannot say.

Q You have named several. Your wagons go all the way to the quarry, do they not?

A Yes.

Q You charge 3s 3d for the whole distance, which is 2s 2¼d per ton per mile?

A No.

Q You charge in the first place 3s 3d for the whole distance?

A Yes.

Q Then there is a rebate of between £400 and £500 in the lump?

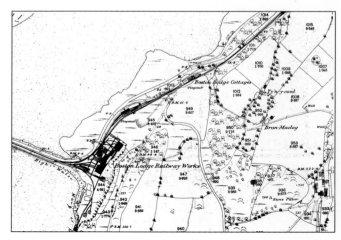

A There is a rebate of so much money but that was under a separate thing altogether.
Q A separate agreement with that company?
A No. It is not a separate agreement. It is a separate clause in the agreement.
Q Between you and the quarry company.
A Yes.
Q Now as a matter of fact – and say 'yes' or 'no' – is it a fact that for the last year, the year ending 30 June 1868, the amount paid for the entire distance from this furthest point to the quarry, when you take the rebate into account it is 2s 2¼d per ton per mile, for the whole distance?
A I never calculated it. I say that the rebate is another affair altogether and was the matter of an agreement the first time they went to make the road.
Q How do you justify your charging the Diphwys Casson Slate Company, which is a much shorter distance, 4s per ton for the entire distance as against what I say, is 2s 2¼d for the other quarry?
A Because we have learned experience. We have found that the amount of rolling stock now is such that we must lay on a larger sum, and recollect that agreement was in the year 1861 and you are now speaking of a company not under agreement at all, who were only asking us to make an agreement last year.
Q (By a lord) The long and short of it is that those companies who come into your agreement pay less than some of the others who did not come into it?
A Certainly.
Q You proposed an agreement with us within the last 12 months, did you not, to bind us down just as you bound down the other companies?
A Yes. Two gentlemen came down from that company and saw us in Portmadoc. We said we would give them certain terms. I was partly interested in making out that agreement and I believe it came under my eye; that is to say, the draft agreement, but we never received an answer to it.
Q You proposed within the last 12 months, did you not, to the Diphwys Casson Company, to charge them 3s 6d a ton above a certain number, 3s 4d if they carried 10,000 tons and not exceeding 15,000, and if they exceeded 15,000 tons 3s 2d. You propose to charge them under the present circumstances 3s 4d as against the 2s 6d you charge the other slate owners.
A Yes.
Q Binding them down to the same conditions?
A Yes. We proposed that, and it was made upon the same basis as Mr Purcell's agreement, adding so much for the increased number of inclines that the Diphwys Casson Quarry Company had.
Q You proposed to bind them down for 20 years from the present time?
A That is if they chose to accept it.
Q You proposed to bind them to carry all the slates by your line for 21 years?
A Yes, certainly.
Q At the price of 3s 4d against the other 2s 6d?
A Yes.
Q When you talk about inclines, do you mean to say that there are longer inclines on the Diphwys Casson than with regard to some of the other quarries under agreement with you?
A No. The longest incline is the one to the Festiniog Slate Company, or Mr Bernard's, but there are a great number of short ones, in fact, the Diphwys Casson Company instead of having only two, have, I believe, five or six.

Charles Easton Spooner. *FR Archives*

Q The same wagon load does not go over all of them.
A You mean to say the mass of the slate is loaded at the lowest incline?
Q Yes.
A What is the use of the upper ones then?
Q Cannot you imagine the use of the upper ones? To get slates from the different portions of the quarry.
A The mass of our wagons go up all the inclines, slap up to the top.
Q And when you proposed to enter into an agreement with them latterly it was after there was a threat of opposition, was it not?
A No, certainly not. It was they that came to us. We never asked them to come to us. They came to us and we said we would draft an agreement for them.
Q You had previously, during the last two or three years refused to let them enter into an agreement with you?
A Pardon me? You are wrong.
Q Give me an answer. Yes or no.
A I say no. We did not.
Q As a matter of fact have they not sent down an increasing quantity of slate year by year, by your line?
A For the last few years they have.
Q (By a lord) Is that the case with regard to all the slate quarries?
A I believe I may say with regard to all of them, I think I may. There may be one or two exceptions but the large increase of traffic has come from Mr Oakeley's quarry.
Q Now, about the number of inclines. Did you take the trouble to enquire, and if so, do you know that out of every 1,000 tons sent down from the quarry on your line 930 only go down two inclines?

A No, I was not aware of that.

Q And still you base your calculation for charging them so much higher upon the fact of your wagons in their quarry having to go over so many inclines?

A You will recollect, whether the slates go down or not our empty wagons must rest upon the inclines. There must be two empty wagons resting on the inclines even if a ton of slates does not go down for three months.

Q I do not understand that.

A Empty wagons must lie there while the full ones are bringing the slates up. You have not practically looked at it I see.

Q They do not get worn if they lie there?

A Would not? I think they would, a great deal worse. They are exposed to the weather and the wheels are not oiled.

Q When did you ever see them lie in that manner?

A I never said I had seen them so, but I was only answering your supposition.

Q I am asking you questions and you are on your oath.

A Yes. I have given everything on oath.

Q Have you ever seen your wagons lying on the inclines in this way at the Diphwys Casson Company's quarry?

A No. I have not.

Q You say the rails on the inclines were narrow. Have you seen the rails?

A Yes, I have, and I objected to them.

Q Did you measure them?

A No, I did not but I saw them. I did not take out a rule and examine them but I saw that they were narrow.

The exchange illustrates well the tensions that always existed between the railway and the quarries. It also demonstrates the reluctance for any quarry to be allowed an advantage over any other quarry even when market forces might be expected to come into effect. The exception appeared to be the Festiniog Slate Company at Rhiwbach, which was paying 3s 3d per ton and received a rebate based on volume in excess of 3,000 tons that amounted to £340 in one year. It may be that FSC was acting as agent and taking slates from quarries served by its tramway and passing them onto the FR for conveying to Portmadoc; Percival implied as much in his evidence. The quarries that were party to the agreement would pay the same rate for transport to Minffordd as for Portmadoc, the railway keeping for itself the 1½d toll, included in the rate, that would have been payable to the Tremadoc Estate previously.

The Festiniog quarries' desire to compete with Dinorwic and Penrhyn on price meant that they not only had to match the price in the quarry but also at the port. The exchange demonstrates, too, that the FR had learned what influenced its costs to work the traffic. A loaded wagon going down an incline, say nearly 3 tons, needed two wagons going up to balance it, which considering the number of inclines in use meant that there was a considerable number of wagons going round the system as dead weight, earning the railway nothing.

The legality of the railway's modernisation was also called into doubt, as the following exchange, still with Thompson, shows:

Q You know now, do you not, that since the opening of the line you have been running locomotives? You cross the Portmadoc & Beaver Pool Road at two places, first of all near the Diphwys Casson station?

A Is that near the school house you speak of?

Q Yes, near the hotel which has been built there, the Queen's Hotel. You cross the turnpike road there?

A I am not aware whether that is a turnpike road or not. We cross a road.

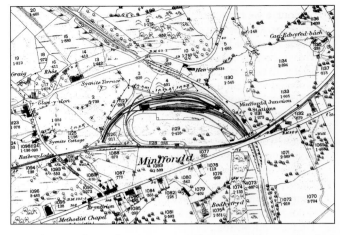

Q When I tell you that it is a turnpike road under an act of parliament that is sufficient, I presume. You also, I think, cross a turnpike road near Portmadoc – near the junction.

A Yes, *here*. That originally was not a turnpike road. It was a private road. They made that private road upon a level crossing, with our permission, after we had made our road.

Q It is a public road under an act of parliament.

A It may be now, but it was a private road then. I recollect when the road instead of going up *here* wound along.

Q We shall never finish if you do not answer my questions.

A It is a matter of dispute as to the facts.

Q You now know, do you not, that you have been running your locomotives over those public roads without any authority to do so?

A Without any authority by act of parliament, but I conceived, until a certain decision in the court of Queen's bench was given that we had full authority, for steam engines are mentioned in our original act of parliament.

Q You are mistaken. Do you not know as a matter of fact that the court of Queen's bench, about a year ago or less, determined that you had no right to run locomotives on your railway – I allude to the case of Jones v the Festiniog Railway Co?

A No, I do not see that. All that that decision of the court of Queen's bench in the case of Jones v the Festiniog Railway Company decides is that we are liable at common law instead of as carriers under the act of parliament.

Q They held, did they not, and you are a lawyer yourself, you were brought up to the bar?

A I did study law at one time but I have not studied it for 30 years.

Q You have read the report of that case I suppose?

A Yes, but not all of it. I read the short judgment of only one of the judges, the judgment of Mr Justice Blackburn.

Q Do you not know that the decision of the court went upon the ground that you had no authority whatever to run locomotives on the line, and that as against the public, they were a nuisance at common law?

A I do not know that that was precisely the ground. You want to put the decision as being that we could not run locomotives. Now the case was another thing altogether; and it was only this – that we were bound to make good the damage done by it.

Q I will not trouble you about it because the case will speak for itself.

A I do not wish to trouble their lordships with law cases indeed.

Q You have nevertheless gone on running your locomotives across these turnpike roads have you not?

A Of course we have, and I would say, if we did not there would be a revolution in the country. How would the traffic get on? I know what it would be in Ireland anyway. They originally made the road with our permission on a level with our line.

Q The road was made over your line after your line was made?

A I think that is not so, I can swear to that, of my own personal knowledge.

Q You know it?

A I know it.

Q Do you mean to say that the road near the Diphwys Casson station was not a public road?

A I am speaking of *this* road.

Q That is only one out of three. You cross a road at Penrhyn, is not that a public road?

A That is a public road.

Q And was a public road when you got your bill in the first instance?

A I think so, but I am not sure of that.

Q That is the one I was asking you about all the time.

A I misunderstood you. I understood you to mean *this* road. I must retract what I said as far as regards the road at Penrhyn.

Q It was a turnpike road at the time your act was obtained?

A No. I don't think it was a turnpike road, I think it was only a parish road.

Q It was a public road, was it not?

A Yes, but not a turnpike road.

Q And the other road at the Diphwys Casson station?

A I don't know. I doubt whether it was in evidence at that time at all.

Q Your railway goes across the turnpike road near Diphwys Casson in a hollow does it not, the ground rises on both sides?

A Do you mean the crossing *there* or *here*?

Q Near the Queen's Hotel.

A The school house?

Q Yes, the road rises up at a sharp gradient.

A Yes, at a very bad gradient, and I should be very glad to have it bridged over.

Q You now propose to get powers by your bill to continue working that road on the level?

A I should be very glad to get powers to bridge it because I consider it a very dangerous thing.

Q That is your opinion, that it is a very dangerous thing and you think a bridge ought to be made there?

A Yes.

Q You will make a bridge there I suppose?

A We do not say that.

Q You propose to take powers to continue the level crossing and I ask you are you prepared to allow that so far as to get a bridge there?

A I think that we tried to arrange that in some way or other and upon considering the matter we found that houses were built so that in fact we could not do it.

Q Are you prepared to do it?

A I am not prepared, single-handed as a director, to say what the company would do, I should have to call together the company.

Q We must know that before the committee sanctions your continuing to cross the road on a level which you admit is dangerous.

A Yes, I think it is dangerous.

The reference to steam engines in the 1832 act concerned the avoidance of smoke nuisance and must have been intended to apply to stationary engines. There was no precedence in the 1830s for steam locomotives being used on such a narrow gauge and they were unlikely to have been in the promoters' minds when the railway was being planned.

The terminating of passenger trains alternately at Dinas and Duffws had been a matter of public complaint, leading to the proposed loop line, called the junction railway on the plan, at Glan y Pwll. For its length, 7 chains 70 links, it took a very long time to build. The plan, incidentally, showed the Dinas route as the main line and that to Duffws as the branch, but the situation had been reversed by the time the authorised works were completed.

Plas Tan-y-bwlch was the Oakeley home, set in about 60 acres with 'very beautiful pleasure grounds' with paths and cascades, rhododendrons and camellias being a feature of the estate. Sheep could get into the grounds from the railway. 'Well, it is a very difficult thing to keep a Welsh sheep out of anything; we have taken every possible means to prevent sheep trespassing' commented Spooner. Oakeley himself blamed the railway for the sheep incursion, apparently overlooking the point that the railway was surrounded by his property and he would not accept that there were breaches in his own boundaries. There had been difficulties in reaching agreement with the Oakeley family over relocating Hafod y Llyn station. The railway had made proposals to W. G. Oakeley's widow, who disliked the steam locomotives, and to W. E. Oakeley without success. The latter had returned a proposed agreement to the railway with amendments calling for demands that could not be met; he wanted a flag station and required that any timber put on a down train there and bound for the quarries should only be charged as if it went directly and not via Penrhyn.

Oakeley believed the station was based on the siding and was there without permission. Replying to leading questions, he agreed that the engines 'go screaming and blowing off their steam', saying, 'the noise is very great and you can hear them all over the house, in the bedrooms and everywhere'. He had a private siding near the Plas that he used to store coal for his quarry. A wagon of coal would be taken past it to Hafod y Llyn and then gravitated back by a porter. When it was needed an up train would not stop to pick it up, because of the inconvenience to passengers, but after the train had gone the porter would take it to Penrhyn and stable it in the siding there to await collection by an up train. There was a water supply nearby that the 1863/4 locomotives sometimes used.

The railway wished to improve public access and make room for a coal siding. There was what Thompson understood to be a 'public right of path' to Hafod y Llyn but it seems that the public preferred to get there by climbing about 20ft from the road and walking along the track or by trespassing on Oakeley's land. Oakeley said that there was no road to it and that it could only be accessed by trespassing. The 1832 act's requirement concerning proximity to Plas Tan-y-bwlch had been breached by several feet. The railway proposed to realign part of the route near the house into a 138 yard-long tunnel to ease the sharpest curve on the railway, less than two chains and indicated on the deposited plans as 'Tyler's cutting'. This had the advantage of moving the line further from the house, although Thompson could not see that Oakeley would get much benefit from it as the railway could hardly be seen from the house which faced away from it anyway. Oakeley agreed that he would not gain anything from the tunnel, especially as 'every engine would naturally whistle before coming to [it]'! A seat had been placed on Oakeley land near the railway, noted Thompson, who had seen children playing near it, and he thought they liked to watch the trains.

Thompson admitted that he knew of three fires started by the locomotives on the estate. He would not object to the railway going past Plas Tan-y-bwlch if it were his property, especially if he 'was getting a large sum of money from every train passing down. There is scarcely a train that goes that has not from £6 to £8 royalty in it.' It was quickly pointed out that this was because of Oakeley's quarrying interests, not because the railway passed close to his house!

Oakeley had submitted two schemes for variations to the route through the estate, but they were ruled out of order because they had not been mentioned in his petition against the bill. One of them required a 550 yard tunnel and a gradient of 1 in 66, at a cost in excess of £11,500 in cash and 7½ tons in reduced capacity on each train. Oakeley himself was not questioned about these schemes when he agreed that he had originally opposed the bill because he was concerned about the effects the limits of deviation would have on the house. He would prefer that no tunnel was made, because of the nuisance of its construction, and if the bill was lost he would do what he could to stop the company using the locomotives: 'I should do so until I got what I required.'

In common with the other quarry owners, Frederick Samuel Percival, co-proprietor of a 'very large quarry', complained about the rates charged by the railway. After ten years of paying 3s 3d per ton the rate had been increased to 3s 9d at three days' notice. He felt obliged to accept the 1863 agreement in consequence. He thought the railway would do very well if it charged only 1½d per ton per mile. In 1868 he had written to the company threatening to repudiate his agreement, describing the company as 'powerful, litigious and unscrupulous' and claiming that the agreement was illegal and unenforceable and that he had been overcharged for years.

Percival was also of the opinion that the railway could be run more efficiently, saying that it could run longer trains more often. The railway had taken, on some occasions, to running up trains with as many as 130 empty wagons but others would have no wagons at all. He thought that the long trains had been put on for show; they had been run over a period of about a year and he agreed that they were for the purpose of making a case before the Lords: 'They are capable of it.'

In horse days there were three sidings (loops) but there was now only one, at Hafod y Llyn, where long trains could pass. The others could not be conveniently worked as 'it would require a larger stock of locomotives'. The line to the harbour had originally been enclosed but the wall had been pulled down '20 or 25 years ago' by agreement with adjacent occupiers. If anything it was safer with steam locomotives than with horses 'because if the slates come down with a rush and touch the horse's heels, he would go on one side'. Pushed to say that it would be better for the railway to be enclosed, to the detriment of the town, Thompson showed evidence of having travelled when he answered: 'You would be quite wrong to fence it in. Look how the railways run through the different towns in Germany.' Later he said: 'The proper thing is to leave it open – going at the sniggling [sic] rate of 3mph there can be no danger.' Probably he meant eel-like.

The Tremadoc Estate was concerned that its rights on the embankment would be lost by the repeal of two clauses in the 1832 act. The estate did not think that the substitute clause proposed for the new act would be specific enough protection. It wanted compensating for the loss of revenue but Spooner riposted that not all traffic would be routed via Minffordd and that the estate would be compensated by the increasing traffic going over the embankment. On one occasion he was asked three times successively if the estate would be compensated. Later, he was told that the embankment had cost £150,000 to build and that 'I believe it is notorious that Mr Madocks and his

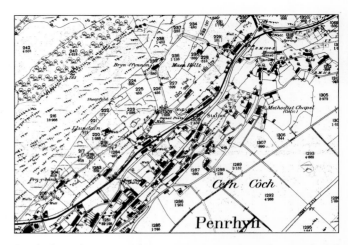

family have been in embarrassment ever since they made it.' When informed of the estate's obligation to maintain the embankment, Spooner replied: '... they have to thank the railway for doing almost everything they do now. The railway company has advanced money towards that lower road, and putting the present embankment in the state it is, and had it not been for that the embankment would have been in the wretched state in which it formerly was.'

There was concern that a wall to be built along the embankment, above the road, to protect other users and their animals from the railway, would be built only if the track was doubled. Thompson explained that the requirement was inserted at the insistence of the House of Lords and the clause had been drafted hurriedly. He pointed out that when he first knew the railway, in 1833, the formation was between 18in and 3ft lower than currently and that the road did not exist; in places the formation was not more than 10ft wide. The road was made much lower than the railway and the proposed wall would increase protection to road users. The railway had increased the width by 2ft and paid £960 to the estate to have the road made, and the company had also loaned the estate £2,000 for the improvement works referred to.

The benefit of developing the inner harbour was the subject of much questioning. Now known as Llyn Bach, it had been built by the Tremadoc estate c1854 and not developed, Spooner describing it as 'perfectly useless'. If it were developed, a movable bridge would have to be installed to replace the Britannia bridge and there was concern that the presence of railway tracks on the site would inhibit the installation and use of a bridge at a later date. Thompson agreed that provision of a swing bridge to open up the inner harbour would be beneficial to the railway by increasing the opportunities for trade.

The railway denied the estate's claim for passenger and some other non-slate tolls and said that it intended to buy out the claim without recognising it and, if necessary, the matter would be resolved in court. Madocks's 1807 act only authorised tolls for animals and pedestrians, while the railway's 1832 act authorised the toll for slate.

One of the examining barristers was clearly not familiar with the layout at Portmadoc and expressed great surprise when Thompson admitted that steam locomotives took wagons to the wharves there. Horses were used to collect them 'and are also used in going up the Croesor line'.

Spooner explained that loaded slate wagons ran by gravity as far as the embankment and were then propelled by locomotive to the port. Later he said that after they had been weighed (at Boston Lodge) they were gravitated across the embankment and then propelled onto the wharves. The passenger carriages could still go by gravity, although the engine was attached to the front to act as a brake. Train lengths varied from 100yd to 400yd – he had known them as long as 440yd. He claimed to have seen 150 empty wagons taken up, coupled behind the passenger carriages and goods and coal wagons. Long trains were a common occurrence and required double-heading. When questioned about the effect of the continuous gradient on the locos, he replied: 'It is a very hard pull for the engines – an engine is very like a horse and requires relief and it gets none going up there.'

The engines had brakes and every sixth 'truck' was braked. To warn of the approach of the gravity trains a brakesman sat on the lead wagon with a horn that he sounded. When the engine was propelling the train 'the engineman always strikes the whistle when the engine is on the south side of the sluice bridge. In addition to that there is a man with a flag that goes in advance of the train right away down to the further end of the line and warns everything to move out of the way.' As Spooner had already said that train speed around the harbour was 4-5mph it can only be imagined that the flag man was pretty fit if that were so!

The matter of the use of sidings (loops) was also raised, the railway only using that at Hafod y Llyn, described as the 'change station'. Spooner said that sidings at other stations, Portmadoc, Penrhyn, Tanygrisiau, Dinas and Duffws, were being used, but clearly not for passing trains – perhaps for stabling while loading/unloading? Hafod y Llyn was shorter than required. Having the second line, Spooner claimed, would be more economic than bringing more sidings into use as passing places. It seems that it was envisaged that the purpose of the second line was to allow loaded and empty trains to be operated without hindrance to each other and regardless of length. Using the sidings as part of the double line, even as a first phase towards developing a double line would, said Spooner, cause delay and increase wear and tear on the rolling stock, apparently demonstrating a lack of understanding of how a single line might be worked intensively.

To convert the railway into a locomotive line had been very expensive, Spooner said, 'We had to alter many of the curves and widen the line in many parts, lay down long sidings, put up stations, signals and various other things required by the Board of Trade.' Some of these works were prerequisite for carrying passengers, others had been carried out many years before locomotives had been contemplated. The sum of £78,000 had been spent from revenue, in addition to the £36,000 original capital (Appendix 1). The net revenue for 1868 was £10,600, a 9% return. The company had wished to capitalise the £78,000

but the House of Lords would only allow £50,000. Spooner produced a document (Table 4) showing how the quarrymen's wages and the value of the slate produced had increased; that the value of the slate had increased by 68%, but the wages by only 63% attracted no comment, neither did the collusion between the quarries over the rates paid for labour and those charged for the finished product. Later, John Whitehead Greaves was to say that the rates for finished slate were governed by the prices charged by Penrhyn. The Festiniog proprietors met annually in the beginning of every year to set the rates, and the Penrhyn and Dinorwic agents also met to decide their prices, but without consulting the Festiniog proprietors, he said.

Between 1865 and the end of 1868, some 392,000 passengers had been carried, rising from 40,000 in 1865 to 94,000 in 1868 (Table 3, p25). Quarrymen had been carried 'gratuitously' for from six to nine months before the locomotives arrived. (This might be an error and may represent the period between the arrival of the passenger carriages and approval being given to open to the public.)

Thompson admitted that he had not participated in any calculations regarding the FR's carrying capacity but thought that the railway could cope with the increasing traffic for a further three years before some action would have to be taken. He thought that doubling the track was a cheaper solution that increasing the number of sidings on the existing line. Spooner said that he had anticipated a big increase in the demand for slate from 1863; 'some of the directors rather thought that I was too sanguine'. The increase in traffic had come about because the quarry proprietors had developed their quarries, he agreed (although the development would have been of no benefit if the railway had not increased its capacity).

The proposed junction with the Cambrian Railways at Minffordd would reduce the rail journey for inland-bound slate by about five miles. Slate routed for the Cambrian via Portmadoc incurred the Tremadoc Estate's toll for crossing the embankment and its port/shipping fee, even though it did not pass into the port and was not shipped from it! There was also a charge by the Croesor Tramway.

Thomas Jarman was the manager of an unidentified quarry that shipped slate via Duffws. The quarry produced 1,000-1,200 tons of slate a year and expected its output to rise to 2,000 tons within 12 months. It was worth between £5,000 and £6,000. He thought the junction with the Cambrian should be made to improve the transportation of his slate to Shrewsbury

Table 4

Table showing comparative increase in wages with the increase value of slates between the years 1851 and 1868

Name of quarry company	Number of workmen	Average daily wages per man	Total annual wages	Amount produced (tons)	Value per ton	Total value	Difference in wages of 1868 and 1851	Difference in value of produce in 1868 and 1851	Difference in favour of producer
Welsh Slate Company									
1868	700	4s 3d	£44,625	37,033	£2 12 3d	£85,631	£17,063	£28,230	£11,167
1851	700	2s 7½d	£27,562	37,033	£1 11 0d	£57,401			
Messrs Holland									
1868	500	4s 3d	£31,875	14,784	£2 12 3d	£38,623	£12,195	£15,708	£3,513
1851	500	2s 7½d	£19,680	14,784	£1 11 0d	£22,915			
J.W. Greaves									
1868	300	4s 3d	£20,250	11,192	£2 12 3d	£29,239	£8,438	£11,892	£3,454
1851	300	2s 7½d	£11,812	11,192	£1 11 0d	£17,347			

and the Midlands. The detour via Portmadoc took time and cost 2s per ton, he said, adding: 'The principal amount of slates from Festiniog will always be sent by sea because the sea freight is cheaper than the railway charge.' He also said: '... with the present arrangement trucks get crammed at the sidings, whereas if it was a double line the empty trucks could go up one line while the loaded ones come down the other line and great time would be saved'. The first part of that statement is probably the most pertinent.

Samuel Holland said that he sent 15,000 tons of slate by rail in 1868, at 3d per ton per mile, and a total of 300,000 tons since the railway opened. He had thought that when the railway was first opened it would have been remunerative carrying 12,000 tons per annum at 6½d per ton per mile; in 1868 it had carried 112,000 tons – an observation that was presumably meant to imply that the railway was profiteering. He had supported the AWCR line to Festiniog but when it was lost he became a party to the 1863 agreement and had not approved of the charges then. He had paid 5s 3d a ton in 1836 and 4s 3d falling to 3s 8d, depending on volume, from 1853. The price achieved by slate had risen considerably since 1852 but the price of labour had increased in a greater proportion.

Holland told how, in 1867, when he 'was driving home [in his dog cart] from Portmadoc, alongside the embankment which is about 10ft higher than the public road, just at the time when I was passing the engine whistled and screamed and so frightened my horse that it jumped against the wall and threw me out, smashing everything, and away it went, although it was a horse accustomed to the railway.' He thought the Duffws level crossing was the most dangerous on the line on account of the population there; a bridge would make it safe and improve the railway's operations because they were sometimes delayed by carts and wagons crossing. The outlay on a bridge would more than offset the crossing keeper's wages.

The railway was making some larger wagons which, said Holland, were '... perfectly useless; too long, too wide and they will not go along the roads within our quarries, and they have been refused by each of the companies'. Although the locomotives propelled the wagons onto the Portmadoc wharves, horses hauled them back to the FR, but he thought that all the harbour work could be carried out by horses. 'In fact, it could be done by gravitation for a very good portion of the way.'

Like the other proprietors, Holland thought that the railway was worked in an expensive manner and that the double line was not required. His complaint over the supply of wagons could be resolved by an injection of capital. He thought the line was worked punctually, largely because it was a single line. He also thought that the port fees were expensive. All the tolls should be reduced, he said, adding: 'The supplies to the people of the neighbourhood ... all of whom are indirectly employed by us and of course if they have to pay more for the carriage of goods we have to pay a higher rate of wages to meet that.' He did not know the current rates for up goods.

Referring to the railway's origins, Holland was asked 'How was it that you were a promoter of the original scheme you are not named in the original act?'

A 'No. I was a promoter so far, that the late Mr Henry Archer and myself, in some measure, got it up and I assisted him at the time. I had nothing to do with bringing in the act.

Q Did you become a shareholder?

A I was a shareholder for some time and I afterwards sold my shares to the late Mr Spooner, Mr Spooner's father.

Re-examined, he agreed that he wished he was still a shareholder, with 30% of the capital!

Table 5

Quantity of slates shipped at Portmadoc

Quarter ending 30 June 1869

	By ship			By rail		
	Tons	Cwt	Qtr	Tons	Cwt	Qtr
Welsh Slate Co	11,038		1	215	5	2
S. Holland Slate Co	5,038	15	1	41	13	
Mathew & Son Slate Co	4,100	2		13		
J. W. Greaves Slate Co	3,600	1	2			
F. S. Percival Slate Co	3,330	4		69	19	
Diphwys Casson Slate Co	2,114	11	3	512	5	1
Festiniog Slate Co	2,098	8	1	412	10	1
Croesor United Slate Co	837	11		14		
Maenofferen	810		3	5	15	
Cwmorthin Slate Co	628	6	2	636	19	
Rhosydd Slate Co	223	5		8	2	
Cwt y Bugail Slate Co	174	16				
New Craig Ddu Slate Co	74	1	1			
Richard Williams & Co	50	14		6	10	
Totals	34,118	17	2	1,935	19	

Questioned on behalf of the quarry proprietors, Spooner had to deal with a claim that they also should benefit, by reduced tolls, from the increased traffic being sent to the FR. The exchange is enlightening:

A As engineer to the company would you not confess that we, the slate proprietors, ought to share in the benefit derived from that increased traffic that we have sent down to you?

Q You do.

A How are we on better terms than we were in 1863?

Q By your increased traffic.

[by the committee] Are they to have lower tolls, the counsel wants to know?

A Yes. I am quite aware that it is that that he wants to know.

Q Will you give an answer to that?

A We granted you very low tolls in 1863 and you entered into a mutual agreement with the Festiniog Railway Company for the carriage of slates, and you had an agreement until the expiration of your lease with Mr Oakeley ... Those terms were before settled on a sliding scale according to the total quantity sent down. That has now reached the maximum of 110,000 tons and therefore anything over that quantity would be charged 2s 6d and you have the benefit of that reduced charge.

Q Are all the other quarries which are not in the agreement on the same footing?

A Except as to terminals.

Q Therefore the only result of having gone into the agreement in 1863 is that we are worse off for it?

A You are better off because you would be charged terminals but for that.

Q What will they be charged for terminal charges?

A That has not been considered – it will be time to consider it when we have our act.

Q Then you do not think that we ought to derive any benefit from the increased traffic that we have brought to you?

A You are deriving it.

The quarries that were parties to the agreement were allowed 18 hours for loading and 12 hours for unloading before demurrage was charged. Diphwys Casson, not a party to the agreement, was allowed 12 hours for loading and six hours for unloading.

There was confusion about the extent of the railway's parliamentary powers at Portmadoc, there being a common misconception that the parliamentary line ended at the bridge; the 1832 act described it as 'from on or near a certain shipping quay at Portmadock, commencing at the north-western end of the sluice bridge there.' The committee chairman adjudicated that the word 'commencing' applied to the quay not the railway and Spooner confirmed that the railway terminated 'at the entrance to the Welsh Slate Company's wharf'. Saying 'I recollect this place since I was a lad of 12 or 13', he explained, with much pointing at the plan, that there was only one quay when the railway was built and it wasn't next to the bridge. The 1830s plans were not as detailed as the plans now required to be deposited, leaving room to question the promoters' precise intentions.

Goods arriving at Portmadoc via the Cambrian, with destinations on the FR, were transported across Portmadoc by cart using the Cambrian's carriers, but in future the transfer would take place at Minffordd. The line on the embankment and around the port was a particular bottleneck. Some time earlier, 12 to 18 months, an inefficient employee 'at the upper end' whose job it was to deal with wagon requisitions had been responsible for the railway having to pay over £200 in demurrage on incoming coal deliveries.

At the time of the hearings, there was considerable concern about how the FR's extra line could be accommodated alongside the Croesor & Portmadoc Railway's line, presumably the unbuilt Borth y Gest extension, the FR hoping to come to an accommodation with the CPR. The local board objected to the railway crossing the road; Spooner said that it did not cross the road, although it did cross the bridge, parallel to the road. There were existing piers that could be used to widen the bridge for two tracks without affecting the road.

On the subject of accidents, Spooner told of one of Holland's miners who jumped off a truck when it was in motion, broke his leg and died subsequently, and about the employee who died after jumping off a loco in 1865. A slate train had been derailed in the dark when fencing had been blown across the line in a winter storm. A passenger train had been derailed once, causing damage to the locomotive tender. The train had run into a slate train that had overrun its section, and if Spooner's response was accurately recorded, he seemed to blame the loco driver for not braking in time, rather than the gravity train brakesman for failing to control his train!

It was, of course, too early for Spooner to assess or react to the impact of the first double engine, *Little Wonder*, on the line. The loco was due to be delivered, but when he said: '... we are working with double engines and heavy trains' as part of his justification for not bringing more passing places into use, he was not referring to the Fairlie, for he went on to say that sometimes there were so many wagons to go back to the quarries that 'we are obliged every now and then to take coupled engines'. About the number of locomotives, he said that there were six; asked if that was sufficient, he answered: 'Yes, we are getting another and that will be seven.' He forecast that the fleet would be doubled in size within five years!

John Whitehead Greaves, the proprietor of Llechwedd slate quarry, had resigned as the FR's treasurer when he had decided to oppose the bill. Livingston Thompson had accepted his resignation but he was still receiving the pay list and he had not heard of anyone else being appointed in his place. He remained a shareholder with 12 £25 shares, and sent all his slate by the FR. He had objected to the dividend because he thought the traders should benefit from reduced rates. The town had grown because of the slate trade and he estimated that £600,000 had

been invested in the quarries. Three years earlier a banker had told him that his branch was paying out £20,000 per month for wages. He did not share his profits with his workforce but paid higher wages when times were good, probably because there would be competition for the labour. After Greaves had been carefully guided through a list of competitive sources for slate, one of the committee members showed great insight when he asked: 'But still, slate has maintained its price, has it not?'

Of the company Greaves said that '... they are here in order to convert a tramway into a railway... I consider they are not a railway company and that they come to get powers to make a railway', agreeing that the FR had gone to Parliament to legalise the locomotive position. He thought the company could pay a satisfactory dividend if it charged 1½d per ton per mile. The line was well managed, he thought, and lower rates would induce efficiency, adding '... low prices produce good management in all cases'. He also considered it reasonable to object to the bill, and perhaps prevent legal approval being given for the use of locomotives, and therefore prevent the company from fulfilling the commitment made in 1863, because the 1863 agreement, that he had been party to, was in need of revision.

Greaves felt that there was no need for the line to be doubled; as a director he had heard no complaints about the way the traffic was handled and he had no complaint himself. He thought that three times the present traffic could be handled with the present engines. There was capacity to handle 140 wagons a day yet 30 wagons could handle the traffic offering. The tolls could be reduced if the line was unaltered. There were complaints from the public about charges for back traffic, which were lower for the quarries. He thought the charges should be the same and he did not think that large traders should get a better rate, and as an example, the quarries paid 2s 2d per ton for coal, the public 2s 11d; the lower was acceptable. He did not believe that the line would be doubled if the powers were given, the promoters were 'men of business and men of sense'.

Table 6

Comparison of tolls and rates

Portmadoc to Duffws 13 miles (Festiniog)	Portmadoc to Pwllheli (Cambrian)
Sugar 6s 8d	5s 10d
Treacle 8s 4d	5s 10d
Grocery 10s	7s 6d
Flour 5s 10d	4s 2d
Soap and candles 6d each or 10s per ton	6s 8d per ton
Bags [of] rice 7d each or 10s	5s 10d per ton
These rates are station to station or in other words the sender or consignee has to perform the cartage	These rates with the exception of flour include collection and delivery

---

Local railways were also keen to contribute to the objections. William Davies was a merchant in Festiniog and managing director of the Festiniog & Blaenau Railway. He also thought that 1½d per ton per mile was a reasonable rate and thought the 2d per ton appropriate for the back traffic. The proposed maximum rates he thought unreasonably high. The FR was proposing a minimum rate of four miles, but Davies thought two miles would be acceptable. The FBR had a short distance rate of 6d per ton, inclusive of terminal charges but excluding delivery. He received beer via the FR at 5s 3d per ton plus 8d per ton for loading: five barrels were rated as one ton and 5½ barrels were loaded on a wagon but when there were 10 or 12 wagons of beer the FR charged him for 1¼ tons per wagon instead, as he thought, of 'lumping' the half barrels together and charging him 'a quarter and a fraction on the total' so on a ten-wagon load the FR charged for 12½ tons whereas he thought it should be 11 tons. He complained but it made no difference. Davies said that the FBR paid no dividend, had only eight wagons and carried workmen, making six return journeys, at 1s per week.

The Cambrian Railways was represented by Elijah Elias, its traffic manager who was its general manager within a year. He too said that the FR's rates were excessive. If the FR charged the proposed rate of 2s 6d on a train of 50 wagons it would earn 15s per train-mile, so allowing 50% for overheads this would give 7s 6d net profit per train mile. He added that the average earnings per train mile by all railways was 5s 3d. He produced a chart comparing the FR's rates with the Cambrian's over a similar distance, Portmadoc to Pwllheli (Table 6, p35); there was no coastal competition with the Cambrian route, although Elias admitted that rates were adjusted to prevent the traffic going by sea. Another chart listed the data for the carriage of slates extracted from 61 Acts of Parliament.

Elias claimed that it was normal for railway companies to provide rolling stock at no charge to the users, 'they are only too glad to find rolling stock where they can find traffic', and that the FR was 'quite exceptional' in wishing to relate tolls to the provision of rolling stock. The FR should charge less, he said, because it only cost £9,000 per mile to build, unlike the Cambrian that cost over £20,000 per mile. He didn't think that the fact of the Cambrian being a general carrier and the FR having a specialised traffic on a constant gradient should make any difference. Having said that the rate should be the same whether the consignor sent 100,000 tons a year or two tons, he was then persuaded to agree that the Cambrian did adjust its rates according to market conditions.

Joseph Kellow was a quarry engineer and proprietor who had travelled widely and had visited many quarries, both abroad and locally. Once again, he did not like the tolls; he thought the FR should be cheaper because it was cheap to build. He had been to see the Penrhyn and Dinorwic railways especially for the hearing. They were both shorter than the FR, he said, and Penrhyn had the same number of trucks, about 720; two trains of 24 wagons, each hauled by three horses, followed each other along the line and made eight return runs a day and carriage cost 5d per journey for six miles. Dinorwic had a locomotive and made five trips per day at a cost of 1s 2d per ton per mile. The lack of rigour in his comparison is noticeable.

Henry Robertson was the high sheriff for Merionethshire and a civil engineer of 'some eminence', 'in practice' he acknowledged. Later knighted, he had engineered the Shrewsbury & Chester Railway and lines in the Dee valley and mid-Wales and attended the hearings to represent the Tremadoc Estate. He thought the railway could accommodate more traffic if it had more sidings at the termini and in the middle of the line. He lived in Bala and imported foreign timber via Gloucester; Portmadoc was, he said: 'the only good sheltered port we have in Cardigan Bay' and called for provision to be made for a lifting bridge to enable the inner harbour to be developed. Improvement of the harbour, together with completion of the railway between Bala and Dolgellau, would allow him to import via Portmadoc. He was also involved in promoting a direct line between Bala and Portmadoc that would be of use in this respect.

Thomas Pritchard had been the FR's traffic manager for five years. At the dinner held to mark the introduction of steam locomotives in 1865, he was acknowledged by Holland as the company's oldest servant, having then been employed by it for 31 years. In Parliament he produced a list of the 1866 tolls and had to read it out. FR trucks were used on the Festiniog & Blaenau Railway without charge, he said, and the gunpowder merchants had 'proper' vans of their own 'for the purpose'. Under cross-examination he was criticised for the omission of slate from the list of tolls:

Q ... How does that happen?
A They are under contract with most of the quarries.
Q Not with all of them?
A Not with all of them.
Q Then that answer will not do. Try again – what is the explanation of slates not being here?
A Well it is clumped in the same as the first one, only it is not named.
Q Do you mean that slates are charged as coals, sand and iron?
A If it is down.
Q But it is not down and I want to know why it is not down. Coals, sand and iron are down but slates are not. You tell me that they belong to the same class. Why are they not down?
A I cannot say.
Chairman
    Is there any provision in your Act of Parliament with regard to slates?
Q Do you know anything about that? Is there any provision with regard to slates in your Act of Parliament?
A I cannot say.
Q You are an odd sort of manager. Do you really manage the traffic of the whole line?
A I do the goods and see that there is a supply of trucks sent up to the quarries.
Q Is there anybody else who manages the line in other respects?
A Yes.
Q Who?
A Mr Spooner.
Q He is the engineer, is he not?
A He is the secretary and manager.
Q Engineer, secretary and manager?
A Yes.
Q Then you are only a manager under him apparently?
A Yes.
Q All that you know about this paper is that it comes into your hands as the company's paper?
A Yes, and that is the rate we charge.
Q But you cannot give me any explanation of it?

Poor Pritchard. Probably the first time that he'd ever been out of Wales and he was attacked in Parliament. As the list had Spooner's (printed) signature on it, it was hardly reasonable to expect Pritchard to be able to justify it. The exchange should have brought home to the committee that the FR was like no ordinary railway.

Edward Vale Bilby was another employee, the Duffws stationmaster. A railway servant watched the trains over the level crossing, he explained. Four or five years previously there had been an accident 'through the carelessness of one of the railway servants who broke the rules by allowing a person to ride with him in a slate wagon coming up'. He gave every facility to traffic bound for the Festiniog & Blaenau line, he said, the question implying that the FR might have hindered the FBR's traffic. He had seen 'more than 120 wagons going under the care of two brakesmen'.

A receipt exists dated 9 October 1869 and signed by a Thomas Roberts. It acknowledges receipt of the sum of £36 5s 8d from Edward Breese as 'the amount due to me for attending as a witness before the committees of both houses of parliament on behalf of the lessees of slate quarries against the Festiniog Railway bill'. Strangely, Roberts is not listed as a witness in any of the minutes of evidence seen by the author. It has to be wondered why he was paid so much and why it took so long to pay him. David Lloyd George was to start his legal career as an articled clerk in Breese's office; the practice is still in business.

Entitled 'an act for enabling the Festiniog Railway Company to widen and improve their railway, and to raise further money; and for other purposes', the Festiniog Railway Act, 1869 gained royal assent on 26 July. By it the 1832 and 1838 acts were repealed, with 13 sections of the 1832 act excluded from the repeal and quoted in full in a schedule.

The company's 1832 incorporation was confirmed, 'notwithstanding the repeal' and for the purpose of the act the company was to 'continue to exist, and accordingly, and as from the passing of the act of 1832, without intermission shall continue to be one body corporate, by the name of "The Festiniog Railway Company"'. It was also allowed to continue holding the property and rights that it owned prior to the passing of the act. All of the company's existing activities were protected, including the employment of all officers and servants. Other aspects covered by the act included:

- The quorum of general meetings should be five persons representing, either in their own right or as proxies, capital shares to the nominal value of £5,000.
- Voting at general meetings was to be one vote per share or per £25 stock.
- There should be five directors and the number could be reduced to not less than three. Directors needed £500 in shares or stock to qualify as a director. The quorum for a directors' meeting was three, unless there were only three directors when it could be two.
- Andrew Durham, Charles Gaussen, George Augustus Huddart, John Graves Livingston and Livingston Thompson were nominated as the first directors, to serve until the first ordinary meeting following the commencement of the act at which time they could be replaced; they were eligible for re-election.
- The original share capital of £36,185 10s was converted into capital stock.
- The capital consisted of three sections: the capital stock, the existing share capital of £36,185 10s; additional capital stock, the capital investment paid from revenue, £50,000; and additional share capital, £90,000 to be raised to fund the works authorised by the act.
- The capital stock, £86,185 10s, was to be allocated pro rata to the holders of the original share capital. This compensated the shareholders for the reduced dividends experienced while profits were being spent on capital works and slightly more than doubled the value of their original holdings! With the dividends that they had received their investment in the FR was proving to be very worthwhile!
- The company was permitted to borrow up to £12,000, including the £5,170 already borrowed, on mortgage. It was also authorised to borrow up to £30,000 when the new capital was fully subscribed and half of it paid up.
- The company could issue debenture stock.
- The line could be doubled throughout its length with the proviso that it should not take more of the Traeth Mawr embankment than necessary; no wharf or building was to be built on the embankment, neither was the company to remove any material from it, nor could it reduce the embankment's height.
- The company could not oppose any application for the old sluice bridge to be replaced by an opening bridge.
- Two branches were permitted. One 'commencing by a junction near the Minffordd level crossing and terminating near the bridge by which the company's railway is carried over the Cambrian Railway [sic]', two furlongs 75 links in length, and the second connecting 'the company's Duffws branch with their main line to Rhiwbryfdir', 7 chains and 70 links long.
- A wall not less than three feet high was to be built along the length of the Traeth Mawr embankment, dividing the railway from the roadway, within 12 months of the act being made.
- The turnpike roads at Rhiw Plas and at Duffws were to be bridged.
- The company was empowered to install aqueducts or pipelines at Rhiw Goch, Creuau and Duffws.
- Compulsory purchase powers were to be exercised within three years and construction completed within five years.
- The tariffs legislated did not apply to special trains.
- For passengers, articles and animals, the minimum charge was set at four miles and for a fraction of a mile over four miles the company could charge as for one mile except 'in proportion to the number of quarters of a mile contained in such fraction ... a fraction of a quarter of a mile shall be deemed a quarter of a mile'. The same logic was to be applied to tons except for stone and timber.
- The company had the right to buy out or commute the 1d per ton toll payable to the Tremadoc Estate on such terms as it could arrange.
- The Crown's rights in the foreshore and all the rights granted to Madocks, his heirs and assigns were reserved.
- The railway was not exempted from any present or future general acts relating to railways.

By this act the company was effectively reincorporated. The procedure of repealing the original acts except for certain clauses that were cited in the new act is unusual. The usual practice, even at the time, is for powers that are no longer required or that have become irrelevant to be repealed.

For the first time the railway was formally brought within the ambit of general railway legislation. Except where expressly varied by the 1869 act, the general acts were incorporated with and formed part of it.

To celebrate, the board declared a 4% dividend for the second half of 1868, having deferred a decision until it knew the outcome of its parliamentary application.

As an aside, in 1870, *The Times* had this to say about the company's financial position: 'The original capital of the company was £36,185, and all the extra money which has been laid out upon the line has been taken from revenue. In this sense, therefore, as the net revenue of the line is £10,622, it appears that the line yields a dividend of 29½% of the original capital. A sum of £50,000, however, paid out of revenue for improvements and reconstructions, has been capitalised, making the total £86,185. In this sense the net revenue of the line yields a dividend of 12½%. Whichever way the fact is stated, it is a most remarkable one, and must fill many a shareholder's heart with envy.'

Had the works been carried out as proposed, substantial parts of the railway would have been realigned. As it was, although the company started to buy property to double its formation, it was overtaken by a significant improvement in its operating technology.

TRANSHIPMENT

Top: **The GWR exchange yard in the 1920s. Judging by the size of the stockpiles, the slate trade has been slow.** *FR Archives*

Above: ***Prince*** **shunting in Minffordd yard on 14 August 1913.** *Author's collection*

Above: **Transhipping slate at Minffordd.** *Author's collection*

Below: **Minffordd yard, seen from the FR main line in the 1920s. Davies Brothers' wharf, in front of the Maenofferen sheds, was the last to remain in use. There are several coal wagons on the rearmost standard gauge siding.** *Author's collection*

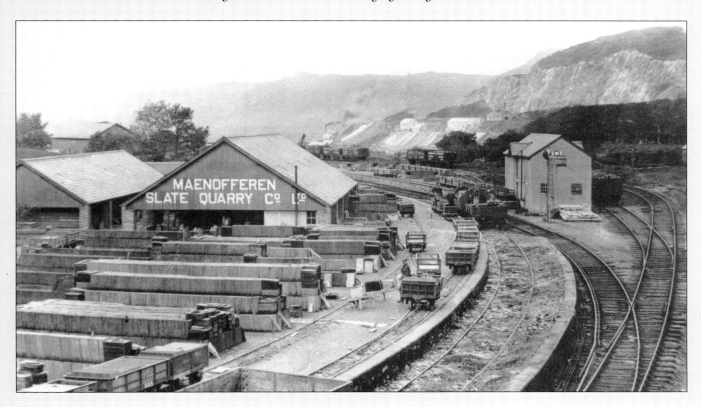

4

The Spooner heyday

1869-1880

Having made some effort to secure the company's new powers with its 1869 Act of Parliament, the board appeared to take a break from business, meeting for the first time under the new regime on 14 September. The directors designated by the act, Andrew Durham, Charles Gaussen, John Graves Livingston, George Augustus Huddart and Livingston Thompson, were present, along with Charles Easton Spooner, manager, secretary and engineer. Durham was 'called to the chair'.

The board resolved to borrow £12,000 on the most favourable terms, to purchase land for sidings and station accommodation at Penrhyn and Tanygrisiau and through the villages of Penrhyn and Tanygrisiau, to treat for land for Creuau station and to give a guarantee to the manager of the National Provincial Bank. The shareholders were circulated that they could take up 4½% preference shares pro rata to their existing holdings.

The directors met again on 17 September to deal with correspondence. Oakeley's agent, Major Johnstone, had written complaining about a fire in the woods; he was informed that improved spark arresters had been installed in the locomotives. The landlord of the Sportsman Hotel in Portmadoc had requested support in maintaining an omnibus service to meet the trains; it was agreed to pay him ten guineas per annum on condition that all arriving trains were met. This arrangement was cancelled by the board in August 1874.

A letter from F. S. Percival suggested that at least one of the quarry proprietors was still unhappy with the rates; Spooner was directed to reply: 'As regards the question you ask, viz: what the directors intend to charge you for the future, they request me to say they are sorry to find you suppose the new act alters your position as they cannot see it does so, in any respect.' The directors decided to take counsel's opinion on the issue.

On 8 October, they resolved to write to Hugh Beaver Roberts, of the Croesor & Portmadoc Railway, advising him that the directors would not entertain his proposal to sell or merge his line to or with the company. The Welsh Slate Company was refusing to pay demurrage for wagons kept over 24 hours. Fifty new slate wagons were to be made to 'the same dimensions as the larger ones'.

By 4 May 1870, £8,740 in preference shares had been taken up; Thompson and Huddart had each placed £4,120 without payment of brokers' commission. When, in September 1871, it had been found impossible to place the remainder, the board decided to agree to a 3% commission being paid on future placings. Given the enthusiasm of the national press for the company this difficulty cannot be explained.

The order to build the branch lines at Minffordd, stipulating that the Cambrian built its own siding, and at Dinas (Glan y Pwll), was given in September 1871. Other quarries were also refusing to pay demurrage and a standard letter was drafted to be sent to them in a spirit of 'liberality and friendly feeling', the directors offered a 50% discount in respect of the amounts outstanding before 31 December. Percival had written again, convinced that the statutory 2s 6d rate included the supply of wagons; a reply was drafted setting out the conditions under which his slate would be carried:

Right: **Dinas was the original Festiniog terminus, serving Holland's Cesail quarry. It was equipped with a station house and, for reasons that will remain a mystery, a two-storey loco shed. The stationmaster's family and *The Princess* pose for a photograph** *c*1870. *FR Archives*

Below right: **Robert Francis Fairlie.** *FR Archives*

Below left: **A classic view of Portmadoc harbour, seen from the Garth in 1879. The FR's zero point was out of view on the left. The station is concealed by the shipping on the right.** *Author's collection*

'... Should you elect not to be under agreement the directors will charge you the sum of 3s 3d per ton which will include all the following services:

1 For carriage of your slates in the wagons of the company from the terminus at Diphwys to the terminus at Portmadoc of the Festiniog Railway.
2 For the use of the company's wagons off their line to the quarry banks for loading only as heretofore.
3 For like use of the company's wagons from Portmadoc terminus to and from your wharf for unloading only as heretofore.
4 For return haulage of empty wagons to upper terminus at Diphwys.
5 For placing the empty wagons on turnouts provided for them so as to be ready for your service.
6 For all services attendant on such carriage of your slates over the company's authorised line but the haulage from the Portmadoc terminus to your wharf for unloading (if preferred by the company) will be charged for separately and in addition to the above sum. And the above sum does not cover any demurrage, the charge for detention of the company's wagons will form a separate and additional item on your account to the company and you will take notice that the above charge of 3s 3d will be subject to revision from time to time and that the directors however desirous cannot undertake that the supply to you of empty wagons shall be continuous and always sufficient for your regular daily traffic.

As regards the terms of a new agreement in lieu of that one at present in force, the directors are prepared to offer you an agreement without any sliding scale, at the simple rate of 2s 10d for each ton, such agreement to be for the entire term of your quarry lease, and the company will not consent to be bound under a penalty to supply wagons within a specified time but will undertake to supply a sufficient number of wagons for your average daily traffic and I am further requested to inform you that the directors will not deem themselves bound by these offers unless you accept them on or before the 26th instant.'

On the same occasion, a letter to Diphwys Casson covering the same ground was much simpler:

'...directors are prepared to undertake the carriage of your slates on the following terms:
1. Length of term – 21 years
2. Rates, including all services as now performed, 3s per ton
3. The charge for haulage from the company's terminus at Portmadoc to your wharf will (if done by the company) be charged for separately.
4. On your company approving of these terms, the matter of demurrage and other details of covenants can be given you.'

It was February 1877 before a settlement was reached with Percival, when the board agreed 'to strike off the difference between £275 and £620 19s 7d or £345 19s 7d in Mr Percival's account'.

A decision to 'dispose of two of the small locomotives', made at the May 1870 meeting provides a hint that something was happening on the railway that was not being mentioned at board level. In fact a development was taking place that was to have a considerable influence on it and its position in the wider railway world. (The disposal decision was reversed in February 1874.)

Robert Francis Fairlie had written to the company on 25 September 1868. He had patented a form of articulated locomotive that had a double boiler with central fireboxes and two four-wheeled power bogies. The benefit was a flexible locomotive with increased traction and distributed adhesive weight; it could be used on existing track and could cope with sharp curves. George England had ceased trading and Fairlie had taken over his works under the auspices of the Fairlie

41

Engine & Steam Carriage Company. He was looking for customers and the FR doesn't seem to have needed much persuasion to try the Fairlie concept as a locomotive was ordered; it was delivered in July 1869.

Named *Little Wonder*, it did not take long for it to become apparent that the loco lived up to its name. Slightly less than twice the weight of two 1867 engines, it was soon established that it was capable of hauling much greater loads than the increase in size might have suggested. Spooner and Fairlie were quick to see the opportunity for promotion and set up a series of public trials, called experiments, in February, June and July 1870.

The trials involved testing for stability on the embankment and running *Welsh Pony* with up to 50 loaded slate wagons to see how far it would get before stalling, then reducing the load and trying to restart on the gradient. A load of 127 tons (50

loaded wagons plus 3½ tons of passengers) was impossible once the gradient was encountered but 63 tons (26 loaded wagons plus 1½ tons of passengers) was possible at 5mph. Then *Little Wonder* took a load of 186½ tons (72 loaded wagons) and walked away at 5mph. *Welsh Pony* and *Little Giant* were tried on a similar load but only got to within 50yd of Minffordd crossing.

On one occasion, *Little Wonder* took a train weighing 141 tons, including the loco, 22 wagons of coal, 21 wagons of slate, two loaded bogie timber wagons, two barrier wagons and a workmen's carriage, 407ft in length, from Portmadoc to Dinas in 70 minutes, exclusive of stops. On another occasion, *Little Wonder* ran from Portmadoc to Dinas with a train of 140 empty slate wagons and seven loaded coal wagons, a total of 100 tons, 1,323ft long; the maximum speed was 16½mph, the average 12½mph. On the return journey the average speed was 25mph

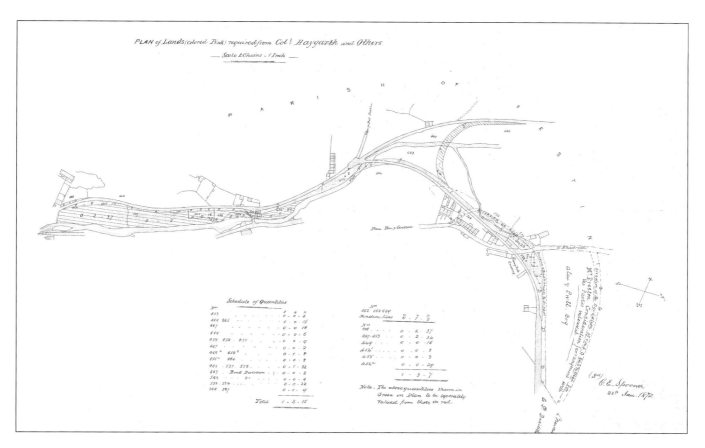

Above: **The land needed for the Glan y Pwll loop line, 23 January 1872.** *Author's collection*

Above left: **The first Fairlie,** *Little Wonder*, **at Portmadoc, probably before the first bogie carriages were delivered in 1872. Four Ashbury carriages are next to the locomotive, followed by three Brown, Marshalls.** *Author's collection*

Left: *Little Wonder* **posed with a very long train at Creuau, the site of Tan-y-bwlch station,** *c*1871. **It is probably Saturday midday, and the quarrymen, travelling home from the quarries, can be seen perching on their so-called carriages.** *FR Archives*

and the maximum 30mph! On 16 June 1870, *Little Wonder* was taken to Duffws in 77½ minutes. The train, described as an 'ordinary mixed one', weighed 95 tons and was 1,245ft long. There was little perceptible oscillation or vibration on the engine, there was drizzle and the rails were greasy, so there was frequent sanding; the speed sometimes reached 20mph. Returning with the passenger stock the speed once again reached 30mph.

There is no mention of these activities in the board's minutes, so one can only assume that they were considered Spooner's private ventures; like his father, Spooner conducted a consultancy business whilst working for the railway. Included in one of the trains was the 'boat carriage', reckoned to be Spooner's private vehicle; it looked like a boat with a prow and a sail mounted on wheels. It is thought that he had it hauled up the line by a service train and then gravitated down in it, using the sail to cross the embankment.

Writing to the Board of Trade on 4 March 1870, Tyler said: 'When the Festiniog Railway was first opened for passenger traffic, the Board of Trade, on my recommendation, made it a condition that the speed should be limited to 10 or 12 miles an hour. And this was done on account of the narrowness and lowness of the works, the condition of the permanent way, and

the novelty of applying locomotive power to so narrow a gauge. Since that time the permanent way has been materially improved, and the greater part of it has been relaid with heavier rails, fished at the joints. The system has also been thoroughly tested, and there appear to have been no accidents to passengers. But the narrowness and lowness of the works remain, and this is now the weakness of the line. ... The speed appears to have been increased from time to time, as the permanent way has been improved, and it would now, I think, be only right to release the company from the obligation which was imposed on them in this respect, on their opening to passengers. As they have hitherto conducted the traffic with safety to the public for so many years, the question of speed might now properly be left to their own discretion, not with the idea that they are to run their passenger trains at the comparatively high speed of which the little line has so curiously shown itself capable, under the system of low centres of gravity, which has so wisely been adopted for the rolling stock, but with confidence that they will keep well within that speed, and allow ample margin for all contingencies...'

It was a consequence of the acquisition of *Little Wonder* that the scheme for doubling the track was never undertaken, although there was no formal decision to that effect. Indeed, in September 1871 the board resolved that 'such land should be secured as speedily as possible'. The work that was carried out was taken at a steady rate. Minffordd station was authorised in April 1873 and work was obviously under way at Tan-y-bwlch; in February 1874 it was minuted that 'no further expenditure to be made on Tan-y-bwlch station'. Four years later, the coal yard there was ordered at a cost of £40; it was to be let out at £3 to £4 per annum. In February 1879 a land exchange took place at Minffordd with Mrs Casson.

The right of approach to Tanygrisiau station was to be inserted in the sale deed in August 1874 and the land purchase, for £300, was agreed in February 1876. Securing the land for the loop line took several years; in 1875 it was resolved to buy

Charles Spooner's house, Bron y Garth, overlooks the Festiniog Slate Company's wharf at Portmadoc. The Oakeley wharf, Cei Newydd, and the FR station are behind, right. *Commercial postcard/Author's collection*

a plot at Glan y Pwll and in 1877 Spooner was to secure the land needed for the loop line near Dinas junction and at Glan y Pwll. It was February 1880 before the board was in a position to consider tenders! Then the board instructed that 'John Roberts contractor be invited to reduce his tender for contract of the loop line to about as low as Owen Edwards's tender for contract before the company can accept it, on his failing to close, then to accept Owen Edwards's tender for the works.' In February 1878, £150 was allocated to lengthen Penrhyn platform, then, in August, Spooner was to produce plans and estimates for both Penrhyn and Tanygrisiau stations, including sidings. The plans were approved and authorised for construction subject to tenders being obtained the following February.

Four accidents were reported to the Board of Trade between October and December 1876. On 3 October, the door of an empty wagon came open in the long tunnel, derailing the wagon and breaking several chairs. Then, on 11 October, seven empty slate wagons and two loaded coal wagons ran away from Duffws and collided with a stop block at Glan y Pwll Junction. The slate wagons and the adjacent wall and fencing were damaged but the coal wagons were unharmed. The accident was caused by the shunting guard not securing the wagons. A locomotive ran into the stop block at Duffws and was derailed, both it and the track being slightly damaged, on 19 October, and finally, on 8 December, a wheel came off a slate wagon in a train near Portmadoc; the wagon was seven years old and there was no sign of any flaw in the tyre, defects in tyres being a cause of concern at the Board of Trade at the time. These must be considered typical and probably to be expected considering the nature of the gradient. Not all incidents were reported to the Board of Trade and of those that were, not all warranted further investigation.

Changes for the railway's main station were in mind in August 1877, when Spooner was requested to prepare plans

and specifications for an addition to the existing station at Portmadoc. Comprising an office adequate to accommodate Spooner and his assistants and suitable for a boardroom, the cost was not to exceed £350. Spooner produced three plans in February 1878, the board approving the building on plan No 3 to be adapted to the site of plan No 2; £800 was approved to be spent. Tenders for the goods shed were to be obtained in August 1878, 'not over £250 if possible', and work started.

Colonel Francis H. Rich made the first of a series of visits to the FR on behalf of the Board of Trade on 25 March 1872, when he inspected Minffordd station and yard. The new mineral siding into the yard started at the station where there was a small cabin for issuing tickets. Although the company intended to replace it with a permanent structure, he was unhappy that intending passengers would have to cross both tracks to get their tickets and then cross them again to board their train. He would not, therefore, sanction the station's use by passengers until the need to cross the railway on the level had been removed. He also expected the pedestrian access from the proposed Cambrian platform under the FR to be built. In addition, the distant signal on the north-east side of the station was to be moved 100yd further way and interlocked with the mineral line points. A crossover between the mineral line and the 'old line' was to be removed and the crossover between the two lines at the south-west end of the station was to be interlocked with the station signals. The work was done to his satisfaction by 16 July.

He inspected Tan-y-bwlch and Dduallt on 14 April 1874, finding that Tan-y-bwlch was acceptable except for want of a repeater for the down distant signal. Spooner had told him that trains would pass 'at the reverse side to what is customary, as Mr Spooner ... thinks it the most convenient and safest method of working the mineral traffic'. Rich did not think it desirable that 'trains should pass each other at different sides at particular stations but as it can be changed without any difficulty or expense at any time that it is found objectionable, I submit that the mode of working be left to the management and not interfered with'. Of Dduallt he said that it 'was taken out a few years since and has since been partly restored by the desire and according to an agreement with the landlord' and that it required signals, distant signals and trap points locked with the main line points and signals before it could be used.

Other capital work in progress in September 1871 was being carried out at Boston Lodge where six coal wagons, six timber trucks, six flour wagons, two bogie ballast wagons and three carriages were to be finished. The carriages were probably bogie brake vans and in August it was ordered that 'the third guards carriage [was] not to be proceeded with till further order'. It was at the August meeting that the order was given to cover the quarrymen's trucks, 'or at all costs 28 of them at first'. A further 25 braked slate wagons were ordered in March 1875 as well as four more coal wagons together with the material for 25 slate wagons in February 1878. Ordering merely the materials suggests that wagons were built whenever there was spare capacity. Also at Boston Lodge, Spooner had been instructed to obtain a new stationary engine in September 1872.

Tyler's advice on the subject of bogie carriages was followed and two vehicles ordered and were delivered from Brown, Marshalls late in 1872. With bogies made at Boston Lodge, they were the first metal-framed bogie carriages to be used on a passenger railway in the UK. The first reference to the bogie carriages in the minutes came in February 1875, when a shed was ordered to be built to house them at Boston Lodge.

Another bogie carriage was ordered in February 1876; requisitioned from Brown, Marshalls & Co, two vehicles were supplied later in the year; it may be that the manufacturer offered a good price for making two. Designed by Spooner's eldest son, George Percival, they lacked the integral wrought-iron frame of the first two. Two more composite bogie carriages 'to replace worn out old ones' were to be ordered and tenders submitted to the directors in February 1879. Gloster Wagon Co got the order and delivered later in the year; the purchase of the wheels and other materials for the bogies and their manufacture was approved in May. The 'worn out old ones' could not refer to bogie carriages as they are all still in service. The board also approved 'two bogie vans to replace worn out stock to be made at Boston Lodge works' at the same time; they were brought into service in 1880. The minutes contain no reference to George Percival's earlier work carried out for the railway, the three smaller bogie vans with the infamous 'curly roofs', delivered by Brown, Marshalls in 1873 (two) and 1876.

In August 1874, Livingston Thompson tendered his resignation due to illness. He had not attended a board meeting since 12 September 1871 and his resignation was accepted with 'deep regret'. Playing a part in the FR's development since 1836, his holding of ordinary shares in 1857 was £4,400. He was replaced by Colonel George Halpin. Chairman Andrew Durham died late in 1876 and on 4 January 1877 John Graves Livingston was appointed chairman in his stead.

There are constant references in the minutes during the 1870s to money due to the company, and not just by recalcitrant quarry proprietors refusing to pay demurrage. In February 1874, Craig Ddu quarry owed £300, required within six weeks, and Rhosydd owed for rail, to pay within 14 days. In March, all outstanding accounts were placed with the company's solicitor for recovery. The Diphwys Casson Company was in arrears for its back traffic by 14 February 1877, when Spooner was instructed to pursue the account.

The first reference to letting wharf space in the new yard at

Minffordd was in February 1874, although the yard can't have been finished. In August 1875, the Cambrian Railways was informed that a charge of £120 per annum would be raised for three wharves, the FR installing the narrow gauge track and turntables and the Cambrian Company to lay down, at its own expense, the 4ft 8½in gauge lines as per a plan that it had been sent. The connection of the FR's line into the yard did not match that shown on the deposited plan, being towards the eastern end of the site. In June 1876 the company offered to buy the land from Huddart for £2,500.

It was agreed in March 1877 to carry mail between Duffws and Minffordd for £275 per annum. For some reason nothing came of this, for in August 1879 it was resolved 'that the company are prepared to carry the mails and that Mr Spooner is instructed to write asking the terms that the Post Office are ready to make with the company'.

Following an auditors' report received in August 1877 it was resolved to open a stores and material account for Boston Lodge. The stock in hand at 30 June 1877 was to be credited to a reserve account and new purchases charged to the new account. When used, items were to be charged to revenue.

The permanent way came to attention in February 1878, when the board decided that future renewals of rail should be in steel, with 20 tons to be ordered immediately.

The company settled several claims for compensation during the 1870s. It is not clear if this was because the railway was inherently dangerous or because the local populace was not acclimatised to the way a railway worked. In August 1874 David Jones at Penrhyn station was paid £25 for an unspecified injury, while 'the old man who was injured at the Duffws crossing' was paid £5. Breese the solicitor, acting for J. D. Jones of Duffws, was to be asked what Jones 'is content to receive as compensation'. It wasn't all personal injuries, for in August 1875 Griffith Owen was given £10 towards the loss of his horse. The widow of Owen Owens, killed on the Cwmorthin incline at Tanygrisiau, was offered, without prejudice, £5 a year for life by a board 'feeling compassion', and in August it was agreed to pay £100, a lump sum presumably. It is not clear why the board felt any obligation in this case.

There were more claims in February 1878, when the board resolved '... £5 donation to the parents of the boy that was killed on line near the Welsh Slate Company's wharf. To give 10s a week for two months ... till the man damaged at the saw mill can return to work and to find employment for him and to give him £2 gratuity at once. The widow of the porter killed at Duffws to have a donation of £20.'

Two accidents that had occurred on railway property in 1872, one of them a fatality, did not appear to result in claims. On 29 August, John Lloyd, a miner of Penrhyn, travelled on the 10pm excursion from Portmadoc. According to an internal report, 'He got out of an open carriage at Minffordd Junction, on the wrong side, and walked over the parapet of the Cambrian Railways bridge there, falling onto the platform below ...' He died of his injuries on 3 September. At the inquest the accident was attributed to the 'want of light and fence on bridge'. If the train had stopped in the station then Lloyd should have been nowhere near the bridge; if there was oil lighting in the station it would have been very dark beyond it – perhaps he had been in drink?

On 28 October, Robert Roberts, a quarryman of Dolgarregddu, broke his leg when he tried to cross between two wagons of a train that was blocking the crossing: '... he placed his foot on the coupling hooks of two wagons but had scarcely done so when the wagons came sharply together ...'

When it came to making donations the board was not consistent. While £25 was given to the new church in

Above: **The second double Fairlie, *James Spooner*, was almost eight years old when photographed at Tan-y-bwlch in September 1880. Both of the 1872-built bogie carriages, two 'curly roof' vans and two 'observation' cars can be seen. The up train, hauled by an England engine, has a good load of back traffic coupled between the locomotive and the passenger portion.** *Author's collection*

Below right: ***Merddin Emrys*, in 1879 the first locomotive built at Boston Lodge, seen at Duffws from the fireman's side. It has only a partial cab roof and square sandboxes.**
John Thomas/FR Archives

Portmadoc in August 1874, in August 1877 a new chapel in Blaenau Festiniog received £5, and the Baptist chapel at Duffws was given only £2 in February 1879; obviously the directors were churchgoers. In the meantime, in 1875, the board decided that it had no powers to contribute towards the commemoration of the coming of age of the Tremadoc Estate's beneficiary, Francis William Alexander Roche.

Discussions about the telegraph took place in 1870 and it was installed the following year. The maintenance contractor was Saunders & Co, a company that had a long, and presumably fruitful, relationship with the railway from c1875. The locking apparatus at Duffws was a McKenzie & Holland installation, however; the £230 tender was approved in February 1879. Portmadoc was the focus of attention in August, when the board was concerned about getting a lease from the Tremadoc Estate for the locking cabin for 10s per annum and instructed that 'tenders be obtained for locking gear and cabin at Portmadoc'. McKenzie & Holland's £205 tender for locking apparatus at Glan y Pwll was accepted in August 1880.

The resolution to purchase a second double engine, *James Spooner*, from Avonside in 1871/2 was not recorded in the minutes. In March 1875, however, the minutes record that 'there be one new bogie engine (single boiler) ordered'. Similarly, in January 1877, it was 'Resolved that Mr Spooner be authorised to build a new double bogie engine, as per estimate, at the company works, that the erecting shed etc be made as suggested ...' Some additional land at Boston Lodge was to be leased at the same time.

The single boiler loco was ordered from the Vulcan Foundry and named *Taliesin,* and like the 1876 carriages, it was designed by George Percival Spooner. The idea that the company should build its own locomotive only 12 years after starting a steam service was quite remarkable and showed great faith in the abilities of the personnel and equipment at Boston Lodge. It was estimated that a saving of £450 would be made, but it is not clear if that calculation allowed for the building work.

An unusual request was acceded to in February 1876: 'To let Mr Bray contractor of the North Wales Narrow Gauge lines one of the small locomotives on hire for six months at £130'. The NWNGR was being built between Dinas, three miles from Caernarfon, and Bryngwyn and Rhyd Ddu. Livingston Thompson had been a director when it was incorporated in 1872; Spooner was its engineer. The locomotive chosen to go was *Palmerston*. It left the FR on 9 May, the date that Spooner signed a contract with the NWNGR in London, and it returned in July 1877.

The directors came unstuck when they tried to enhance their fees at their August 1874 meeting. They resolved that in future, receipts would have to be produced when claiming any expense in addition to the usual three guinea fee, but for this occasion they could claim two guineas, making five guineas in total, regardless. By the time of the following meeting they had been informed that they were in contravention of the 1845 Companies Clauses Act that required directors' remuneration to be set by the company in general meeting! The resolution was rescinded. They could fix Spooner's pay and expenses, however, and in January 1877 agreed to pay him 'travelling expenses attending meetings or other business in London etc and £1 a day for other expenses'.

The issue of the tolls for carrying slate was still not resolved despite the clarification of the 1869 act but that was not the only matter concerning the quarry proprietors, as this letter dated 29 January 1875 from the solicitors, Breese, Jones & Casson, shows:

'Mr Holland MP and Mr Greaves have consulted us on the subject of the tolls which you charge them for the carriage of the slate over your line and the fares charged to their workmen.

'They have three complaints to make: First – that you charged them at 2s 6d per ton for the carriage of slates to the port whereas you make a much less charge to the Welsh Slate Company and they demand to be put on the same footing as the latter company.

'Secondly – you charged them and their partners being quarry proprietors in the meaning of the 117th section of the 2 and 3 William 4 cap 48 whereas they claim to be carried free of toll in accordance with the provisions of that section.

'Thirdly – you charged their workmen more than the farthing per mile stipulated for by your agreement with them on the ground as they understand that you provide different carriages to those mentioned in the agreement.

'They demand that the agreement shall be adhered to both as to the carriages and the amount of fares. We are therefore instructed by them to ask you for an answer as to whether you are prepared to meet their requirement on each of the above points and to say that if you should decline to do so it is their intention to take the matter before the Railway Commissioners and obtain their decision as soon as possible.

'We must request a definite reply on or before 8th proximo and in the event of our not receiving one we shall assume that it is the intention of the company to comply with our clients just requirements.'

It is obvious that the quarry proprietors, or their solicitors, had been giving the 1869 act close attention, for they had noticed article 117, which had been retained from the 1832 act and which had previously been overlooked. The article was primarily to permit the Tremadoc Estate to make use of the railway for maintenance purposes but buried away in the middle it declared that quarry proprietors who paid tolls to the railway for carrying their slate could personally 'pass and repass to and from the several slate quarries over and along the said railway without being subject to the payment of toll'. The company resisted this claim vigorously, and at some expense, without justification for the wording is quite unambiguous unless the company perceived a difference between toll and fares.

The railway's solicitors had replied to the letter before the deadline but no response had been received when the board met on 16 February. It appears that the quarries had taken their complaint to the Railway Commissioners, for the following entry appears in the minutes for February 1877: '... it was found that the decision of the Railway Commissioners of the 31st December 1874 was to the effect that not only the rates for slate but that of up goods was to be as charged as to others (under agreements). The decision by Judge Field subsequently made was to the effect that the charge for slate was to be 2s 6d a ton and the rate for up goods be as per the order of the Railway Commissioners of the above date (same as charged to the quarry companies under agreement.)'

The reference to a decision by Judge Field and the timing of the minute suggests that the railway had appealed the 1874 decision. Even if the company was, as the proprietors saw it, brought into line it didn't stop them trying for more. In February 1878 the Cwmorthin company was advised: 'the charge for carriage of up goods to be the same as heretofore'.

It was Oakeley's turn to seek a reduction in June 1879, the company replying to his agent in February 1880: 'Since writing to you the 15th September last in reply to yours of 17th June 1879 asking for reduction in rates charged for carriage of slates from Mr Oakeley's quarries to Portmadoc, and Minffordd, it was only at a meeting of the directors held in London on the 17th instant that I had the opportunity of bringing your request to their notice. I am desired by my directors to inform you that your application has been duly considered, and to say that they are not in a position to comply with your wishes, inasmuch as existing contracts with other quarry proprietors will not admit of any reduction being made in the already small rate charged Mr Oakeley for carriage of his slates.

'On making use of the expression "small rate" it should be borne in mind that the charge by the railway company does not

only embrace the prosecution of the traffic between the termini of the railway, of providing rolling stock, and keeping in repair, but they have to supply and maintain the extra carrying stock for outside services beyond their line, over Mr Oakeley's quarry inclines and platforms, at Dinas, and at his wharves at Portmadoc; hence they feel sure that upon your mature consideration, you cannot fail to admit that the charge now made is but moderate and such as cannot bear a reduction compatible with the heavy cost the railway company necessarily have to sustain in carrying on the traffic effectively.'

Greaves, at least, had continued to pursue his 'rights' for free travel, in February 1878 being informed, rather cryptically: 'in answer to your letter of the 28th ultimo that as they have been advised that no such right as you refer to exists under the company's act they regret they must decline acceding to your request'. He didn't let up, though, and in August 1879 the board instructed 'Mr Spooner to write to Mr Greaves, that his application in regard to Section 117 in company's act has been considered by the directors and they request him to say that they see no grounds to alter the decision already communicated to him in their secretary's letter of February 1878'. Greaves wasn't going to let go and by February 1880 both parties had taken counsel's opinion on the issue. Breese, writing on Greaves' behalf, had suggested that a special case for the proprietors to travel free be put to the court and the decision be binding, the matter of costs also to be put to the court!

There were other minerals being carried apart from slate. In August 1875 it was resolved 'to charge 8d a ton for carriage of granite from tunnel to Duffws or Dinas and 6d to Tanygrisiau'. In February 1879 a Mr Simpson was informed that the directors were willing to reduce his rate from 1s 8d to 1s 6d per ton, 'the Granite Sett Company ... finding their own wagons'. The rate for carrying setts from Tan-y-bwlch station to Minffordd and Portmadoc was set at 1s 3d per ton in May.

In June 1875 there were several issues concerning the use of the company's wagons under consideration. Could the Cwt y Bugail Slate Company be charged an extra 1s for use of wagons in respect of the extra 2½ miles to their quarry, or should the charge be applied to the Festiniog Slate Company, the Rhiwbach Tramway's owner? Should the Festiniog & Blaenau Railway Company be charged for the use of slate wagons and trucks required for slate companies, and goods trucks required for the public, and did the FBR have any power to retaliate by making stock and charging the FR?

The Craig Ddu Slate Company, the Moelwyn Slate Company, Morgan Lloyd, and Carters, and the Wrysgan Slate Company were also making use of wagons that the company felt was outside the terms of normal usage. Twelve months later it was decided 'to make a charge against the quarry proprietors for all goods running up the inclines from the foot of their lowest incline at a fair and moderate rate. To allow as a special arrangement the coal trucks to go up the inclines of the quarry proprietors at the same rate as lately allowed to the Welsh Slate Company and to charge other parties the same as the Welsh Slate Company excepting in cases of greater service rendered.' In August 1877 the WSC had not paid £1 2s 8d for the use of FR wagons on its own property; the FR informed the WSC that in future 'all goods delivered to your company in slate wagons and slate trucks at the foot of the lowest incline must be unloaded and not permitted to be taken up in the railway company's slate wagons ...'

The oldest part of the Gorseddau Tramway had been a non-statutory 3ft gauge line just over a mile long between Portmadoc and the ironstone mine at Llidiart Yspytty near Tremadoc, established in the early 1840s. In Portmadoc it ran down Madoc

Street to get to the harbour. It was taken over by the Bangor & Portmadoc Slate & Slate Slab Co (BPSSS) in the 1850s and extended to Gorseddau slate quarry in Cwm Ystradllyn, a distance of eight miles.

The FR built at least four wagons, one of them braked, for the BPSSS; 'the remaining four wagons (which complete your order) I had delivered at the end of the embankment on Saturday last ...', Spooner wrote on 11 February 1858, charging £18 each for them. In September 1858 the board agreed to BPSSS, referred to as the Gorseddau company, having 'the use of the rail of the railway company's railway subject to the payment of 3s 6d per month'. Spooner's letter on 21 September specified that 'the Gorseddau company are at their own expense to lay down what rail they may require, the Festiniog Railway Company not wishing to undertake the laying of the rails'. It is not known if the BPSSS ever did create any mixed gauge track on the harbour side.

The quarry was closed and the tramway became disused in the late 1860s, the BPSSS going into liquidation in 1870. The New Prince of Wales Slate Company, developing a quarry in nearby Cwm Pennant, wished to acquire the tramway to reconstruct and extend it, but found that the land ownership position was unclear on some parts of it. Therefore a bill was deposited in 1871 and the Gorseddau Junction & Portmadoc Railways Act received Royal assent in July 1872. In addition to authorising and defining the railway as 2ft gauge with a new 5-mile-long branch, the act enabled the GJPR to change its route in Portmadoc as the Tremadoc Estate didn't want it in Madoc Street, so as to make a junction with the Croesor & Portmadoc Railway near the gasworks and to use the CPR between the gasworks and the harbour. It was also permitted to use the CPR's extension to Borth y Gest when built.

None of this appeared to affect the company until 1875, when the GJPR applied for further powers, including running powers over the FR. In November 1875, the board delegated Huddart and Livingston to deal with the matter and in June 1876 a special meeting of the shareholders was called to approve the FR's clauses in the bill. The only issue to reach the board thereafter came in May 1879, when it was resolved to charge the GJPR '3d per ton for right of running over FR between distant signal at Portmadoc station and the lower terminus near to the Welsh Slate Company's wharf'.

Oakeley got permission to stop the goods train at 'Plas' and passenger trains at Bryn Mawr, provided he signed an indemnity, in October 1875. He and his friends were to be allowed to ride in 'goods and other trucks' and the following month the board agreed that 'Mr Spooner arrange to fix the charges for coals to Tan-y-bwlch at a rate that will compete with the Cambrian Company from their Penrhyn station to Maentwrog and he is to take care that any alteration will be such that will pay the company'. In February 1878, the board decided that Oakeley deserved no special favours and that he was to be charged the same as the public for the carriage of coal and goods.

The board rarely commented on expenditure, either capital or revenue. It was obviously informed by the twice-yearly reports to shareholders but they were never the subject of comment. The figures shown in table 7 were entered in the minutes without remark in February 1877. A year later, a resolution was drafted to raise fresh capital, £6,000 5% preference shares. In August 1878 it was 'Resolved that a sum of £5,000 in preference shares of £10 each bearing a fixed dividend at the rate of 4½% per annum be issued when it may be found necessary, and offered to the share and stock holders of the original and preference stock and shares at par and in proportion to the amount of such held by each, bearing interest

from the date of payment – £2 per share to be paid on allotment and balance by calls not exceeding £2 each at such times as may be hereafter decided upon by the directors: not less than three months notice being given by them of each call'. In February 1879 the board decided 'to make a call on the new preference shares of £2 per share on 1st April and 1st July' and to write to Messrs Sandilands, the solicitors, 'that there is no commission allowed on the preference shares taken by Miss Swete and that the preference shares were merely offered to the shareholders'.

Table 7

Works etc

Capital

Shed	300
Wall at Portmadoc	80
Engine shed	320
Land at Tanygrisiau and Glan y Pwll	1,930
Total	£2,630

Revenue

Carriages	652
Rails	120
Tools in engine house	225
Law costs	400
Engine	1,000
Total	£2,397

The board was *very* interested in expenditure when it met on 19 August 1879, however, and the minute, reproduced in full, gives a flavour of the tension: 'That Mr Spooner's attention be particularly directed to the urgent necessity that exists for effecting substantial reduction in the several departments of the working expenditure, no reduction having as yet been effected, at all commensurate with the falling off in traffic. That as the item of wages in particular shows an actual increase on the

amount expended last year, Mr Spooner be requested to report what reduction in the staff he can recommend. That the remaining 500 £10 4½% preference shares created August 1878 be now issued and offered in the first instance to the shareholders of original stock at par, calls being made in same way as the last issue and that subscribers have the option of paying their calls in advance, getting interest at 4½%.'

The board met again the next day, when it adopted Spooner's cost-cutting proposals 'reducing the expenditure on the line, ... (so far as can be effected without risk or injury to the service) ... – reduction for month: permanent way £10 0s 0d; masons £16 10s 0d; carpenters £15 10s 0d; smiths £13 0s 0d; locomotive department (running shed) £6 0s 0d; engine house £18 0s 0d; traffic department £13 0s 0d; total £92 0s 0d'. Unfortunately, there is no indication as to how many personnel were affected by this cull; those concerned were not likely to have been impressed by the news that Spooner's son, George Percival, had been appointed locomotive superintendent on £100 per annum, backdated to 1 July. The reduction in staff numbers does not appear to have held too well; there was an increase in five over the ten years from 1874 (Appendix 3).

In the event, George Percival held his position for less than a year, being forced to resign, probably by his father, in June 1880 after he got a housemaid pregnant. Charles Easton offered to undertake the duties, along with the other positions already held, and the board resolved that 'Mr Charles E. Spooner's salary be increased by £50 per annum, making it £650 and that Mr Hughes be appointed his assistant in these and the other duties connected with the company at a salary of £50 per annum. The foregoing arrangement to take effect from the first day of July next.' John Sylvester Hughes had worked for Spooner since 1864, when he served a four-year pupillage, and had been in partnership with him since 1873.

Still very concerned about the cash position, in August 1880 the board instructed Spooner 'to dispose of old iron, brass and other old stores ... on satisfactory terms'. Spooner was also instructed to limit expenditure on the capital account to the balance available on that account, as the board was determined not to raise more capital.

PERSONNEL

Left: **Duffws station staff, 1901. 'General inspector' Hovenden is seated between two personnel with braided loops on their sleeves; to his right is the stationmaster – their titles are woven onto their jacket collars.** *FR Archives*

Below left: **Station staff and train crew pose with** *James Spooner* **at Duffws,** c1890. *Rowland Hughes/FR Archives*

Above: **Loco shed staff and crews pose with their charges –** *Taliesin*, *Merddin Emrys* **and** *Prince*, c1900. *FR Archives*

Below: **National Shell Factory and FR personnel in 1917. There are over 70 people in this photograph; one wonders how they were accommodated.** *P. G. Thomas/FR Archives*

5

Connecting to the outside world – losing the monopoly

1871-1881

The Festiniog Railway Company built its business because it had a monopoly of the Festiniog slate traffic. As the word spread that this small company was paying large dividends it will have come as no surprise to the company that there were others interested in taking a share of the market. What might have surprised it is that the promoters of the proposed competitors were some of the same people who promoted the FR in the first instance. The likes of Samuel Holland, who played a key role in the FR's establishment, and was keen to boast of it in his memoirs, had been a key player in the founding of the Festiniog & Blaenau Railway (Chapter 2).

It is clear that the quarry proprietors thought that the FR was there to serve them at the lowest possible price and that although it had already given them big reductions in their transportation costs, improved their chances in the market, and justified investment in their own expansion schemes, they did not like the company's surpluses being spent either on improving the FR or on paying dividends to shareholders. If there was any surplus in the equation it was theirs, they thought. What has to remain a mystery is why they did not seek to control it by becoming influential shareholders themselves. Had they controlled the FR they could not only have influenced the company's policy on rates but also shared in the profits earned by carrying their competitors' slate!

Whilst the FBR had a (possibly marginal) viable role as transport for quarrymen living in Festiniog village and for slate from Manod, and brought traffic to the FR, it was designed to facilitate the export of the FR's traffic by routes unbuilt and maybe unthought of when the FBR company was registered in August 1862. Had the Aberystwyth & Welsh Coast Railway's 1863 scheme been built it would have been connected to the FBR and competing with the FR for Portmadoc-bound slate.

The Merionethshire Railway was similar in concept to the AWCR scheme. An Act of Parliament obtained in 1871 specified a line just over ten miles long, between a junction with the FBR at Festiniog and the Cambrian Railways at Talsarnau, where a double junction would have allowed traffic to go either north or south. It was intended to be 2ft gauge. The chairman was Samuel Holland, and Charles Menzies Holland was engineer for a few months. Two of the directors, James Hassell Foulkes and Hugh Owen, were also directors of the Diphwys Casson slate company. The MR was allowed to enter into traffic arrangements with the FBR and/or the Cambrian. Three acts for extension of time were obtained, in 1876, 1879, the only occasion that the FR board recorded discussing the MR, and 1882, but no construction was undertaken, the MR remaining a bargaining tool. An abandonment order was obtained in 1887.

The Bala & Festiniog Railway came into being by Act of

The Merionethshire Railway.
National Archives

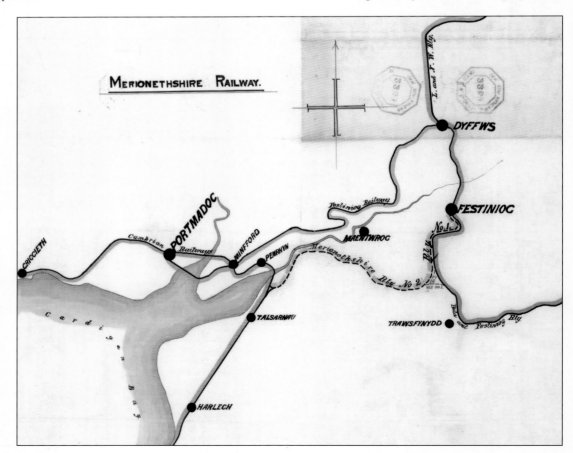

Parliament in 1873 and was another line that involved Samuel Holland; it also had the Great Western Railway behind it. It was to be 22 miles long, connecting with the Corwen & Bala Railway near Bala and terminating in the 'Festiniog station ground' of the FBR. There would have been a triangular junction with the Merionethshire Railway four miles from Festiniog. The Great Western Railway, Vale of Llangollen Railway, Llangollen & Corwen Railway and Corwen & Bala Railway (the contributing companies) were all permitted to subscribe to the BFR, the last three being sponsored by the GWR. Holland shared the BFR directors' table with, amongst others, the GWR's Daniel Gooch. It was permitted to enter into working and traffic arrangements with the contributing companies and/or the GWR, and the BFR and/or the BFR and the contributing companies could make working and traffic arrangements with the Merionethshire Railway; they had reciprocal running powers. Neither railway's gauge was specified in the legislation but plans show that where they shared the common route there would have been mixed, 2ft and standard, gauge track, despite the routes being legally separate.

The relationship between the FR and the FBR was symbiotic: they both got something out of it, although the FR must have sometimes felt that the FBR was taking advantage of it as the following minute entries show:

August 1875   Not entertained (As to charge the Festiniog & Blaenau for the use of slate wagons over their line.) To reply that the 3d is charged for extra distance and the 8d from Portmadoc is a less charge than legally authorised by the company's act.

August 1877 That Mr Spooner be instructed to write to the secretary of the Festiniog & Blaenau Railway intimating that this company will be obliged to charge 4d per ton for all goods and timber wagons sent by the Festiniog Railway over Festiniog & Blaenau Railway in consequence of them having failed to adhere to the agreement with regard to a supply of wagons.

A year later, the charge was reduced to 3d per ton for more than 3,000 tons in six months, while 6d per ton was charged for carrying goods from Festiniog to Blaenau. Materials carried for J. P. Edwards, the contractor who converted the FBR to standard gauge, were charged at 1d per ton. The FR charged £1 per day for the use of a locomotive and driver.

Apparently at the FBR's request, an agreement was reached in 1876, whereby the FBR would be purchased by the BFR, leading the way to giving the GWR access to Blaenau Festiniog's slate. In 1880 the GWR obtained an act that gave the BFR powers to absorb the FBR, although the GWR had been in correspondence with the FR concerning the FBR's operating for some time. In August 1879, the board considered a request from the GWR that the FR should operate the FBR, resolving that 'Mr Spooner be instructed to state in reply that the board would be willing to enter into such an arrangement provided satisfactory terms could be arrived at and that Mr Robertson be invited to propose terms, but that a preliminary condition be

Above: **A 1936 view of the GWR exchange platform, looking towards Portmadoc and showing the footbridge installed by the GWR. There is another FR train underneath it.**
S. W. Baker/FR Archives

Right: **The FR accessed the GWR yard by this crossing over the GW headshunt. Seen after 1939, with the main line overgrown, the vantage point was the weighbridge.**
R. M. Casserley/ Author's collection

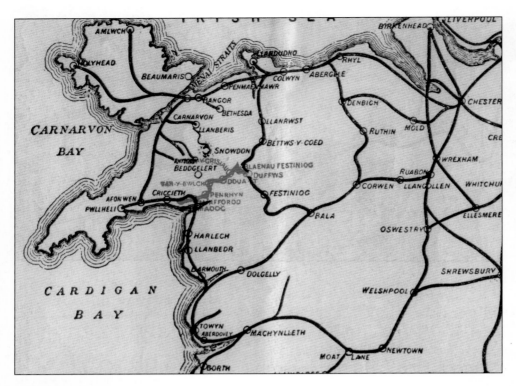

Left: **The FR and surrounds – a location map used in company promotional materials.** *Author's collection*

Right: **The LNWR station, probably *c*1920, with two motor cars in view. The FR tracks entered at the lower right; slate was transhipped at the wharf in the centre.** *Author's collection*

Below right: **The LNWR exchange platform, Stesion Fain.** *FR Archives*

that the permanent way be put into proper working order and that the sidings, requested for the interchange of traffic be put up in [a] manner approved of by our own engineer'.

The FBR obviously hadn't been well maintained and as nothing came of the proposal, presumably the FR's conditions were seen as being too onerous. The FR transactions to be found in the last of the FBR's account books give a further insight into the nature of the relationship (Appendix 4).

The line from Bala was completed in 1882 and conversion of the FBR to standard gauge was finished the following year, the GWR opening its Blaenau Festiniog terminus on 10 September 1883. Developing an exchange yard to the south of the FBR's former terminus, the GWR was in a position where it could tranship slate from Manod bound for Portmadoc, via the FR, and, as it undoubtedly hoped, attract inland-bound business from the other Festiniog quarries. If there were any traffic in the latter direction it would have to be transferred to the GWR yard via the FR.

Another attack on the FR's monopoly came from the apparently impregnable northern end of the town, where a railway was built with the capability of having direct access to two of the FR's biggest customers, Oakeley and Greaves.

The Bettws & Festiniog Railway was a London & North Western Railway-backed scheme floated in 1870. The need for a tunnel more than two miles long was responsible for it being promoted in 2ft gauge. It would have been an extension of the standard gauge Conway & Llanrwst Railway that had been extended to Betws y Coed in 1868; the CLR had been incorporated in 1860 and was taken over by the LNWR in 1867. Had this line been built as planned, along with others proposed by the North Wales Narrow Gauge Railways or the Portmadoc, Beddgelert & South Snowdon Railway, Betws-y-coed would have been a centre for 2ft gauge lines radiating out to Portmadoc, Blaenau Festiniog and Corwen.

The LNWR submitted a bill for the line to Blaenau in 1871, causing a Mr Bell to express his concern to the FR. In January 1872, the board noted that he should be informed that 'the directors ... are aware of the LNWR Company's bill but they have not yet determined on the course of action'. J. G.

Livingston, Huddart and Spooner had already met the LNWR to discuss the issue on several occasions. The company's policy appeared to be to keep the LNWR as close to the tunnel mouth as possible and to give it running powers from Dinas to Duffws and the connection to the Rhiwbach Tramway.

The LNWR (Additional Powers) Act, 1872, which received royal assent in July, specified that the line 'should be constructed on the same gauge as the other local railways'. Work started on a narrow gauge formation but in 1873 the LNWR decided to avoid the need to build special locomotives and provide special facilities at Betws-y-coed and adopt the wider gauge.

There was continued communication between the two companies while the invading line was being built, a meeting in March 1874 with the LNWR's George Moon about land appearing to be particularly fraught. By August 1877 the LNWR's traffic department was obviously planning its commercial strategy when the board agreed this letter to be sent by Spooner: 'I brought the matter of the tonnage to be charged by the Festiniog Railway Company for the conveyance of slates from the quarries to the interchange station at your terminus before the directors at their meeting on the 8th instant. They expressed their willingness to co-operate with the LNW Company in every way in their power but they are under the impression that your line to Duffws cannot be completed before the summer of 1879 and therefore that it is premature to ask them to bind themselves to a specific scale of charges. If however you feel confident that your line will be completed and opened for traffic next summer they will then be prepared to take these charges into consideration and let you know their decision. In the event of Mr Spooner being satisfied that there was a reasonable probability of the LNWR's line being opened in 1878 he was authorised to offer a rate of 10d per ton for the slate from the quarries to the new yard, the FR supplying the wagons, or 6d per ton using LNWR-supplied wagons, the rate in each case being exclusive of terminals.'

The Cambrian and the slate merchants Ashton & Green, at Minffordd since 1874, also wanted to know what the FR was going to charge in the face of competition, the former writing in December 1880 and seeking to establish terms for through

traffic. The company sought details of proposed rates for different classes of goods to London, Birmingham, Manchester, Liverpool and Chester, showing how they would be calculated and how much would be attributed to the FR, including the ever-essential terminals. In the case of the merchants, Spooner was instructed to write that 'they are not prepared to enter into the question of a through rate via Minffordd until they know what course will be adopted by the LNWR and to point out that the present rates via Minffordd are not more than those charged by the LNWR and further to state, that in case of the LNWR making a reduction this company would be prepared to consider the propriety of making an alteration in their rate in conjunction with the Cambrian Company ...'

In February 1881, the Cambrian's proposals were rejected, but the board was prepared to resolve 'that while declining to adopt through booking arrangements proposed by the Cambrian Company, the company is prepared to join the Cambrian in making a reduction in rates for goods as will bring the sum of the local rates of these two companies to the through rates that may be charged by the LNWR for the same traffic. Such reduction to be divided between the Cambrian and Festiniog companies in the proportion of the mileage the goods may be carried by these companies respectively... '

The LNWR opened to a temporary terminus near the tunnel mouth in 1879 and extended to its permanent terminus in 1881. The FR was ready to face the inevitable; in August 1880 it had

By the tunnel mouth, the LNWR could take slate from both Oakeley (left) and Greaves. The Oakeley wharf is well stocked in this 1930 view. *J. Valentine/ Author's collection*

accepted the tender for the roof 'for new passenger station opposite the LNWR's station at Blaenau Ffestiniog'.

As expected, the LNWR did set a lower rate, 13s 9d per ton from Blaenau Festiniog to London (Table 8) against the FR/Cambrian rate of 14s 7½d. In August 1881 the board instructed Spooner '... to make an arrangement with the Cambrian Railways Company as regards the rates for mineral traffic, similar to that already adopted regarding goods' but then in February 1882 repudiated the (unspecified) terms that he negotiated, countering that company would forgo one 1½d of its 2s 1½d share if the Cambrian was prepared to reduce its 12s 6d share to 11s 9d.

Table 8

Breakdown of LNWR rate for slate

Blaenau Festiniog–London

From quarries to Blaenau	10d
From Blaenau to Betws y Coed	5d
Betws y Coed to London	12s 6d
Total of aggregate rates by LNWR route	13s 9d

The rent payable by the Cambrian for use of the sidings was set at ¾d per ton on traffic handled there in August 1881.

The Cambrian's traffic manager, George Lewis, met the board and Spooner on 3 May 1882 and a formal agreement over rates was agreed and signed by both parties. It was agreed that the combined rates should match the LNWR's and the FR agreed to reduce its rate to Minffordd to 2s as proposed. The Cambrian, however, agreed that 'the rates charged by the Cambrian Company from Minffordd continue to be the same as at present but that the Cambrian Company shall allow out of such rates a rebate to such an extent as will reduce the combined rate, in both these lines, to the rates via the LNWR route, such rebate to be paid monthly by the Cambrian to the Festiniog Railway Company and credited by the latter in the traffic accounts with the several consignors'. Subject to confirmation by both boards, the agreement was backdated to 1 February 1882.

While these efforts to tap in to the Festiniog slate business were coming to fruition the board was faced with another possible incursion into its sphere of influence, this time at Portmadoc. Bills for a standard gauge Portmadoc & Beddgelert Railway and an extension of time for the Merionethshire Railway had been deposited in Parliament and at a meeting in February 1882 the board considered whether it would be preferable to support or operate the existing 'Croesor, Portmadoc and Beddgelert Railway', actually the Portmadoc, Croesor & Beddgelert Railway, which had powers to extend to Beddgelert with its 1879 act.

As the LNWR had running powers to Festiniog 'over the Blaenau line, and if a broad gauge line was made to Beddgelert, and the Merionethshire Railway [was] constructed, that company could book through from Blaenau station and other stations on the system to Portmadoc and Beddgelert, hence the traffic would be diverted and lost to the FR'. On the other hand, 'If the Portmadoc & Beddgelert 4ft 8½in gauge bill was thrown out, and the narrow gauge line made, passengers would book at Blaenau by the FR for Beddgelert over [a] continuous narrow gauge line ... Coal, lime and goods could be brought from the LNWR and the Great Western stations at Blaenau, via the Festiniog line for the Beddgelert and Llanfrothen district, on the narrow gauge railway being constructed to Beddgelert. Coal, lime and goods coming over the Cambrian for Llanfrothen and Beddgelert, would be transhipped at Minffordd and then taken over the Festiniog line, via Portmadoc to Beddgelert &c, and slates, minerals &c vice versa.'

The memorandum noted that 'It is important that the FR oppose both the foregoing bills, and to prevent, if possible, either of them being carried, and that advice be taken with their parliamentary agents, as to their chances of opposing the bills and the best mode to proceed'.

In considering whether to work the PCBR it was noted that 'the trains could work through to Beddgelert instead of stopping at Portmadoc and passengers would not change. The additional cost would be only in extra wear and tear of rolling stock and for fuel and grease.' Notwithstanding any possible benefit, the board followed precedence when it had determined not to take over or amalgamate with the Croesor & Portmadoc Railway, and decided it did not want to be involved with the PCBR either.

There is no evidence that the board ever made such a structured examination of the effects of the LNWR and GWR activities in Blaenau Festiniog on its business, but it might have thought that it could not defeat them. In Portmadoc it evidently thought it could win.

In less than three years the FR went from being very much a monopoly supplier to being in a position where the quarry proprietors had three choices when it came to deciding which way to route their slates. By the time the GWR completed its route to Bala in 1883 the FR had already peaked on the indicators of passengers carried, profit, and slate and merchandise tonnage. It was by no means the end for the FR, but it really was the beginning of a long drawn-out finale.

6

Coping with competition

1881-1890

Whilst the efforts of the LNWR and the GWR to undermine the FR's domination of the Festiniog slate traffic came to their inevitable conclusion, the railway's operating environment remained much the same as it had been during the previous ten years. There were some works arising from the 1869 act, which should have been completed within five years, but which were only just being completed! Land purchase for the Glan y Pwll loop line was obviously a problem (Chapter 4), but Spooner and the board must have forgotten about the time limit.

The railway came to the attention of the Board of Trade again when a contract clock-winder called George Westley was killed in Portmadoc goods shed on 4 March 1881. Colonel Rich conducted an inquiry and found that the goods shed had been shunted by a locomotive that had then gone to Minffordd, taking the shunting guard and leaving the points set for the shed instead of for the harbour. A slate train of 53 wagons entered the goods shed, at two-three miles per hour, colliding with two empty coal wagons and a loaded slate slab wagon stabled there. The impact occurred with such force that the slab wagon and one of the coal wagons were pushed through the 2ft thick rubble-masonry wall!

According to witnesses, Westley was in the goods shed reading a letter. He was found crushed between the slab wagon and the coal wagon. The shunting guard, John Owen, said that he had set the points back after the engine had left the goods shed before joining it to go to Minffordd. Signalman William Newell, who had been employed by the company for two years, also said he had set the points back for the harbour after the loco had left. He had looked at them again a few minutes before

the slate train was due and they were still set correctly. The brakesman applied the brake on the leading wagon when he realised that his train was headed for the goods shed. Rich did not comment on the inconsistency of two people claiming to have reset the points, neither did he consider if the rain that day had played any part in the accident, nor ask Newell the basis of his speed estimate. He found that the collision was caused by the neglect of Owen and Newell.

Following a coroner's inquiry, Newell was prosecuted and found not guilty at Carnarvon Quarter Sessions; in August 1882 the board agreed to award him £10 towards his legal expenses. In February it had instructed its solicitors to repudiate any liability to Westley's widow.

As is so often the case with railway accident reports, Rich's provided a window into conditions at the time. The 53-wagon gravity slate train had come to a stand at the distant signal and had been split into three portions, destined for the wharves of the Welsh Slate Company, Oakeley, and Votty & Bowydd, by the guard; no evidence was given as to the number of wagons in each portion. The division had been done before the loco reached the train. Driver David Davies, an employee for eight years and driver for eight months, whistled for the signals to be cleared and restarted the train. Robert Griffith was the leading brakesman; he thought he had adequate brake power. Owen was brakesman for the middle portion. Stationmaster John William Wheeler said that the waybill showed the train had consisted of '52 slate trucks and a slab truck' and that eight of the wagons were braked.

Rich was back to inspect new arrangements in Blaenau Festiniog on 31 March 1881. He found half a mile of new line

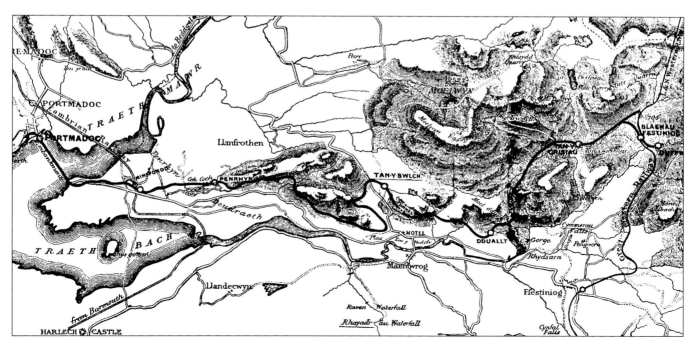

A map of the line used by the company for many years, first produced in the 1880s. *Author's collection*

This busy view at Tan-y-bwlch pre-dates the installation of the waiting shelter in 1883. *Taliesin*, with no cab roof, arrives with a down train that consists of a 'curly roof' van, bogie carriages Nos 15 and 16, five Brown, Marshalls and an Ashbury. *James Spooner* waits at the water tower. Loads in the 14 wagons include coal and beer. The closed Brown, Marshalls carriage has been uprated from 3rd to 2nd class. The bogie carriage is either No 17 or No 18 and is not fitted with the window bars required by Captain Tyler.
Frith/FR Archives

running eastwards from Dinas Junction that was to be used by passenger trains and serve the new interchange station while the 'old line' was to remain in use for minerals and goods. At the east end of the station the passenger line was crossed by an incomplete branch line from the goods line into the LNWR goods yard. He had several requirements: gravel was needed on the platform area, as were a clock, waiting room, booking office and urinals for the station; level crossing gates at Glan y Pwll required stops to prevent them being opened outwards; an up signal was required on the gate; the down stop signal was to be brought near the gate and a down distant signal was to be provided; the up distant signal at Dinas Junction should be lowered for the goods line or a second distant signal should be provided, and the junction diagram, in the signalbox, required correction. Considering them to be incomplete, he refused to approve the works.

When he returned on 8 June he found the situation to his satisfaction and gave approval for the new line and station to be used by passenger trains. He was dissatisfied, however, with the interlocking on the branch into the LNWR yard and made proposals for rectifying the situation. He also inspected what he called Glan y Pwll Junction, where the Dinas branch diverged. There, he found the distant signal too close to the junction, requiring it to be moved 200yd further west, and repeated. He also called for the junction to be protected by two up home signals that should be interlocked with the points. In a postscript he required that the company should submit an undertaking to work the new passenger line by train staff and block telegraph.

Spooner put the work in hand without delay and on 15 June

was able to report to Rich that it had been done with the exception of the second home signal. He explained that the signal engineers thought the signal unnecessary as there was no up traffic on the Dinas branch; the empty wagons were all worked through to Duffws and any required for Dinas were worked back over the loop line, which junction was fully signalled. He hoped this would be satisfactory and sought an immediate approval to bring the LNWR yard branch into use. Rich gave his approval, pointing out that an inspection would still be required when an officer was in the area.

Rich himself was in the neighbourhood on 23 July 1881 and gave his formal consent, to be effective as soon as the undertaking over the method of working was received. Spooner and Livingston signed the undertaking and stamped it with the company's seal on 30 July. Shown in the timetables as Blaenau Festiniog, the station earned itself the Welsh appellation of *Stesion Fain*, narrow station; the second Welsh word is often misspelled as *Fein*.

The author suspects that the company was being rather flexible with its powers for these works. As noted earlier, the period for construction for the works in 1869 had expired in 1874. Rich was not, incidentally, asked to approve the loop line.

A new source of problems in unloading and returning wagons became apparent in April 1881, when the company decided that if the situation didn't improve it would refuse to supply the Croesor & Portmadoc Railway with wagons after 1 June. A request to reduce the rate to 4d per ton for the CPR was refused in August.

The Festiniog proprietors did not let up on their complaints against the railway. In August 1881, Oakeley's agent submitted a claim for compensation in respect of the alleged loss of time by his loaders due to the railway's failure to supply wagons. The board instructed Spooner to write: '... they desire me to inform you that they cannot entertain it.

'The company have supplied wagons to you as to the other quarry proprietors, with as much despatch as possible, and they have never had any claim from other quarry proprietors, similar to that now made by you.

'As the amount of your requisition for wagons is so very much in excess of the supply required to meet the output it is evident that it affords no reliable criterion of the efficiency of the number of wagons supplied. I am also in a position to satisfy you, if you will call here to examine the returns, that my company's wagons are occupied by your traffic for a much longer time than by that of other companies.

'While, therefore my directors are most anxious to meet your requirements in the matter, as far as it is in their power... they feel that [it] is quite out of their power to entertain the claim you have made.'

Oakeley also required a reduction in the 10d per ton rate for transporting slate between the quarries and the LNWR sidings, threatening to ask the LNWR to make a connection that would avoid the FR. The company felt that the business barely covered its costs and refused a reduction.

However, the following February, having spoken to Oakeley's agent, Spooner wrote: 'with a view however to retain the existing relations with the quarry proprietors and afford them no ground for making separate connection with the LNWR', and offered 9d per ton. Oakeley refused the offer, and further negotiation, and went to the LNWR for a connection.

As if in answer to the complaint about wagons, the board then ordered that 'Mr Spooner be authorised to proceed with the making of 25 more slate wagons', adding that 'the number of hands employed in the workshops be on no account increased beyond those at present employed'. The material for the wagons had been ordered in February.

A few months later, in February 1882, Diphwys Casson's complaint that it had been overcharged was considered. The board had taken legal advice and decided to reduce the rate on two outstanding invoices covering the second half of 1881, Diphwys Casson being advised that the company would not reopen earlier accounts.

On the same occasion, the board decided to draw a line under the issue of the proprietors' free travel, having Spooner write to the company's solicitors: 'The directors of the FR at their meeting on the 16th instant took into their consideration the question of the free passes to the quarry proprietors, and seeing that the litigation on the question is likely to be protracted, and the point in dispute is not of much consequence to the company, in a pecuniary sense, they had decided that they will accede to the request of Mr Greaves and give him a free pass. This they will do without prejudice to their legal rights. They will grant one free pass for each quarry to the owner thereof, or someone nominated by the owner or owners thereof and as regards the present pending proceedings with Mr Greaves, it is to be understood that each party pay their own costs.

'You will be good enough to communicate this decision of the directors, to Mr Greaves' solicitors (Messrs Breese, Jones & Casson) and inform me whether they will agree to this solution of the difficulty.'

Back to the routine, the quarrymen had found a champion, Arthur Osmond Williams of Barmouth, to promote their cause for daily trains and even-cheaper fares. It was decided, in February 1881, to run a daily service for them on a three-month trial basis. The fare would be 5d single and the existing 6d fare for the Saturday/Monday train would be reduced to match. Williams was to guarantee any loss arising from running the extra trains or from the reduced fare. His request to the company to agree a 2s weekly fare was refused in April. This would equate to one-sixth of 1d per mile and the directors were prepared to run the trains for 3s per week, at ¼d per mile a quarter of the legislated minimum rate. By the time an agreement was drawn up in August the directors had agreed to a 2d single fare between any two stations and a weekly ticket of 2s, also between any two stations. The guarantee was to cover any deficiency between the receipts and the sum of £376 10s, with the service starting on 5 May 1882.

By August 1882 the company was willing to continue the daily service provided the quarrymen's committee indemnify the company against any personal injury claim and guaranteed revenue of £185 per month. Finding that the service was not profitable, although there is no record of the guarantee being called in, the company gave the committee the option of continuing with the existing arrangements or of increasing the fare to 2s 6d and doing away with the guarantee. The latter being preferred, the company commenced to provide fully enclosed vehicles. Distance-related fares were introduced in 1885.

In February 1881, Spooner had been authorised to establish a new weighbridge and office at Duffws; with incidental works it was not to cost more than £60 but the estimate was £66 10s. In August, a new a new weighing machine for Portmadoc 'in place of old one, cost not to exceed £40' was approved. Messrs Pooley were ordered to install a new weighing machine, 'in lieu of the old one', near the market hall at Blaenau Festiniog in August 1883; the tendered cost was £65.

Changes to the signalling at the junction with the Festiniog & Blaenau Railway were to be carried out by McKenzie & Holland in August 1883, the GWR agreeing to pay half of the cost. Whether this meant the removal of the junction is unstated, but the conversion of the FBR to standard gauge was completed in September.

On the personnel front, William Williams had been appointed locomotive superintendent in February 1881, with a 10s per week increase in salary. There was no suggestion that Spooner should forgo the £50 increase he had been awarded in return for taking on this duty the previous year! Sydney Crick, a traffic officer who had been with the company since at least 1875, was awarded 10s a week extra from 1 March.

The work to install the additional sidings in Minffordd yard for the Cambrian had been carried out at the expense of one of the slate merchants, J. L. Prichard, who had lost some space. When he complained in August 1881, the company undertook to allocate him an equivalent amount of space in a different part of the yard. It also decided that the cost of the new sidings be charged to capital.

Major Francis A. Marindin was the next officer of the Board of Trade to become acquainted with the FR. On 15 November 1881 the down passenger train had been derailed near Dinas junction, injuring four passengers. The train consisted of a double-engine, brake van, two bogie carriages, a 'short' third-class carriage, and seven quarrymen's carriages. Five of the carriages were derailed and two of the quarrymen's carriages turned on their sides. The cause was found to be an axle on one of the quarrymen's carriages that 'was bent and nearly broken through'. The axle had been made by Caine & Kitchen, Liverpool, in 1875; new wheels had been fitted three weeks earlier and the carriage had made only six journeys between Portmadoc and Blaenau Festiniog. Examination showed that the carriage had derailed as it passed over the Dinas branch points.

Marindin reported that he found the track to be in excellent condition and correct to gauge but for a distance of about two feet near the point the outside rail on the curve was about ¼in low. The axle was broken through in his presence and he considered that the metal was of good quality but that there was a hair crack extending into the metal for more than half of its circumference. He thought the crack should have been detected when the new wheels were fitted. Of the quarrymen's carriages, he said: 'they are nothing better than slate wagons with covers to them, and I am not aware that any parliamentary or other sanction has been given for the conveyance of passengers, even at reduced fares, in such vehicles, which are undoubtedly less safe than the third-class passenger carriages in use upon this line'. He concluded that 'it should be remarked that this is the first accident to any passenger train which has taken place upon this line since it opened more than 16 years ago'.

Further use of the Oakeleys' private station was discussed in May 1882 when the board agreed: 'That the application from Captain Spencer to use Mr Oakeley's Flag Station for travelling by the down trains be allowed conditional that he has the privilege only to stop down trains and to limit the number of stoppages all [sic] possible and that no trains are to be kept waiting at the Oakeley station on any account. That he will be liable to the ordinary fare as from Tan-y-bwlch station. That he obtain permission to use Mr Oakeley's Flag station and "stopping signal" but that immediately after stopping any train the signal is to be placed back at "all right" and locked. The company reserves to itself the power of withdrawing the above privilege at any time.'

The new station building at Portmadoc having been built, Spooner was asked to produce a plan and tenders for covering the platform and the two sidings next to it in August 1882. The drawing showed an elegant iron structure that would cover four bogie carriages on the two lines. It was decided not to proceed in February 1883, although on that occasion the board approved a platform roof and goods shed for Tan-y-bwlch that were to be completed before the summer.

The company's confidence in the skills of Boston Lodge were confirmed in August 1882, when the board resolved 'That Mr Spooner be authorised to commence building a new double bogie locomotive to be completed in three years time, on the plan of the *Merddin Emrys*, to replace the *Little Wonder*, the expenditure to be equally distributed, if possible, over three years'.

The agreement with the Cambrian Railways concerning the combined rates had fallen apart by February 1883, with the Cambrian refusing to pay the rebate the FR was entitled to. The amount outstanding was £472 7s 10d and the board gave a great deal of attention to the matter over the following years.

Despite its decision in February 1882 that it was not interested in taking over the Portmadoc, Croesor & Beddgelert Railway, the board did consider a letter from Hugh Beaver Roberts of 15 February 1883 requesting that it should enter into a working agreement. Some of the conditions in Roberts's proposed agreement were unacceptable, notably the percentage of gross receipts proposed as the FR's share for working the line was too small. After a meeting with Roberts the board agreed to accept 50% of the gross receipts subject to a minimum of £3,000 per annum.

The company's slate tonnage had peaked at 132,244 tons in 1881, reflecting the opening of the LNWR line to Blaenau Festiniog. Things must have got off to a slow start in 1884, forcing the directors to panic to the extent of reducing their own fees before cutting staff! In February, they cut their fees to two guineas per day spent on the company's business, plus travelling expenses, with the chairman receiving a salary of £50 per annum. Graydon, the auditor, offered to accept £50, plus one guinea a day and travelling expenses, as his fee instead of £125. Spooner offered to reduce his salary to £617 10s, from £650, and volunteered that Hughes would have his salary of £50 reduced to £47 10s. The board restored Spooner and Hughes's salaries with effect from 1 July 1885.

At a second meeting in the same month, Spooner reported that he had made staffing reductions: permanent way platelayers, reduced by four, from 15; locomotive department,

fitters Boston Lodge, reduction of three, carpenters, reduction of one, from three; painters, reduction of one, from three. He estimated a saving of about £500 a year, 5% of the wages budget. He could not see any way of reducing the number of employees in the traffic department. Notice given to those being dismissed was 14 days. Spooner's proposals for an increase in fares were rejected, 'this not being an opportune time for making such a change'. The number of passengers carried, 215,455, goods tonnage, 35,843 tons, and profit, £10,351, had already reached their zenith in 1878, the best year in the company's history for revenue.

The railway had continued upgrading its track with steel rail, 50 tons from the Dowlais Iron Company in February 1881 and another 40 tons in August 1882. Although 4½ miles had been relaid with the steel rail the remainder could not wait until the company could afford more, Spooner reported in August 1884. At a time of stringency, it was necessary to find ways of containing costs and he had taken the best of the old 49lb double-headed rail, laid in 1869/70 and '71 and in need of renewal, and planed the bottoms smooth: 'the burr or indentation on them caused by impact with the chair bed would not otherwise admit of their further use'.

Following an experiment with rail from the embankment, he had treated a further five miles in like manner. He calculated that the cost of planing the iron rails, inclusive of labour, machine time, new sleepers where required, lifting and re-laying, was £66 per mile, compared with steel rail delivered to site ready for re-laying at £462 per mile. By this method he thought he could extend the life of the iron rails by six to eight years; they were already 14 years old. A half-mile would need re-laying in the next 12/18 months and the remainder of the main line would last about three years. He thought that the iron rail on the loop line, Dinas and Minffordd branches and the Duffws mineral line would last for several years without attention. Saying 'I must hope that the advantage secured in prolonging the life of these old rails for the permanent way may be appreciated by the directors as beneficial to the company's interest', he sought approval to buy 15 to 25 tons of new rail for renewals over the next three years.

The board resolved to create a reserve fund to finance both the re-laying and the new quarrymen's carriages that would soon be required. A year later Spooner received approval to purchase a further 50 tons of steel rail.

In another money-saving move, the board resolved, also in August 1884, to extend the telegraph from the long tunnel to Dduallt and to dispense with the services of one of the tunnel signalmen as soon as the work was completed.

The sale of the railway was the subject of a brief private correspondence between Spooner and Roche, beneficiary of the Tremadoc Estate, in 1885. On 4 April, Roche wrote that he had been asked the price of the harbour and the railway, but did not identify the would-be purchasers. He wrote again on 27 July, saying that he had met the would-be purchasers in London and had expected them to call another meeting; he would write to them and advise Spooner of the outcome. There obviously was no outcome and the matter was not put before the board.

A resolution of the Cambrian rates affair seemed in sight at the same time, when the directors authorised a letter rejecting the latest proposals from the Cambrian and said that they would be happy to maintain the *status quo* established in April 1884, whereby the Cambrian allowed a rebate of 1s per ton, but in future the FR wanted the rebate paid directly to the quarry proprietors instead of via the FR. The following February, the amount of the outstanding rebate was still in dispute. The Cambrian had declared that the rebate would be the same

whether the slate was shipped at Minffordd or via the Croesor sidings. Presumably, the quarry proprietors expected that as the Cambrian paid a tonnage to the FR on slate transhipped at Minffordd, tranship costs at Portmadoc should be cheaper and they wanted the benefit of any saving! This would relate to slate that had been stored on the Portmadoc wharves.

In August 1885, Spooner sent the Cambrian a very strongly worded letter of complaint over the handling of the rebate. Diphwys Casson had transferred its output to the LNWR because it had been unable to get any response from the Cambrian about its own shipments.

A traffic agreement made with the GWR in 1885 required only a fraction of the management time; in February the board declared that it was willing to enter into a similar agreement with the LNWR and the terms for shipping slate to Deganwy were agreed in August. An agreement with the GWR to locate an FR ticket office on the platform of its Blaenau Festiniog station was approved in August 1885, but before the agreement was signed in February 1886 the company complained to its solicitors for failing to produce documents that reflected the requirements of the parties.

Both Portmadoc residents and quarry proprietors expressed concern about fees and tolls levied for using the harbour, a public meeting being held on 19 February 1886. The rates were seen as high and discouraging of traffic, especially with the LNWR being able to ship via Deganwy. The board spent some time on the issue, although it was really a matter for the Tremadoc Estate. Cwmorthin and Greaves both wrote to the railway: '... I would urge upon you sir and upon your company directors the advisability, nay the necessity of meeting and forestalling, while yet there is time, this threatened competition. A comparatively small sacrifice now will in my opinion suffice to keep the trade and traffic in its old groove; but once allow the traffic to be diverted it will require a much greater reduction in the rates to recover it. I would also suggest that your board should communicate with Mr Roche with a view of inducing him to reduce harbour dues and other port and estate charges which are under present circumstances untenable and which unless they are reduced all round will surely drive the trade away from Portmadoc. Pressure also ought to be brought to bear

upon the tug boat company to reduce their charges and also upon the lessees of the ballast bank ...'

The company accused Cwmorthin of not making a valid comparison, as the proprietors would have to invest in facilities at Deganwy, which they already had in Portmadoc, and also pay dues there. The board, however, was prepared to make concessions, including agreeing to forgo the 2d per ton charged for haulage on the wharves.

The residents had also addressed their complaint to the Cambrian Railways, which called a meeting with the FR on 28 July 1886. Two of the Cambrian directors met Livingston, Cairnes and Hardy in London. The Cambrian directors thought that Portmadoc was 5d per ton more expensive than Deganwy, not because of the rail rates, which were identical, but because of charges for harbour dues, tug dues and rent and taxes of wharves, which latter charge was remitted to shippers at Deganwy by the LNWR. It thought that the FR should make an effort to remove the discrepancy without affecting the rail rate.

The Cambrian also thought that in the situation where slate had been stored on the wharves at Portmadoc, it should be able to ship it via the Cambrian without further charge. Slate stored at Deganwy would, of course, be sent on via the LNWR without incurring an additional transfer fee. The Cambrian thought that if the Croesor & Portmadoc Railway 'was improved and made fit to carry locomotives this might afford a means of removing this difficulty'. This proposal would result in the closing of the transfer facility at Minffordd, 'entailing a serious loss to both companies', and had not been put to the Cambrian board.

In response, the company decided that it would make an allowance of 1d per ton towards rent provided the Tremadoc Estate and the tug boat company made similar allowances. It countered the Portmadoc transfer proposal by offering to

Whistling curve, near Tan-y-bwlch, in 1887, a view that is unrepeatable due to tree growth. *R. H. Bleasdale/Author's collection*

reduce the 6d Portmadoc–Minffordd rate to 3½d provided the Tremadoc estate would reduce its tonnage rate by 1s 2d to 1s. It confirmed its position on the 2d wharf haulage rate. Spooner was instructed to send a copy of the resolutions to the Cambrian and to bring them to the attention of the Estate and the tug boat company 'with a view to ascertain whether they would be prepared to enter into the arrangements proposed'.

The Cambrian's response must have come as a shock to the board when it received a letter dated 11 August 1886 from John Conacher, the Cambrian's company secretary. The FR's proposal had been put to his board, he wrote, and 'I am instructed to state that, in their opinion, the proposals contained in those resolutions are entirely inadequate to meet the circumstances of the case, and, that while the directors consider no satisfactory settlement can be arrived at on the basis of such proposals they have instructed me to seek another interview with you for the further discussion of the matter'.

Following a meeting with Spooner in Portmadoc, Conacher wrote on 16 August 1886 to explain that the Cambrian had been losing 5d per ton on its slate traffic when compared with the LNWR and GWR rates to London. In 1884 it had started transferring the 5d 'loss' to a suspense account pending a settlement with the FR over the combined rate; the amount in the suspense account had reached nearly £2,000 and the Cambrian was expecting to recover this amount when it had completed an agreement with the FR. This explanation of the Cambrian's position was in contradiction of what the Cambrian directors had said on 28 July.

The board requested Spooner to inform the Cambrian that the FR had done all it could on the rates; it had already reduced the Portmadoc–Minffordd rate and agreed to allow 1d per ton on the wharves; it could not do more: 'if they did, no margin would be left for remuneration'. The Cambrian was also informed that the FR could not move on the Blaenau Festiniog–Minffordd rate, otherwise slate would be shipped to

Minffordd and then separately to Portmadoc at the reduced rate, breaching the whole-line rate.

On 6 September 1886, the parties with an interest in the harbour had met: Roche, its beneficial owner; Prichard of the Portmadoc Steam Tug Company; Conacher of the Cambrian, with Spooner and Hughes for the FR, the latter probably as note-taker. Based on the average of the previous three years, the reductions proposed earlier would amount to £704 by the FR and £386 by the Estate, a total of £1,090 per annum. Roche proposed that this should be borne four-fifths by the FR and one-fifth by him, which appeared to mean, on the basis of the average figures, that the FR should forgo £872 instead of £704! For the Steam Tug Company, Prichard said that it was prepared to reduce its rates in a range of 20% to 50% provided other port charges were reduced as well.

The part played by the ship owners in the price of slate delivered is never mentioned; perhaps the parties, particularly the quarry proprietors of course, thought their charges equitable. According to Hughes, again, in 1890 the barque *Prince of Wales* carried 520 tons of slate from Portmadoc to Hamburg, 1,000 miles, for 10s per ton.

What happened during the next few weeks is not explained in the minutes but when the board met on 27 October 1886 Spooner was 'instructed to express the regret of this board that Mr Roche and Mr Prichard will not make the reductions in their charges of 1d per ton in each case proposed by the Festiniog board as a condition of making the reduction on their part...' The board decided to act unilaterally and introduced the changes previously considered. The board's distress over this outcome is manifest by the minute that concludes '... this board consider there is a strong claim on Mr Roche as the person representing these charges to make a substantial reduction in them'.

The company's general meeting had been held in London on 18 August, when the full dividends on the preference shares had been approved. Only 1½% was voted for the ordinary stock, however, and this might have led to some of the shareholders requesting 'that a committee be appointed to enquire whether the working expenses of the line cannot be reduced without interfering with its efficiency and safety'. The proposal was accepted and 'J. G. Livingston, T. P. Cairnes, C. H. C. Huddart, J. W. Elliott and a scientific gentleman chosen by the committee' were appointed. On 26 October 1886, John Stevenson Macintyre was appointed consulting engineer, to inspect the line and recommend savings. He had worked for the Eastern Counties Railway and played a key role in developing Harwich harbour for the Great Eastern Railway; he was regarded as being careful and methodical in his work.

Macintyre's review and the committee's report were competed in time for the company's general meeting on 23 February 1887. The committee found that the company's reduced earnings arose from two causes: depression in the slate trade and competition from the LNWR for goods and mineral traffic. The depression was beyond the board's control and its effect was countered by increased economy; there appeared to be a slight improvement in the demand for slate. Competition from the LNWR had '... received the careful attention of the board and they have endeavoured to meet it so far as practicable so as to retain the traffic ...' The board also considered that 'it was inevitable that a considerable portion of the goods traffic should pass into the hands of the London & North Western Company but in the mineral traffic which is the item of first importance, this company occupied a more advantageous position and by reducing rates, entering into through booking arrangements with the Cambrian Company and meeting as far as practicable the wishes of the quarry proprietors they have succeeded up to the present in retaining the great bulk of this traffic'. The passenger traffic had been only slightly affected, having benefited by increased through traffic almost to the extent of the loss sustained by reduced return traffic to Portmadoc.

On the matter of expenditure, Macintyre had informed the committee that:

- Permanent way costs were comparable with those of other similar lines except that chairs and fish bolts could probably be obtained more cheaply by contract; they had been produced at Boston Lodge.
- The cost of the new locomotive had inflated the cost of locomotive power; considering the costs of repairs and renewals, the costs of the carriage and wagon departments were slightly above those on other lines in the neighbourhood.
- Traffic expenses and general charges were moderate, being considerably less than those of the GWR and about the same as those of the Cambrian.
- Operations at Boston Lodge should be restricted to ordinary repairs and renewals; savings might be made by obtaining locomotives and passenger carriages by contract.

It is apparent that, encouraged by Spooner, work was being undertaken at Boston Lodge because it had the capability, rather than because it was the most efficient or cost-effective way. The committee made the following recommendations to the board which agreed to put them to the general meeting:

I   That the operations at Boston Lodge should be confined in future to ordinary repairs and renewals so far as the engines and passenger carriages are concerned; that the building of new rolling stock be limited to goods and mineral wagons, quarrymen's carriages and vehicles of this class and that the staff employed be proportionately reduced and the expenses kept as low as may be practicable, consistent with maintaining the rolling stock in good and sufficient working order and repair.

II   That the building of any more new engines should not be undertaken without consulting the shareholders.

III That tenders should be obtained at least annually for the

The company's crest embossed as an envelope seal and used from Spooner's office in the 1880s. The original is 1in diameter.

supply of the various stores for the permanent way and locomotive departments so as to ensure that the supply is obtained on the best terms possible.

The recommendations were accepted and the tendering procedure put into immediate effect, with Spooner instructed to obtain tenders under the headings of stores, coal and rail. When considered on 23 February 1887, the price of coal from the Vron Colliery Company at Wrexham was 13s 8d per ton delivered to Minffordd. J. G. Jones, the colliery's representative, had been informed 'yesterday by telegram' that the directors were dissatisfied with the price and required a reduction of 2s per ton, Spooner being told not to purchase through Jones unless he could supply at 12s per ton delivered at Minffordd. The New British Iron Company of Ruabon offered to supply at 10s 11d per ton to Minffordd; two months supply to be tried.

Concerning rail, Spooner reported that about 30 tons was in stock and recommended that a further 50 to 60 tons should be obtained. The last delivery from Dowlais Iron & Steel Company was £5 4 0d per ton delivered at Cardiff. Tenders were to be obtained from the Dowlais company and from the Barrow-in-Furness Iron & Steel Company and Spooner was authorised to contract for from 50 to 60 tons if it could be obtained for not more than £5 5s 0d delivered to Portmadoc or Minffordd. If the best price was higher he was to order only 25-30 tons. He was allowed to order 120 tons in February 1888.

When it came to the 100 steel or Low Moor iron tyres required for the slate wagons in August 1887, Spooner was instructed to obtain a second tender before ordering; their purchase was approved in August 1888.

In October 1886, Oakeley had complained about being charged 1d per ton extra for slate produced from his middle quarry. This charge had been levied because the quarry could not accommodate the 3 ton wagons and the company incurred additional expense in marshalling 2 ton wagons for him. The board agreed to cancel the charge with immediate effect. In a similar vein the following February, the company decided to reduce the charge to the Welsh Slate Company for goods carried up one incline in FR wagons to 9d, but to retain the rate at 1s 3d if more than one incline was involved; it also decided that these rates should be applied to all quarries.

Palmerston, 'the shunting engine', was the subject of an unusual example of a particular locomotive receiving board attention in February 1887. It had been dismantled and found to be in good condition except for the boiler. With a new boiler costing £150-£170 it could be repaired at a total cost of £250-£300. 'This is important as at the present time the company have no spare shunting engines and should be done gradually (say in two years).' Spooner was instructed to have the work done, tendering for the boiler from Adamson & Co and Vulcan Foundry. Adamson's tender of £162 was accepted in August. A tender for a new boiler for *Little Giant* was issued in February 1888 and a new tank was authorised to be made at Boston Lodge in August, at the same time as a contract for Neilson & Son to supply a new boiler for *James Spooner*, at £390 delivered to Minffordd, was awarded; three tenders had been requested. There was a hiatus when *James Spooner's* boiler was delivered in February 1889, because Neilson had gone into receivership and the solicitors were asked for approval to pay the trustees. A new tank for *Welsh Pony* was authorised in February 1889.

When the General Post Office circularised railway companies on 1 April 1887, warning against breaching the state monopoly for carrying letters, the company sought advice from the LNWR. In August Spooner was instructed to see that the company did not contravene the instructions in the circular, the rider 'letter bags not to be carried for quarry proprietors' suggesting that they had been! A contract to carry mail bags for £30 per annum had been agreed in 1881.

Along the line, the railway's largest structure, Cei Mawr, was giving cause for concern when Spooner found that some of the original stone cladding was being crushed by the weight of the structure. He was told that he could 'carry out the works which

may be required for making the Big Quay safe' in February 1886. He then found that an existing buttress at the north-east end required attention and was told that 'the abutment may be commenced and proceeded with gradually', on 23 August 1887. In February 1888 he had found that it would be necessary to build an abutment at the south-east end so he was authorised to spend the not inconsiderable sum of £1,250, in total, on the structure. Although the work was to be carried out as quickly as Spooner thought necessary, the expenditure was to be spread over eight half-years. The original estimate had been for £750.

A fine record of how the FR appeared to contemporary eyes was made in August 1887, when photographer R. H. Bleasdale visited the line on two occasions and made 44 exposures. Although, apart from the photographs, there's no record of his visits, considerable effort was obviously made for his benefit. At least one train was run and locos and rolling stock were posed for him, *James Spooner* and *Merddin Emrys* were turned so that he could photograph the driver's side on the embankment, and he travelled the length of the line and photographed many of its features. The reason for his visit is now unknown, but he did appear to have some status, at least, as a semi-official photographer for several main line railway companies, so it could be that the board, or Spooner, wanted to commission an official record of the railway's achievements from someone with established capability.

Another meeting with Conacher took place in August 1887. The Cambrian had tried to make an agreement with all of the slate-carrying railway companies and had published rates as though it had full agreement, when the FR had objected. He explained that the slate traffic paid poorly for his company, the route was longer than either of the LNWR's or the GWR's and was expensive to work as there were heavy gradients against the load. The suspense account now had £3,000 debited against it and his company was anxious for a resolution. It did not get one that day, and it was pointed out that the FR had made concessions worth £700 a year in shunting the Blaenau traffic and he would have to wait for a decision.

That came in a letter from Hughes on 9 November 1887.

James Spooner arrives at Portmadoc on a Saturday afternoon in 1886. In its train are an 1880 van, both 1872 bogie carriages and a Brown, Marshalls four-wheeler. On the right is a train of second generation quarrymen's stock. This is probably the oldest known picture of a moving train on the FR. *FR Archives*

A meeting had been arranged in London only to be cancelled at short notice by telegram; the directors' anger is apparent. Hughes explained that the quarry proprietors' practice of consigning slate to Minffordd or Portmadoc and then forwarding it to its ultimate destination via the Cambrian actually precluded through-booking as preferred by the Cambrian. Under the existing arrangements, he went on, there was no difference in the through rate and none of the proprietors complained about it. 'Under the circumstances my directors with the information placed before them are not prepared to disturb the existing arrangement.' It was left that the matter would be held over until the FR's next general meeting in February 1888.

The appointment of John Sylvester Hughes as secretary is rather a mystery. Spooner was in post at a meeting held on 24 August 1887 but at another meeting held three days later, Hughes was the secretary. In February 1888, the board decided to pay him £125 for the current half year, and if he was satisfactory at the end of that period his salary would be increased to £150 per annum. He was required to retire from his partnership with Spooner but could undertake consultancy work with the directors' approval. Spooner continued to attend board meetings. Presumably in preparation for the change, Alfred G. Crick was appointed assistant clerk at Portmadoc at a salary of 24s per week from 1 October. Members of the Crick family established a lesser-known dynasty in the FR's administration, Sydney having worked for the company since 1875, while F. G. Crick had joined two years earlier.

The locomotive superintendent, William Williams, applied for an increased salary in February 1888, his present remuneration being £190 15s 0d, including extra for inspecting carriages. Spooner was instructed to tell him that he could have his living accommodation rent free.

A request from Portmadoc traders for a late train to/from Blaenau Festiniog was considered in February 1888, when Spooner was authorised to timetable one for a three-month period from 1 June. At the end of August a trial of operating the winter service with one passenger train instead of two was approved to start from 1 October. The trial was reported on 31 December that year as having been satisfactory and in August 1889 approval was given for it to be repeated.

An unusual demand was made of Hughes in February 1889, 'to report whether it is possible to arrange to interlock the points at Portmadoc station so as to secure greater safety, but so as not to necessitate any interference by the Board of Trade'!

Greaves had asked for a special rate to carry 50 tons of coal to his quarries in February 1888, to which the board had agreed, provided Greaves gave an indication as to the amount of discount he required! Twelve months later the minutes noted that ten new 3 ton coal wagons were needed. Hughes was instructed to inform the quarry proprietors that the railway would supply them with coal wagons if required, 'making the same charge as at present if taken to the quarry'.

Other matters arising from the quarry proprietors at the same time was Oakeley's request to lease a wharf at Minffordd (approved and lease to be prepared), and Craig Ddu's request for a reduction in rates for slate. This last might have been unexpected as the quarry was connected to the GWR at Tan y Manod; its proprietor, Richard Bowton, was to become a company director in 1906. The board agreed that he should pay the same as the Blaenau quarries, from 1 March 1889.

The board was getting a good grip on the tendering process by February 1889, when it agreed to take 12 months' supply of steam coal, about 1,200 tons, from the Vron Colliery Company at 13s per ton, delivered to Blaenau Festiniog as required. In February 1890, the agreed price was 15s 6d per ton less 1s per

FESTINIOG RAILWAY.

TIME TABLE

From FEBRUARY 1st, 1888, until further Notice.

Up Trains	1, 2, Ply. 1. A.M.	2. A.M.	3. A.M.	4. A.M.	5.	6. P.M.	7. P.M.	8. P.M.	9.
PORTMADOC dep.	BK5 45	7 0	8 35	10 30	..	C1 0	3 30	4 50	
†MINFFORD JUNC.	5 55	7 10	8 45	10 40	..	1 10	3 40	5 0	
PENRHYN	6 0	7 15	8 50	10 45	..	1 18	3 47	5 5	
TAN-Y-BWLCH	6 18	7 35	9 7	11 10	..	1 40	4 7	5 22	
DDUALLT	A	A	..	..	..	A	..	A	
TAN-Y-GRISIAU	6 38	7 55	9 28	11 27	..	1 55	4 27	5 43	
§BLAENAU FESTINIOG JU.	6 44	8 3	9 33	11 33	..	2 0	4 33	5 48	
•DUFFWS arrive	6 46	8 5	9 35	11 35	..	2 5	4 35	5 50	
L.&N.W. Blaenau depart	7 0	..	9 55	12 20	..	2 30	..	6 20	
L.&N.W. Llandudno J. ar.	8 14	..	11 9	1 32	..	3 45	..	7 35	
L.&N.W. Chester „	9 58	..	1 8	3 45	..	5 15	..	10 0	
G.W.R. Blaenau depart.	..	8 5	11 45	12 42	..	2 10	..	7 5	
G.W.R. Bala .. arrive	..	9 13	Not an Sat. Festiniog only	Sat. only Trav-fyaydd.	..	3 19	..	8 13	
G.W.R. Chester .. „	..	11 38			..	5 31	..	10 26	

Down Trains.	A.M.	A.M.	A.M.	A.M.	A.M.	A.M.	A.M.	P.M.	P.M.
L.&N.W. Chester depart.	..	2 30	..	6 30	..	..	10 0	..	2 30
L.&N.W. Llandudno J. „	..	4 25	..	8 38	..	..	11 40	..	3 55
L.&N.W. Blaenau arrive.	..	6 10	..	9 50	..	..	1 0	..	5 10
G.W.R. Chester depart.	..	..	..	7 10	..	..	9 0	..	From Festiniog
G.W.R. Bala .. „	..	..	..	9 27	..	..	11 20	..	Sat. only
G.W.R. Blaenau arrive.	..	..	..	10 40	..	..	12 30	..	5 30
DUFFWS depart	..	H7 5	8 40	10 45	..	12 28	H1 10	3 40	G5 50
BLAENAU FESTINIOG JU.	..	7 7	8 42	10 47	..	12 30	1 12	3 42	5 52
TAN-Y-GRISIAU	..	7 12	8 47	10 52	..	12 38	1 18	3 47	5 57
DDUALLT	..	A	A	A	..	A	A	A	A
TAN-Y-BWLCH	..	7 35	9 7	11 10	..	12 58	1 40	4 7	6 15
PENRHYN	..	7 54	9 27	11 28	..	1 23	2 0	4 25	6 37
†MINFFORD JUNC.	..	8 0	9 35	11 33	..	1 28	2 5	4 30	6 45
PORTMADOC ar.	..	8 10	9 45	11 43	..	1 38	2 15	4 40	6 55

†Change for Cambrian Railway.
§Change for L.&N.W. Co.
•Change at G.W. Platform for Festiniog, Bala, &c.

(A) Stop by Signal to take Up and set Down when required. Notice to be given to the Guard at the preceding Station.
(B) On Mondays will leave Portmadoc at 6 a.m. (C) Leaves Portmadoc at 12-30 on Saturdays. (E) On Saturdays only.
(F) Will leave Duffws 1-20 p.m. on Saturdays. (G)-Not Parly. on Saturdays.
(H) On Mondays will leave Duffws at 7-15 a.m.
(K) On and after the 14th will leave Portmadoc at 5-35 a.m.

Return Tickets are available for return on the following day.
The Company cannot guarantee these times being kept under any circumstances, nor will they be responsible for delay.
☞ Omnibuses run between the Portmadoc Stations of the Cambrian and Festiniog Railways, meeting every train.
The Village of Festiniog is 3½ miles by G.W. Railway from Duffws.

E. Jones, Printer, Portmadoc

ton rebate, delivered to Minffordd, on 'the understanding that 2cwt per truck be given as overweight'.

It was resolved to transfer Spooner's responsibilities as engineer and general manager to Hughes on 21 August 1889, a move made without recorded comment. Spooner was in attendance but he was to die on 18 November and was buried with his wife and maid in the churchyard at Beddgelert. The railings around his grave are said to have been made at Boston Lodge. Hughes took over on 1 October, with a salary of £300, inclusive of his secretarial duties.

When the board met next, in February 1890, no one thought to place on record any tribute to the man who had transformed the Festiniog Railway from a horse tramway to a sophisticated steam railway with imaginative solutions relative to its special position in the landscape. Before Charles Easton, the railway was a little-known curiosity in a backwater; with him it was at the forefront of technical development and became known the world over; after him it became, once again, a curiosity.

Mrs Tiddeman, Spooner's sister Harriet, asked that 'the allowance made to the late Mr Spooner be continued to Miss Spooner', the latter probably an unmarried sister, Amelia, who he had been supporting. Although the request was refused, the board agreed to make a payment for the period from the date of his death until the end of the year.

In the ten years that the FR had been exposed to competition its dividends ceased to break records, falling to 2¼% in 1886. The 132,244 tons of slate and 179,286 passengers carried in 1881 had become 95,381 tons and 144,327 passengers by 1890, the net receipts falling from £8,841 to £7,667 over the same period.

SIGNALLING

Far left: **The McKenzie & Holland double-arm slotted post signal at Minffordd.** *Author's collection*

Left: **A distant signal, probably at Minffordd.** *Author's collection*

Below left: **Portmadoc signals with the locking box. On the left, an Ashbury carriage is stabled with a quarrymen's carriage.** *Author's collection*

Below: **The signal arrangements for the Dinas loop line submitted to the Board of Trade on 26 March 1881.** *National Archives*

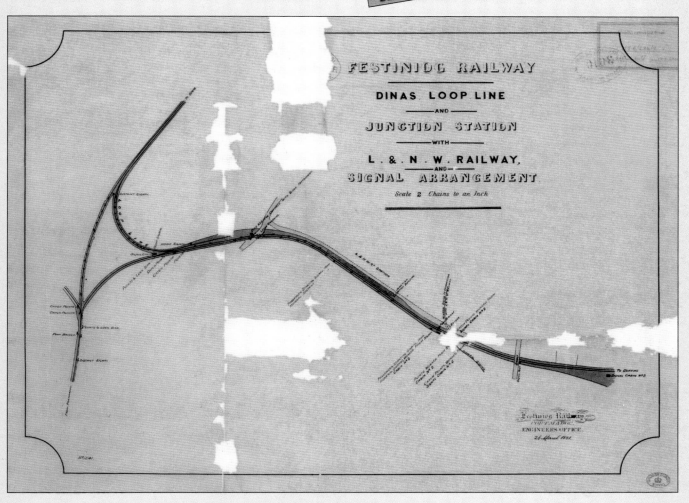

7

After the Spooners

1890-1899

After the death of Charles Spooner the FR carried on much as it had done before. The board might not have been aware of it but the railway had actually entered a period of gradual decline. The big weakness in the accounts was the level of debt; the debentures and preference shares needed nearly £3,000 a year to service. A 3½% dividend on the ordinary stock, the average in the last 20 years of the 19th century, required a similar amount again. While the railway was doing well this was not a problem, with shareholders more than happy to receive their interest twice a year, but with no policy in place to reduce or eliminate the debt, and set against falling revenues, it was a millstone. The directors' priority was always to preserve the interest/dividend payments, even if the long-term result was to weaken the business.

Complying with the Regulation of Railways Act of 1889 was an issue that faced all railways during the 1890s. In the interests of public safety, the act gave powers to the Board of Trade to order railways to adopt the block system of signalling to provide interlocking of points with signals and to install continuous brakes on all passenger trains. The company could apply to the Board of Trade for a certificate to authorise any capital required, thus avoiding the need for further parliamentary powers.

Livingston Thompson, **the second locomotive built at Boston Lodge, at Tan-y-bwlch c1890. The trailing load on the up train is quite substantial considering that it is being hauled by** *Taliesin.* **The screen in front of the door to the right of the station building conceals the urinals.** *Author's collection*

Receiving the Board of Trade's 24 October 1889 notice concerning the act, the company's instinct was to apply for an exemption. Hughes replied on 21 December 1889, describing the railway in some detail and making a number of points about the railway's operation, including the following:

- The up trains running up the gradient are mixed trains arranged with goods trucks in front of the passenger carriages and van and empty slate trucks behind the van.
- These trains are composed generally of one double engine, four to eight goods wagons, two four-wheel carriages, two bogie carriages, one bogie van, and 50 to 80 slate wagons.
- The engines and vans are supplied with powerful screw brakes.
- It has been considered that having the loaded goods wagons in front has been conducive to safety more than otherwise. This arrangement gives also an advantage that the wagons can be detached at any of the stations and the train started without shunting the passenger carriages.
- The slate wagons are attached and detached at different stations on the line.
- The down passenger trains are worked separately from the minerals and goods, they run down by gravity, engine and van in front, but the down mineral train has no van attached … and is controlled by two brakesmen.
- The line is single and worked with the train staff. There is a single needle block between Boston Lodge and Minffordd, … as there is a good deal of shunting done on this portion; also from Dduallt to the top end of [the] tunnel ... and from Tanygrisiau to Duffws ... where there is a good deal of shunting going on.

- There are speaking instruments at all the stations.
- The signals between Portmadoc and Dinas Junction are wood semaphore for home signals and iron disc distant signals and the points are worked with a bolt by the same wire which works the signal.
- There are point signals on all the points.
- Between Dinas Junction and Duffws where there is much shunting there are home and distant signals with the points interlocked with rods and worked from cabins.
- The trains stop at all the stations and run at a speed of from 15 to 17 miles an hour between stations and can be stopped in a distance about equal to their own length.
- The brakes can be applied quickly and effectively, especially as the wheels are small in diameter.
- Any arrangements of continuous automatic brakes would be very expensive and impracticable to work.

Concluding 'My directors beg to submit', he said:

- That the proposed requirements would entail a large expenditure to provide for which their company has no available funds and which in their present position could only be raised at a very serious disadvantage.
- That the line is different in so many important respects from other railways.
- That the trains are very limited in number.
- That the train speed is quite unusually low.
- That there is ample brake power at present provided to secure safety.
- These facts, together with the safe and satisfactory working of the present arrangements, as shown in 25 years' experience, will, they trust, be sufficient reasons to induce the Board of Trade to exempt their company from having to carry out the requirements of the act.

When the board met in February 1890, it decided that if an exemption could not be obtained then it would seek a three-year period to complete the works from the date of any order. In the meantime, Hughes was to produce estimates of the cost of complying with the act.

Submitting the draft order to the Board of Trade on 4 March 1890, Hughes wrote that in addition to the reasons he gave in his application for exemption dated 21 December 1889, the board should also consider that 'the trains, which are nearly all mixed trains, run in and out of stations at a speed of about five miles an hour'. In the draft order he proposed that the company be allowed one year to install the block system and 18 months for each of the interlocking and the continuous brakes; under the heading of exemptions he asked that 'the portions of the line not already supplied with the block system be exempted from the order'.

The Board of Trade's responses to these documents have not survived but it asked Rich for his opinion, which he gave on 12 November 1890. He thought that 'it appears desirable to prevent the company following the present practice of running trains of six or seven goods wagons in front of about four or five passenger carriages and from 70 to 85 slate wagons behind'. Saying that he thought the company should comply with both block and brake requirements, he added: 'There will no doubt be some difficulties to overcome in fitting up the vehicles in consequence of the little room available but we think these can be overcome. We do not think the wagons that go into the quarries could be piped. They are so low the pipes would be broken by the rollers and the loose slates ...' concluding, 'we would suggest that four four-wheeled coaches or five quarrymen's carriages or four goods wagons should count as one. Each large bogie passenger coach should count as one and the large bogie engines, which weigh 24 tons, as three ...'

An amended draft order was submitted to Hughes on 14 November 1890. Responding on 18 November, he detailed the distances of the sections he wished to be excluded from block working as: Portmadoc–Boston Lodge, 1,320yd; Minffordd–Tan-y-bwlch, 10,120yd; Tan-y-bwlch–Dduallt, 3,960yd, and north end of the tunnel to Tanygrisiau, 2,200yd. He explained that the company would wish to run six mixed trains up and one down in summer and four mixed up and one down in winter. For the purpose of counting, he submitted the following: engine – one vehicle; tender, four-wheeled carriage or four-wheel truck – ¼ vehicle; eight-wheel carriage or van – ½ vehicle.

The estimate for compliance totalled a suspiciously rounded £2,000 (Table 9). The order was made on 18 December 1890 and was accepted by Hughes on 22 December. The company had one year to adopt the block system and two years were given to complete the interlocking and the installation of continuous automatic brakes on passenger trains. Hughes's method of counting was adopted. A proportion of vehicles, not exceeding one in four, could be run unbraked provided they had through pipes and that the last vehicle in the train was braked. A limited number of mixed trains was permitted, subject to certain conditions:

- The engine, tender and passenger carriages be provided with continuous brakes worked from the engine.
- Goods wagons to be conveyed behind the passenger vehicles, with one brake van for every ten wagons or part of ten wagons.
- No mixed train to consist of more than 25 vehicles.
- Maximum speed not to exceed 25mph.
- All mixed trains to stop at all stations or at intervals not exceeding ten miles.

In a return made to the Board of Trade in 1896, the company declared that it had equipped nine locomotives, 28 passenger carriages and five vans with vacuum brakes and had piped 26 carriages.

Table 9

Estimate for compliance with Regulation of Railways Act, 1889

1	12 sets of Tyers block instruments complete with batteries	£300
	11 miles of wire with the necessary brackets, insulators, leading in wires and extra poles required	
	Necessary additions and alterations in block stations for fixing instruments etc	
2	Adding eight additional levers at five different stations with necessary signals and connections	£150
	No spare levers	
3	Fitting the automatic vacuum brake to:	£1,550
	3 double-bogie tank engines	
	6 tank engines with tender	
	6 bogie carriages	
	35 four-wheel carriages	
	5 bogie brake vans	
	Total	£2,000

Three consequences of compliance with the 1889 Regulation of Railways Act are shown in this photograph. *Livingston Thompson*, on the left, has vacuum brake equipment; the loaded goods wagons are coupled behind the passenger stock; and the centre track to the goods yard has been cut back. The tail load for the up train includes both 2 ton and 3 ton slate wagons and iron- and timber-bodied coal wagons.
Commercial Postcard/Author's Collection

Returning to the board's February 1890 meeting, Hughes submitted an in-depth report on the railway's condition. He said that since he had taken control of the FR he had examined all 'the papers and plans of the railway' and made 'a careful examination of the whole of the buildings, works, bridges, culverts, breastwalls, fencing, and permanent way and signals, also the machinery and rolling stock and made notes respecting same for present and future guidance'. He also had the wagons counted to ensure that the number given in the returns was accurate. 'The results were satisfactory.'

Other points in the report:

- Only 2½ miles of the main line required renewing with steel rails.
- The works at the Big Quay had been completed at a cost of £1,079 2s 4d.
- A new carriage shed had been built at Boston Lodge.
- *James Spooner's* overhaul had been completed at a cost of £769 15s; the loco had cost £2,135 10s when new.
- A decision was needed on the future of *Welsh Pony*; plate was in stock for a new tank and it would cost £420 to return to service. *Little Giant* required new frames.
- The coal trucks approved in 1889 had not been made and there had been complaints; they would have cost £35 each. The railway had 20 low-sided trucks that were not in use so he had had 16 adapted to carry coal, costing £18 each. He was also adapting six slab trucks to carry coal, costing £9 10s each.
- One new quarrymen's carriage had been made and two wagons for carrying pigs and calves had been made from two old workmen's carriages.
- Oakeley and Greaves had decided to have a private telegraph between the quarries and the Portmadoc wharves; the wayleave had been agreed at 7s 6d per mile and the work was completed in January.
- He had rearranged the company's insurance, gaining £2,935 more cover for £5 13s less premium.

- Summer traffic had been poor due to wet weather, but circular tours had done well.
- Coal traffic from the port to the quarries was doing well. In the second half of 1889 the quantity of slates sent by the LNWR had been 5,671 tons (5,187 tons), by the GWR 9,178 tons (7,497 tons) and by the Cambrian 17,503 tons (17,065 tons). Also, 58,158 tons (54,785 tons) had been shipped from Portmadoc.
- Princess Beatrice and Prince Henry had been passengers from Minffordd to Plas Tan-y-bwlch.
- Hugh Williams was the oldest workman on the line; too much of a liability to use as a platelayer, he was kept on for weeding and helping with the repairs of the fencing and other jobs.
- It had been necessary to increase some wages to retain personnel; the other railways had increased wages and there had been increases in the area.

The royal visit had taken place on 27 August 1889. Escorted by Spooner, the royal visitors were presented with an album of photographs, possibly those taken by Bleasdale in 1887. Queen Victoria was to have been the principal guest but was indisposed, remaining at Palé, near Bala.

The board decided to invite tenders for *Welsh Pony's* new boiler and to have *Little Giant* repaired. Adamson & Company tendered £240 and the Vulcan Foundry Company £227 15s 0d, both inclusive of delivery; the Vulcan tender was accepted in August. A decision to have *Prince* rebuilt 'gradually', including a new boiler, was taken in August 1891. New tyres were required for *Merddin Emrys* in August 1892; the tender from Vickers & Co was 24s per cwt and Bolton Steel Co, 18s per cwt, the latter being accepted. At the same time, *Princess* was considered 'worn out' and it was to be 'remade by degrees' and three tenders obtained for a new boiler. Vulcan's tender of £190 was accepted in February 1893, while the Hunslet Engine Co had quoted £220 and W. G. Bagnall & Co £180, so presumably the FR preferred to deal with a company that it knew. *Merddin Emrys's* boiler was worn out by August 1895, when a new one was approved; the Vulcan Foundry's tender of £454 10s was accepted six months later. Beyer, Peacock & Co had tendered £700. The Vulcan Foundry's tender of £295 for a new boiler for *Taliesin* was accepted in February 1899.

No steel rails were to be ordered unless the price fell, Hughes was instructed. The price was five guineas when 100 tons were ordered in August 1890, £4 15s when 60 tons were ordered in August 1891 and £4 5s in August 1893, when a further 40 tons were ordered, all from the Dowlais Iron Company. In February 1891, a second platelayers' gang was to be recruited, the £300 cost to be charged to reserves. Consideration was given to re-laying in the tunnel in February 1893.

The final item of business in August 1890 was Hughes's salary. The board resolved to increase it to £450, backdated to 1 January 1890, and to increase it to £500 at a rate of £25 per annum. It was declared that Hughes's interests would be protected in the event of a sale of the railway. In August Sydney Crick's salary was reviewed, when the board decided that he should be paid £220 per annum from 1 July 1890, 'but that he is to supply all clothing'.

At Dinas, Oakeley was running out of tipping space and sought to encroach on company property. In August 1890 the board resolved that 'the secretary write to Mr Dunlop [Oakeley's agent] that the diversion could proceed without prejudice as to the legal ownership of the land by the FR Company on his paying £60 for the cottages and leaving sufficient room for a siding for the FR Company and also being liable for any damages to the railway caused by such diversion'. Little progress had been made by February 1894, when the board resolved that 'Mr Dunlop be asked to submit a plan and section of the proposed diversion, the curves and gradients not to be worse than at present and the line to be double throughout and made so, up to Rhiw and new buildings needed instead of those at Dinas station should the latter be done away with and the necessary signals etc fixed as required by the Board of Trade, the land and works handed over to the railway company free of expense'.

To authorise the diversion, the company obtained a Board of Trade certificate issued under the Railways Construction Facilities Act of 1864 and the Railways (Powers and Construction) Acts 1864 Amendment Act of 1870. These acts provided a facility for a railway company to obtain approval for a branch or deviation where there were no objections and without being required to obtain a special act. The Festiniog Railway (Deviation) Certificate 1898 was made on 23 May 1898 and published in the *London Gazette* on 31 May. The certificate authorised the deviation line and declared that it would be deemed to be part of the railway authorised by the 1869 act. The company was empowered to abandon the existing railway on completion of the deviation and to convey it to W. E. Oakeley and the Oakeley Slate Quarries Co Ltd.

Returning to the matter of the Regulation of Railways Act, Hughes reported, when the board met in February 1891, that he had seen Sykes' block instruments in use on the London, Chatham & Dover Railway and, having also met Sykes, recommended that system. The board accepted the tender of £210 for providing and installing 12 instruments, including a 12-month guarantee, rejecting tenders from Saunders & Co and the Telegraph Manufacturing Company.

When Saunders heard the news, they objected, claiming that their existing contract with the company gave them priority. By the time the board met in August it was in a position to reconsider Saunders's tender, which had been amended and was now lower than those of its competitors(!), and accepted it. Regarding the vacuum brakes, Hughes was instructed to negotiate with the Vacuum Brake Company for improvement on that company's £1,019 16s tender.

David Ellis, a 65-year-old tailor from Criccieth and a regular user of the railway, met his untimely end on it in 1890. At Duffws on 17 November, he bought a ticket for the 6.20pm departure three minutes before the train was due to leave. Running to catch it, he fell; his leg was caught and two carriages were derailed. He died of his injuries on 6 December. Although an inquest returned a verdict of accidental death, the coroner complained that the lighting was inadequate. Afterwards, the company paid £32 in 'full discharge of all claims', which suggests that it accepted that it was culpable. The board must have been aware of the incident for the settlement to be made, but it was not recorded in the minutes.

Rhiwbryfdir, looking towards Portmadoc. The ground at the rear centre was due to be buried in Oakeley slate waste, the cause of the 1899 deviation. The LNWR carriage shed is on the centre left. The prominent building in the centre foreground is the Oakeley quarry hospital. *FR Archives*

A slate train derailment at Bryn Mawr in the 1890s. The sheep being held in the centre of the picture might have been the culprit. *FR Archives*

The Railway & Canal Traffic Act, 1888, was an issue when the board met on 18 August 1891. Under the terms of the act the company had submitted its tariffs, including any terminal charges, in order that the Board of Trade could make a provisional order that, in turn, would be submitted to Parliament as a bill. The company was now faced with the Board's proposed rates that, Hughes had calculated, would produce a loss of £118 13s on coal and slate traffic when compared with existing rates. Hughes was instructed to negotiate to improve the position; if he was unsuccessful then the 1d per ton rebate on slate would be discontinued.

Five petitions were entered against the bill: Lancashire & Cheshire Conference of Municipal Corporations; Mansion House United Association on Railway Rates; The Traders of Carnarvon; The Corporation of London, and the Oakeley Slate Quarries Limited. The board recognised the last as being the most important as it represented all of the railway's quarry customers; Oakeley was fearful that the company would be able to increase charges and wanted it to guarantee the existing rates for 21 years. At a meeting, Hughes persuaded Oakeley to withdraw its objection in exchange for a written undertaking that the company had no intention of applying the charges contained in the bill, unless unforeseen circumstances warranted a change. Hughes also met 'Mr Lloyd George, the member for the Carnarvon Boroughs, and Mr Ellis, the member for Merionethshire, in regard to their not opposing the bill on the third reading in the House of Commons and received satisfactory assurance that there would be no opposition'.

Gaining royal assent on 20 June 1892, the Railway Rates & Charges No 6 (Festiniog Railway &c) Order Confirmation Act, 1892, also applied to the Gorsedda Junction & Portmadoc Railway, the North Wales Narrow Gauge Railways and the Portmadoc, Croesor & Beddgelert Tram Railway Company, classifying merchandise and specifying the maximum rates and charges that could be made for its carriage.

Passenger comfort was rarely an issue for the company, although in August 1891 it decided that the 3rd class compartments in two bogie carriages should be 'cushioned' when convenient. At the same time it was decided that two old 3rd class carriages be converted into opens 'if found advisable'.

Approval was given to fit cushions in the remaining 3rd class compartments of the bogie stock in August 1896.

In February 1892, £2,000 4% debenture stock was authorised. Sanctioned by the Board of Trade, this extra capital was to pay for the work necessary to comply with the Regulation of Railways Act, 1889. The company received two offers to place the debentures. Mr Herbert of the Stock Exchange offered 4½% at par free of brokerage at a week's notice, whilst Mr Armstrong, who worked for the company's solicitors, offered 4% at par with a commission of ½%, in tranches of £1,000. The latter was accepted.

When the sick pay entitlement of stationmasters and clerks was considered in February 1892, the board decided to follow the example of the LNWR. A head of department could certify for up to one month; after one month the head of department was to report to the directors with a recommendation; if the efficiency and conduct of the individual merited, then a further two months could be paid. At a time when no pensions were payable and men carried on working as long as they were able, the rule allowed 'That in regard to the old men they be paid when ill or unable to work at 9s per week'.

The performance of two stationmasters was found wanting in August 1892, when the board resolved to dismiss the post holders at Dinas and Duffws. Their replacements would be paid 25s (Duffws) and 22s (Dinas) per week, with increases promised for satisfactory performance.

The wellbeing of staff received attention in August 1893, when Hughes reported that one of the offices at Portmadoc was very cold in winter, the board resolving 'that the same be heated by hot water or some other satisfactory arrangement'. Alfred Crick's pay was increased to 28s per week and Sydney Crick's to 24s; the latter is odd, because he had been awarded £220 per annum in July 1890. They both received another 2s per week in February 1895 and in February 1896. In recognition of the effort made by Hughes to meet the Board of Trade's requirements, the board awarded him a bonus of £50; his salary was increased to £600 per annum in February 1895, backdated to 1 January, and another £50 bonus was awarded in February 1898. William Williams, the works manager, had his salary increased to £200, but no clothing, in August 1894.

The board decided to formalise the workforce's holiday arrangements in February 1899, when it realised that there was no record of the existing practice of paying for holidays taken on Christmas Day and Easter Monday.

As previously noted, the availability of wagons was a regular cause of friction with the quarry proprietors; both Greaves and Oakeley complained in August 1892. Oakeley's agent said that he had sent a cargo to Deganwy because of a lack of FR wagons and at a meeting the board promised that changes were being planned 'at the upper terminus' which it was hoped would improve the situation. Greaves complained about being unable to send coal up the line, although a further six coal wagons had been authorised in February 1891. In a rare example of self-help, Greaves intended to build a store at the port so that coal could be sent to the quarry as required. Ten more coal wagons were approved in February 1896.

What the changes planned for 'the upper terminus' were is not known, neither is it known if they were effected, but in February 1893 complaints were still being received about the availability of wagons. The board decided to order 20 'additional wagons of the smaller type', to be 'gradually constructed, as they could be done without increasing the number of hands'. It also resolved that slate companies despatching via the LNWR should use that company's wagons when there was pressure on the FR to transport slate to Minffordd or Portmadoc. Twenty more slate wagons were ordered in August 1894, following complaints from the Wrysgan Slate Company and Diphwys Casson Slate Company. They were to be made 'with due regard to other work and without increasing the number of men'. A further 20 wagons were approved six months later.

Changes to the board were not consistently recorded in the minutes but such an example occurred in February 1893, when John Graves Livingston resigned as chairman. His letter, to Hughes, of 10 October 1892, was quoted in full, saying that 'I am getting old and feel that I have not the strength nor energy sufficient ...' Thomas Plunkett Cairnes had refused to accept his resignation but John W. Elliott had agreed to undertake the duties. Elliott proposed a vote of thanks, hoping that Livingston, who was present, 'may be spared for many years to act as a director and so continue to give them the benefit of his advice and experience'.

In February 1893, the board gave attention to the first lineside incident to come to its notice for nearly ten years. The platelayers' trolley 'ran against' two children at Penrhyn station and one was 'rather seriously injured'. Her father was seeking compensation and threatening legal proceedings and the board resolved that 'the matter be amicably settled by paying him a sum not exceeding £20 in full discharge of all claims'. In May 1882, the board had 'decided that the woman Gabriel, wife of the man killed at foot of the Welsh Slate Company incline be paid a gratuity of £10' and in August 1883 had agreed that '£15 be paid as a gratuity to the widow of Robert Jones, who was killed on our line'.

The Cambrian Railways were still trying to attract traffic via Minffordd, writing twice in 1893 to suggest that the FR give a further 5d per ton rebate to Oakeley and Greaves. 'Having already made such heavy sacrifices towards keeping the traffic via Minffordd' the board had no hesitation in refusing, in both February and August. The Cambrian wrote again in August 1894, when the board resolved 'that they be informed that the company does not consider it advisable to move in the matter until the question is raised by the slate companies themselves'.

The Moelwyn Mining Co needed access over land the company leased from the Bankes estate at the long tunnel to develop a lead mine during the 1890s. In 1893 the board decided that it would not renew the lease when it expired in 1899 and was prepared to relinquish it, except for the signalman's cottage and garden. The Moelwyn company was to agree to make the siding connection with the FR at its own expense, to supply its own wagons and to submit a draft agreement. The normal rates would apply to any traffic.

Communications were a matter for the board in February 1894, when it considered installing a telephone exchange for the use of the quarry companies and the public between Portmadoc and Duffws at a cost of £290, replacing the single-needle telegraph at stations by telephones for £70, and making a telephone connection between the general manager's office and Boston Lodge at a cost not stated, only the latter was approved. Raising awareness of the railway, it also accepted a tender from Ward Lock for a full page advertisement in 65 guides for eight guineas, but refused to advertise in a Llandudno newspaper. In August 1896, the Ward Lock advertisement was supplemented by station advertisements (£10) and 10,000 leaflets (£14 15s), both the latter supplied by Riddle & Couchman.

The slate companies' application for a telephone connection between their wharves at Portmadoc and at Minffordd was considered in August. Saunders & Co having tendered £162 15s for installation and £12 10s for annual maintenance, the board resolved to pay £100 and £5 on these amounts, the slate companies paying the remainder. By February 1895 the quarries had telephone connections to Duffws, the board confirming an arrangement to charge the £5 a year each for use of the trunk line wayleave and attending to the switchboard.

The expansion of the company's telephone network, which seems to have happened more by accident than design, came to the attention of the General Post Office, which complained that the company had no authority to provide a public telephone service. In August 1895, the board resolved 'that no action be taken until we hear again from the Post Office'. There had been no recorded activity on this front by February 1897, when 'it being found advisable to have telephone communication between Duffws and Dinas so as to arrange about empty wagons and slate trains it was resolved that the same be erected at a cost of £13 10s'. By November, however, the company had received another letter on the matter, to which it responded that it was prepared to meet any reasonable requirements. By August 1898 a draft licence had been received, the company agreeing to accept it and to pay the £35 annual royalty.

The quarrymen complained about overcrowding on the trains and wished the capacity to be reduced from 16 to 12 passengers per carriage. In February 1894, Hughes was instructed to assess the number and cost of the additional carriages required to meet the request, the board thinking the fares should be increased from 2s 4d to 2s 6d, weekly, and from 6d to 7d, daily, to cover the outlay; a 2d increase on the weekly and daily fares was agreed in February 1896 because the LNWR, GWR and Cambrian Railways charged more! Hughes was instructed to investigate methods of lighting the carriages in August 1894 and report on the various options available, 'including electricity', and 12 months later he was instructed to apply the most economical manner.

Two new bogie carriages were ordered to be 'built under contract or at the company's workshops, as may be cheapest and most advisable', in August 1895, the 'stock of carriages being found inadequate for the requirements of the quarrymen and for excursions.' The Ashbury Carriage & Wagon Co's tender of £188 each, complete, was accepted in February 1896. The Gloster Wagon Co had offered to supply the bodies only for £305 15s. By August 1897 the board decided that accommodation on the quarrymen's train was still inadequate and resolved 'that two new carriages be built and that a tender be got for the body of another third class bogie carriage' but nothing more was done.

The Railway Regulation Act, 1893, came to the company's attention in June 1894. The act allowed railway employees to complain to the Board of Trade if they thought their working hours were excessive, and it enabled the board to require railway companies to bring the hours of work within reasonable limits. The board had notified the company that it 'understood the drivers and stokers were working too long hours' and requested a statement of the book and actual time worked for 14 days ended 23 June. The statement having been submitted, the company was informed that the hours of duty were unreasonable and that the drivers and stokers should not work more than ten hours daily. In August 1894, Hughes was instructed to produce a compliant schedule and submit it.

It was probably not unrelated to this issue that Boston Lodge employees requested a reduction in their working hours in February 1896. They wanted 15 minutes a day less, starting at 6.15am, and 30 minutes on Saturday, finishing at 12.00; the board agreed to give them the 30 minutes.

When the company tried to recover the £50 expenditure incurred in signalling the siding that served the powder magazines and sett quarry near the tunnel, the Elterwater Powder Company refused to pay its share. In August 1895, the board resolved to inform the company that the lease was quite clear about their liability.

Operations at Minffordd had been subject to delay and passengers missed their FR connection because of the distance and gradient of the path linking the Cambrian with the FR. In August 1895, the board resolved to ask the Cambrian to pay half of the cost of installing a path and a vertical luggage lift on the east side of the bridge, but nothing more was said of this. In February 1892, the GPO had been given permission to install a letter box at the station. Several changes for stations were approved in February 1896: a goods shed at Penrhyn; a waiting room on the down line at Tan-y-bwlch; and a waiting room at Dduallt. Permission was to be obtained from the landowner to build a footpath from Dduallt to 'the waterfalls in the dingle below it'.

The board decided to define the railway's responsibilities at the Penrhyn and Tanygrisiau level crossings by relocating the gates to the boundaries in February 1896. The Festiniog Local Board had tried to get the railway to take responsibility for road maintenance beyond the boundaries at Tanygrisiau since 1893. In November 1896 Hughes told the board that the crossing was dangerous and produced a plan for a proposed deviation of the road, whereby the crossing would be replaced by a bridge under the railway. Progress was slow but in February 1899 the company asked the council if it would take over the diverted road and keep it in repair.

Further down the line, Penrhyndeudraeth Parish Council sought permission to construct a bridge under the railway for an approach to a proposed cemetery at Lloc Meurig. Considering the request in February 1899, the board gave its approval subject to the bridge meeting the company's requirements.

Hughes wanted to keep up with the times and obtained approval to spend £15 on a 'typewriting machine' for his office in February 1896.

Also approved in August that year was the purchase of a Lee & Hunt wheel press and pump for use at Boston Lodge at a cost of £52; Tangye's tender was £171.

The GWR proposed to construct a footbridge from its Blaenau Festiniog platform over the FR to connect with the streets beyond, in February 1898. It was resolved to accept it subject to plans being approved and a nominal rent of 1s per annum being charged.

In 1894, £1,000 had been placed to a reserve fund; in February 1896 it was decided to liquidate the fund and to raise £4,000 of additional capital by issuing 4% preference shares at par, to be offered to shareholders pro rata. The new capital was to fund new works and improvements. The decision appeared to be against the rules, for at the next meeting it was rescinded in favour of a new motion, 'that under the powers conferred by the Festiniog Railway Act of 1869 £1,000 additional 5% preference shares being part of the balance of £10,000 unissued of the £35,000 preference shares created in January 1872 be issued (subject to confirmation at the general meeting of shareholders) and that the same be issued at a premium of 25% each or to be £12 10s 0d for each £10 share'. Being able to place these shares at such a high premium is surely a demonstration of the regard in which the company was held, even if its underlying weakness was being ignored. The premium, £250, was allocated to the reserve account in February 1898. The £1,000 originally in the reserve fund was invested in 3½% New South Wales government stock.

An accident that had occurred at Penrhyn on 28 August 1896 was not a subject of comment by the board. The loco, its tender and a quarrymen's carriage of the 10am passenger train were derailed as it approached the station. In addition to the derailed vehicles, the train comprised two four-wheeled carriages, two bogie carriages and a bogie van. The train had vacuum brakes throughout and the equipment was found to be in good order; the engine, tender and quarrymen's carriage were damaged, but there were no injuries. The derailment had occurred on a 7-chain-radius right-hand curve some 75yd long. The straight sections either side of the curve had been resleepered four months previously, but the curve had not received attention for some time.

Lt-Colonel H. Arthur Yorke conducted an inquiry and his report was submitted on 7 October 1896. Evan Morris, the permanent way foreman, said that he had been employed by the company for five years and had been foreman for six months. He was responsible for the line between Portmadoc and east of Penrhyn station, about 4¾ miles. On the day of the accident the brakesman of a gravity train had told him that the line was 'shaky' near Penrhyn. He went to investigate and found a slack joint, so set off for Minffordd to fetch his gang, passing the 10am train as he did so, obviously not on the embankment at Gwyndy! He did not think to caution the driver. It had rained heavily during the previous 24 hours. Attributing the blame to Morris, Yorke said that he attributed none to the driver, Jarrett Davies. However, he did say that he was surprised to find that the driver was only 22 and the stoker, Rowland Owen, 17 and that, 'it does not seem right to entrust passenger trains, which doubtless are often heavily loaded during the tourist season, to lads of so little experience'. Davies had worked for the company for seven years and had been a driver for 12 months; Owen had been an employee for 12 months and a stoker for 3½ months.

When the board met on 23 February 1897, Hughes produced a list of works that needed attention along the line. This included replacing Penrhyn crossing with a bridge; repairing the retaining wall near the crossing; extending the platform at Tanygrisiau; a footbridge was required over the line near Glan y Pwll crossing; buttresses were required at Coed y Bleiddiau and Pant Coch; girders for culverts at Doppog, near the tunnel and underbridge at Bryn Nazareth; a culvert under the line at Pant Coch; a footbridge over the line at Highgate; relaying the passing siding at Tan-y-bwlch with steel rails; fence railing at Boston Lodge curve; broken stone ballast for wet cuttings, and creosoted sleepers to be used throughout the line as in the tunnel. The board resolved to leave it to Hughes to carry out the works as and when he felt best, some of which, notably the replacement of Penrhyn crossing with a bridge, the slate slab underbridge with steel girders at Bryn Nazareth, and the Highgate footbridge, were never carried out. The proposal to use broken stone ballast in wet cuttings implies that the imported ships' ballast was not good for drainage.

The Rhiwbach Slate Quarry Owners used the Railway & Canal Traffic Act of 1888 to make a formal complaint against the company on 10 February 1898. It objected to the practice of giving no reduction from the 10d per ton charged for the carriage of coal 'from Blaenau Festiniog to Duffws' even when it used its own wagons. The company responded that that it could charge 10½d for conveyance plus 4½d for using its wagons but it charged 10d regardless, a long-standing practice; traders who used their own wagons did so for their own convenience. No further action was taken.

The Workmen's Compensation Act of 1897 came into effect on 1 July 1898. This required the company to compensate any workman injured in the course of his employment. In August 1898 the board considered seven offers to insure the company at rates ranging from £64 to £128. Not unnaturally, the lowest, provided by the Ocean Insurance Company, was accepted.

Lt-Colonel Yorke returned to the railway on 18 August 1897 to investigate a collision that had occurred at Dinas Junction on 23 July. A passenger train waiting at the down home signal was run into by an up goods train that should have gone into the mineral line. The couplings on both engines were broken and one wagon was derailed. There were no injuries. Signalman Owen Morris, employed by the company for 36 years and a signalman for 21 years, said that he had forgotten about the passenger train and had set the road for the goods train to go on the main line. Realising his mistake at the last minute he put the signal to danger, although he said that it was to caution the driver who he thought was going too fast, but was too late to prevent a collision at about 5mph.

Yorke said that no blame could be attributed to either of the drivers and that Owen was responsible for the accident. He criticised Owen's sloppy use of train tickets; he was in the habit of removing several tickets from the ticket box early in his shift and would issue them without necessarily having the staff to hand; the ticket box required the staff to unlock it and the staff should have been shown to the driver when issuing the ticket. On the day of the accident the staff was still on the down train while Owen was ready to pass a ticket to the up train.

Yorke found fault, too, with Owen's admission that he would use the home signal to caution a driver who he thought was going too fast. 'This is a totally wrong method of using signals,' he said; 'a signal, other than a distant signal, when in the danger position, should have no other meaning than an imperative direction to the driver of a train approaching it to stop.' He was also critical of the company's lack of rules concerning the use of the Duffws main and mineral lines, saying that the staff and ticket should apply only to the main line and the company should devise special regulations for the use of the mineral line. The signalmen were in the habit of allowing the staff and tickets to apply to both lines. He also criticised the goods train crew for having no memory of what signals had been cleared for them. Upon reflection, it seems odd that when Rich examined the installation in 1881 he did not examine the method of working.

There was some upset amongst the board during 1898/9, for both C. H. C. Huddart and G. A. W. Huddart resigned as directors but were persuaded to rejoin. At the first meeting they attended after resuming their places, in August 1899, C. H. C. Huddart proposed, and G. A. W. Huddart seconded, a motion that the chairman's honorarium be £100, backdated to 1 January! At the same meeting Hughes informed the board that the purchase of the land occupied by Minffordd sidings, which had been leased from the late G. A. Huddart, had been completed.

In a sign of the times, in August 1899, Hughes reported that 'the public was making use of the Traeth Mawr embankment for cycling and thereby endangering the safety of the traffic. It was resolved that a notice be put up at each end of the embankment that anyone doing this would be prosecuted.'

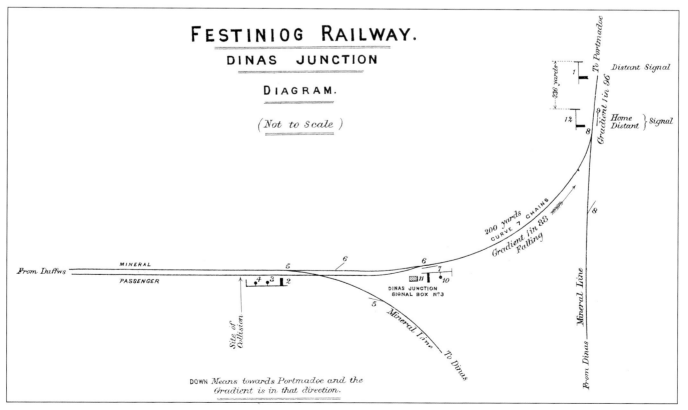

The diagram that accompanied Col Yorke's report into the collision that occurred at Dinas Junction on 23 July 1897.

THE HARBOUR TO BOSTON LODGE

Above: **A general view of Portmadoc harbour in the early years of the 20th century; ship building has finished, but there are still sailing ships in evidence, although in reduced numbers. The wharf next to the station is well stacked with slate.**
Lilywhite Ltd/Author's collection

Right: **Prince shunting close to the FR's zero point in 1934.** *R. W. Kidner/Author's collection*

Below: **A view of the harbour from Ynys y Towyn, *c*1900. One of the port's steam paddle tugs is on the left.**
Commercial postcard/Author's collection

Above: **Livingston Thompson** with an unusual train at Portmadoc. The presence of the 'curly roof' van in the centre of the train indicates the use of two train sets, the leading set consisting of a quarrymen's carriage, three Ashburys of two types and the van. The normal set is behind, starting with a Brown, Marshalls followed by a 'bowsider'. *Kingsway/Author's collection*

Left: The harbour branch, and WHR route, where they leave the FR for the street, showing the relationship between the railway and the embankment road, 1930s. *FR Archives*

Below left: The doors of the four-wheeled stock have been opened ready for the anticipated passengers on 6 August 1936. The leading bogie Ashbury is one of the 1894 vehicles built for the NWNGR; heading the train is *Taliesin*. *W. H. Whitworth/Author's collection*

Right: **The original *Taliesin* taking the route to the Portmadoc 'new' station, c1923/4. The carriage stabled behind the signal may be an ex-NWNGR vehicle.** *Author's collection*

Below: ***Taliesin* arrives at Portmadoc in the mid-1930s. Platform staff still have uniform to wear despite the annual issue being cancelled in 1924.** *Commercial postcard/Author's collection*

Bottom: **A train hauled by *Taliesin* crossing the embankment towards Boston Lodge.** *Author's collection*

TOY RAILWAY, PORTMADOC

Above: **Tourists watch the photographer as their** *Taliesin*-**hauled train leaves Portmadoc.**
E. O. Jones/Author's collection

Left: **Grass-covered track on the embankment, 1948. The concrete kerb had been built in the later 1930s.**
J. Valentine/Author's collection

Below left: **Palmerston's boiler was repaired in 1933 by using the dome section from** *Little Giant's* **boiler barrel.**
H. W. Comber/FR Archives

*Above: **Taliesin** taking water on the main line at Boston Lodge on 3 June 1932. H. C. Casserley/Author's collection*

Right: There was little to interest enthusiasts in the top yard until 1940, when ***Palmerston*** was installed as a stationary boiler. The wagons were awaiting repairs that never happened. An unusual view of the yard was captured in August 1952. *J. B. Snell/Author's collection*

Below: The erecting shop on 24 July 1946. ***Prince's*** frames and new boiler stand in front of ***Taliesin***. The use of electricity in the works is vague and surrounded by myth, but there is evidence of it in this photograph. Notice that the floor is wooden. *B. B. Edmonds*

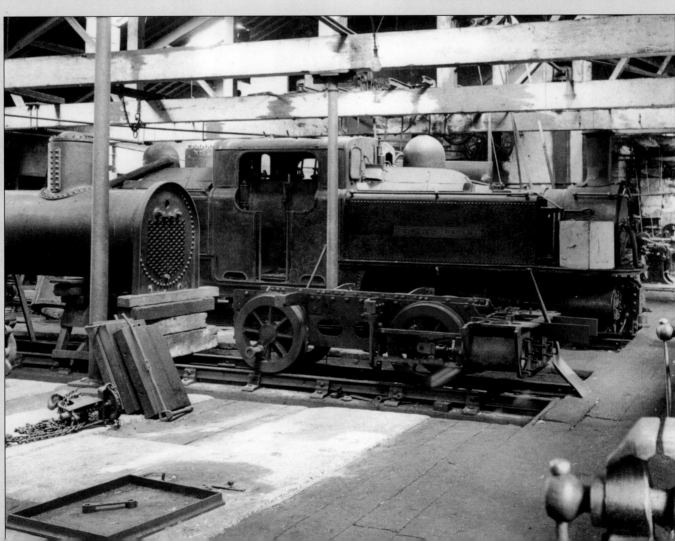

Above: **Running repairs, and sometimes others of a more substantial nature, were carried out in the loco shed, which was equipped with a small machine shop. In 1933, *James Spooner's* boiler was jacked up in the loco shed and plate cut out of the barrels as part of a proposed repair that failed.**
H.W. Comber/
FR Archives

Left: **Merddin Emrys had probably steamed its last for the old regime when photographed on 24 July 1946. Also in sight are *Moel Tryfan* and the 'Simplex'.**
B. B. Edmonds

81

8

Descent to war

1900-1914

The FR experienced a brief recovery during the 1890s, with the indicators of passengers, tonnage and revenue peaking in 1897, although none of them reached the level achieved 20 years earlier, and all fell away immediately. The average dividend had been just over 3½% during the decade. As the 19th became the 20th century, the decline became more pronounced. Two-thirds of the merchandise traffic, 9,200 tons, and 12,000 passengers were lost in 1900, never to be recovered. A 3½% dividend was to be paid in 1900 but it never reached 2% thereafter.

Changes to the board were discussed in August 1904. H. M. Felkin, a director since 1899, submitted his resignation 'by reason of his not being able to do justice to the post through his increasing deafness'. John W. Elliott, the chairman, proposed his son, also John, who was elected but who could not act as a director until he had acquired a qualifying shareholding. H. A. Cowper was also elected, taking the place of C. H. C. Huddart who had died in 1900, apparently at the Royal Sportsman Hotel whilst *en route* to a board meeting.

Elliott senior's resignation from the board was accepted 12 months later; a letter was to be written to him, 'conveying the cordial thanks of the directors'. R. Norman Thompson had taken over as chairman, without comment, in February 1905.

Further boardroom changes were on the agenda on 16 August 1907, at a meeting attended only by Richard M. Greaves and John Elliott, so inquorate. Richard Bowton had submitted his resignation by letter dated 29 July; Greaves was to write and tell him that his resignation had been rejected, that George A. W. Huddart was to be invited to be chairman with an honorarium of £50, that the directors were to be paid one guinea for each attendance and that meetings would be held monthly in future; Thompson had recently died; board meetings had been held at least twice yearly, usually coinciding with the general meetings, but were often held more frequently.

Greaves and Elliott discussed the poor attendance at general meetings and the non-availability of shareholders suitable to be directors. They would have been concerned about the share price, too. In 1909 A. G. Crick was to inform Breese, Jones & Casson, executors for Charles Edwin Spooner, that he understood the value of £100 ordinary stock to be £4; it wouldn't have been so different two years earlier. The outcome was that Elliott met two of the Irish shareholders, Messrs Cowper and Bewley; the former having been a director from 1904, attending his last board meeting in February 1906. They introduced him to Frederick Vaughan, who had applied to be the company's auditor. Vaughan had worked for the Cambrian Railways and for several Irish railway companies and was looking for a new position.

At a meeting that was quorate, on 28 August, the board was introduced to Vaughan and, following an interview, he was elected a director. At this meeting the board considered a letter from one of the shareholders, saying that it would be more convenient if the general meetings were held in London instead of Portmadoc; he was to be informed that the change to having meetings in Portmadoc was done to save money and that more shareholders attended the meetings there!

Despite the declining revenues the board was still prepared to consider developments but in February 1900 a scheme for a new fitting shop at Boston Lodge was rejected because the tenders were too high. On the same occasion Hughes told the board that he was having difficulty in operating Tan-y-bwlch station because there was no accommodation for the station-master and staff; the board agreed that a house was wanted but left it for the time being; just how long it was left is not clear but the house had certainly been built by 1905 although a photograph suggests that it could have been built as early as 1897/8; an extension was approved in April 1910.

At Tanygrisiau the bridge in lieu of the level crossing was

ordered to be installed in February 1900. The company's seal was affixed to the agreement with Penrhyndeudraeth Parish Council regarding the cemetery access bridge under the railway near Lloc Meurig in August 1900.

The future of the Portmadoc station site was considered in August 1903, when Hughes heard that the Tremadoc Estate was intending to sell its ground rents. Although the board felt that the company was in no position to make the purchase, it thought that it should consider setting up an insurance or sinking fund that would generate sufficient to purchase the freehold when the lease expired. On hearing, subsequently, that the purchase would be 33 years rental, £4,125, the board decided to take no further action.

In May 1910, following representations from Festiniog Urban District Council, repairs to the Duffws overbridge were approved. Changing circumstances are indicated by this stark minute dated 12 November 1912: 'Dduallt station – agreed that it is closed for part of the year'.

The railway's cottage at Coed y Bleiddiau had a new occupant from May 1913, when a bank manager, J. W. Sudbury, from Wylde Green, Birmingham, took up a lease at £5 a year. The cottage had been occupied by J. A. Hovenden, who had been with the company since 1841, its 'general inspector' since 1884. Described as 'policeman's cottage' on the 1869 plans, it is not known why the railway had felt the need to build a house in such a remote location where there is no road access. The existence of a station house at Portmadoc is known by a 1913 reference to it being let at a nominal rent to James William, Boston Lodge's foreman carpenter, its previous occupant having left.

A Stock Exchange listing for the ordinary stock was initiated in February 1900. In August, a 20 guinea fee was agreed to be paid to the stockbrokers Woolner & Co for their services in securing it.

The scope of the railway's promotional activity broadened as the years went by. The August 1900 issue of *The Railway Magazine* carried an illustrated article about the FR, probably the first significant feature to be published since the promotional activities of Spooner, Fairlie and Tyler in the 1860s/'70s. No 34 of a series of 'illustrated interviews' with railway managers, although not an interview as the term is now usually understood, was illustrated with Bleasdale photographs. It told much about the railway and its history, some of it quite fanciful, but less about Hughes; he was a Welshman, much travelled, had designed railways to the summits of Snowdon, Skiddaw, Ben Lomond and Snaefell and had held a commission in the 2/3

Volunteer Battalion Royal Welsh Fusiliers for 23 years, retiring with the honorary rank of lieutenant-colonel. The company paid £5 for a full page advertisement in the same issue.

In 1909, Vaughan, then managing director, arranged for the Cambrian to display 50 photographs of 'scenery on the Festiniog Railway' in its carriages and 2,000 copies of a pictorial poster were ordered in April 1910. This was the well-known impression of a train on a ledge, 500 copies of which were to be framed and glazed. Also, 20,000 'pictorial pamphlets ... similar to those of the Cambrian Company' were ordered from Wyman & Co in March 1911. On 19 June 1914, the railway was host to a group of journalists from both the UK and overseas.

On 12 February 1901, the Portmadoc, Beddgelert & South Snowdon Railway bill was considered. The PBSSR was seeking running powers over the FR at Portmadoc. As it was taking over the Croesor & Portmadoc Railway, which connected to the FR, it probably considered the powers as a matter of inheritance. The board instructed Hughes to consult with the company's parliamentary agents.

Hughes was also instructed to obtain legal advice concerning the Croesor & Portmadoc Railway and others who were making use of the FR's harbour sidings and refusing to pay for the privilege. The Rhosydd Slate Quarry Co and Park & Croesor Quarry Co both complained about the rate charged for taking their own wagons from the CPR to the wharves, and in August 1901 it was resolved to charge 3d per ton 'without prejudice'. The same rate was notified to the Carnarvonshire Granite Quarries Co that wished to carry setts and metalling from the CPR to the public wharf in their own wagons at the same time. However, when the Moel-y-gest Granite Co made a similar application in August 1904 the company offered 2½d per ton up to 10,000 tons and 2d per ton on any quantity in addition to the 10,000 tons per annum.

The occasion of Queen Victoria's funeral on 2 February 1901 had been treated as a public holiday, the board afterwards agreeing that wages should be paid for it. On hearing the news, the Boston Lodge staff held a meeting during the 'dinner half hour' and resolved 'that the heartfelt thanks of all the employees be sent to yourself [J. S. Hughes] and the directors for what has been done for them with regard to the funeral day of the late Her Majesty the Queen Victoria'.

For most employees, their FR pay was never going to be much above subsistence level, especially for those with large families. W. M. Roberts, a foundry moulder, must have felt quite

Left: **A typical FR passenger train at Portmadoc, *c*1893. The 1879 building gives a certain dignity to the railway company's status in a small town where it might well have been the largest employer. By this time *Merddin Emrys'* cab roof had been fully enclosed.** *J. Valentine/Author's collection*

Right: **An Edwardian family and the uniformed stationmaster await the train at Dduallt. The screen to the right of the building suggests the presence of a urinal – there was probably no facility for the ladies. The tunnel distant signal can be seen behind the young man standing on the rails.** *FR Archives*

aggrieved when he wrote to Hughes on 10 March 1900: 'Sir. My duty is, I think is to give you this notice that I will quit your employment on Saturday next, the 17th inst, so long that you won't give me 18s a week. If you can get a man to do my work for this money I will work in Boston Lodge for nothing for you.'

Owen Griffith, a carpenter, 'had quite broken down that he could put no work through his hands'; he had submitted a doctor's certificate and applied for a pension. The board resolved, in February 1901, that he leave the company's service and 'be allowed 5s a week for a short time'. Another employee came to the board's attention in February 1902, when John Jones, who had also been a moulder in the foundry, at the age of 76 had given up work, the board resolving to pay him 5s per week 'for a short time, same as given to the other old hands'.

The activities of particular employees sometimes reached the board, as demonstrated by the case of stationmaster Roberts at Duffws in February 1905. He had somehow come to the attention of G. A. W. Huddart, who proposed that he 'be put into a position of greater responsibility so as to combine the duties of stationmaster and railway agent and that his salary be increased by 6s per week and that he be told that he will receive a bonus at the end of the year if his work is satisfactory'.

Major E. Druitt had cause to visit the railway on 22 October 1901, to investigate a derailment. On 4 October, the 6.15pm passenger train from Duffws became completely derailed near Coed y Bleiddiau. Slight damage was caused to the engine, and a spring on one carriage was broken. The rails were dislodged from the chairs for about 60yd, 79 chairs were broken and some sleepers were damaged. The ballast was river gravel and shingle with 'a good deal of earthy matter contained in it'; half-round larch sleepers were in use with 50lb double-headed steel rails resting in cast-iron chairs fixed with two spikes. Druitt found that there was no direct evidence as to the cause of the accident but concluded that it was caused by the 'faulty condition' of the track. Hughes had informed Druitt that he had already commenced a programme of track improvements before the accident, including re-laying the whole line with rectangular, creosoted Baltic pine sleepers and improving ballast and drainage.

The track was obviously in poor condition. Druitt had also commented on the lack of supervision of the track gang, but the evidence also suggests that the wagon fleet was not being adequately maintained. In August 1901 there had been two occasions when goods wagons attached to passenger trains had derailed below Tan-y-bwlch, attributed to a mechanical failure and overloading. In 1902 three more derailments occurred on three successive days! All of them involved wagons, two of them on passenger trains below Tan-y-bwlch and one on a down goods train entering Tan-y-bwlch station. The August 1901 incidents appear to have been reported 'after the event'; two of those in 1902 were reported on the appropriate forms, while the third one was reported in the *Cambrian News,* which commented on another derailment that had taken place at the same location 'at the end of last year'!

Arising out of this incident, the Board of Trade entered into correspondence with Hughes over the running of mixed trains. Hughes took the view that the schedule of mixed trains submitted with the draft 1890 Regulation of Railways Act order had been sanctioned with the making of the order, while the board felt that the company should have obtained approval for them after the order had been made!

The following September the Board of Trade was sent a cutting from a Welsh-language newspaper that was highly critical of the FR; the board had it translated. The anonymous author said that the stations, carriages, permanent way and signals were out of date and that the carriages were dirty. The question 'How many times has an accident happened on this line during the last two years, through an engine breaking down, axles breaking and carriages going off the rails?' obviously wasn't rhetorical. The first comment on the board's file was that as the article was anonymous it need take no action. However, it decided to take the subtle approach, and asked Hughes how the FR was getting on with its track improvements. Replying on 24 October 1903, he gave the following figures of renewals:

- 7,530 sleepers
- 4,170 chairs
- 23,728 keys
- 6,190 fishbolts and nuts
- 13,040 spikes
- 534 pairs of fishplates
- 36 points totally or partially remade and resleepered
- Broken stone ballast in some places
- Changes made in the gangers
- New inspector of permanent way and works appointed

A breakaway had occurred on the Rhiwbach incline on 16 September 1905. The Rhiwbach Slate Quarry Owners, successors to the Festiniog Slate Co, claimed £108 from the FR, saying that the accident was caused by a defective link on an FR wagon. Richard Bowton, a slate merchant who had just become an FR company director, negotiated the claim down to £85, apparently on the basis that Rhiwbach could still make use of the damaged cables!

The Rhiwbach Owners afterwards gave notice to the FR, and the LNWR and GWR, that their wagons would not be accepted to go over the Rhiwbach inclines and tramway unless they would be responsible for accidents. Representatives of the three companies repudiated such liability, saying that they would accept only their legal responsibility, that all precautions were taken to ensure that the wagons were in proper condition, and that each case must stand on its merits. In June 1906, Rhiwbach asked the FR to supply it with wagons and to reduce the rate from 7d to 5d per ton, but the board decided that as the slate was not being routed via the FR the rate would stay unchanged!

A horse belonging to the owner of the Maenofferen Hotel, Blaenau Festiniog, was injured in an accident at Glan y Pwll level crossing on 23 September 1908. The owner claimed £25 but settled for £17 10s following Vaughan's intervention.

Two accidents were recorded in the minutes for 1910: at Dduallt on 4 July and near Tan-y-bwlch on 13 September. Details of the first were not given but the second involved a slate train, with Greaves, Maenofferen and Bowton claiming, and being paid, for damage to slate. *Palmerston* was involved in an accident at Glan y Pwll in 18 July 1911, but the details were not recorded. When the 6.35am passenger train to Duffws derailed at Tan-y-bwlch on 22 January 1912 the board ordered 'full enquiries to be made'.

A report on the boilers of *James Spooner, Livingston Thompson* and *Little Giant* was considered in February 1904. It was resolved that a new boiler for *Little Giant* be ordered at once and new boilers for the others be obtained in future half-years. Purchase of *Livingston Thompson's* boiler from the Vulcan Foundry was approved a year later and *James Spooner's* in February 1906. The latter was tendered at £674 complete and £510 without tubes, the board opting for the latter, the railway supplying the tubes from stock, 'which had been in use but a short time'. Davies & Metcalfe had tendered £814 complete and £615 without tubes. Two old copper fireboxes were ordered to be sold in June 1096. Adamson's tenders for new boilers for *Palmerston* and *Welsh Pony* were accepted in July 1909 and October 1911 respectively.

Left: **Merddin Emrys at Portmadoc in the early years of the 20th century.** *Author's collection*

Below: **The FR's practice of running mixed trains was not always trouble free. At least one incident has been recorded of a goods van overturning on a curve because it was overloaded. That might be what has happened here; not having the van next to the brake van would have aggravated the situation if it was overloaded;** *c1902. FR Archives*

A storm that had derailed a carriage in a passenger train going over the embankment, near Boston Lodge, was considered in February 1904. The board resolved to call on the Tremadoc Estate, as landlord, to build a windbreak as the location was very exposed. At the other end of the embankment the siding had become unusable by July 1906 because the structure was in poor condition. The Estate had started work on repairing the sea-side face of the embankment by February 1907, when the board decided that 'a small charge be made for carrying the stone for repairs'. It was February 1908 before the board could note that the windbreak had been built.

Along the line, Hughes reported several retaining walls required attention following heavy rain and severe frosts during the winter of 1906/7; reinforcing buttresses were authorised. The walls continued to be a problem, with permanent way engineer Rowland Jones writing twice to the board about them in 1908; repairs were approved in November. Jones, incidentally, was always referred to by name in the minutes, never by position. Obviously well thought of by the board, he alone was awarded a £5 gratuity in February 1909 for 'zealous service'! He and Robert Williams were similarly rewarded in 1910 and Jones again in 1911.

A landslip occurred at Llechwedd Coed on 26 October 1909, when 30 tons of earth fell into the cutting during the night. The driver of the first up train saw it in sufficient time to stop his train without damage.

The company's telephone system continued to be expanded. In February 1905, the board had approved a connection to the GWR's Blaenau Festiniog station at an annual rent of £10 provided the GWR paid for the installation. The board realised, in February 1907, that it would lose some of its subscribers when the GPO commenced installing public telephones and resolved to ask for a set-off in the royalty charge in compensation.

Accommodation on the quarrymen's train continued to be an issue, with the quarrymen submitting a list of demands in February 1905. Following the board's refusal to entertain any of them, the Penrhyndeudraeth Workmen's Committee complained to the Board of Trade citing the Cheap Trains Act, 1883 on 10 January 1906. Hughes submitted a rebuttal on 3 February.

Colonel Yorke held an inquiry in Blaenau Festiniog on 8 December. In his report he noted that neither party said anything different at the enquiry from what they had already put in writing. The formal complaints were:
- That the accommodation provided in the trains was improper and insufficient as regards space, light and cleanliness.

- That the fares were too high.
- That in the case of a weekly ticket not wholly used no refund was made.
- That excess fares were charged if a workman wished to return home by any train other than the ordinary workmen's train.
- Absence of waiting accommodation at stations.
- Inconvenience caused by smoke from the engine while passing through the tunnel.
- Absence of ventilation in carriages.

Yorke pointed out that several of these matters were beyond the scope of the Cheap Fares Act. He found that the accommodation provided by the company, 18 or 19 carriages, each with 12 seats, for an average of 190 men travelling, was sufficient. Witnesses admitted that they sometimes crowded 16 into a carriage, not because there was insufficient room on the train but because some groups preferred to travel together. Hughes said that on one occasion a guard had found 21 men in a carriage and the extra men had refused to come out when requested. No comment was made by either side about Nos 21 and 22, the bogie Ashburys introduced in 1897 for quarrymen and tourists, and despite being rough-riding, they would have resolved this problem. The fares, unchanged since 1896, were less than ¼d per mile, except from Tan-y-bwlch where it was a small fraction more. Hughes having provided him with a very comprehensive table, he found these fares to be slightly less than those charged by the other companies serving Blaenau Festiniog. One of the quarrymen, who had been using the daily train since it was introduced in 1882, said that as the wages had been reduced the fares should be reduced also. Hughes believed that the company was the first to introduce workmen's cheap trains; the men often damaged the carriages, cut the window straps and threw the experimental oil lamps out of the windows, because they were too hot for the enclosed space. Revenue in 1905 had been £2,070.

Concerning the complaint that the accommodation was too poor for the fare charged, Yorke found that it was reasonable in the circumstances, and the men admitted that they would prefer cheaper fares to better accommodation. The excess was charged to quarrymen using their cheap tickets but travelling on ordinary trains, which all included a quarrymen's coach in the formation for this purpose. One man claimed he had got wet and wanted to go home at 10am but he had no money for the 4d excess and was not allowed to travel, and had to wait all day for the 5.50pm quarrymen's train. The miners worked overnight so always travelled at different times to the majority and always had to pay the excess. Hughes denied this; afterwards, it pained him to have to point out that even with the excess, the fare was still only half of the parliamentary rate of 1d per mile. Yorke had said that it equated to the ordinary 3rd class fare. The quarrymen also wanted the age of a boy to be raised from 16 to 18; they said that it had been 18 in the past. The company had offered 17 but this had been refused, although Yorke thought this a reasonable compromise that should be accepted.

Of the issues that were beyond the act, Yorke summarised his observations. On lighting, he said that candles were used, the carriages were too small for ordinary oil lamps, but it ought to be possible to design a smaller oil lamp, otherwise a glass shade protected by a wire mesh should be provided for the candles as the men were entitled to a reasonable amount of light, especially during the winter months. On cleanliness, he said: '... the men, by their expectoration, make the floors a disgusting state'. The company washed the carriages weekly, the men wanted them washed daily, which the company said would make them damp and unhealthy, especially in winter. Yorke recommended twice-weekly washing.

As an aside the 1895 Merioneth Slate Mines Inquiry into the health of Festiniog quarrymen had attributed chills to the daily railways journeys 'three-quarters of an hour in damp clothes in a draughty railway carriage may easily lay the foundations of disease', especially crammed 12 or more in a small carriage, the committee might have added. Men were often seen waiting for their train sitting on the ground, sometimes in wet clothes, for want of sufficient bench accommodation. On the other hand, one of the witnesses said that, in his opinion, lower house rent in Penrhyndeudraeth and a better climate there more than made up for the possible risk of catching a chill when travelling, a view not shared by the committee's medical members.

On shelter, Yorke said that it was unreasonable to expect the company to provide it. The company had said that shelter was available at all stations, but the men said that 120-150 joined the train at Penrhyn, where the shelter would have been inadequate, as it would have been at any of the Blaenau Festiniog stations at going-home time. On smoke in the tunnel, he said it could not be avoided so long as steam locomotives were used as traction and the journey through the tunnel was less than two minutes. On ventilation, he pointed out that although it was largely in the men's hands as the windows could be opened whenever they chose, roof ventilators could be installed. He had been told that they had not been introduced because of the risk of blowing the candles out but that would be avoided with a suitable shade.

On 13 March 1907, Hughes said that in future refunds would be given for unused tickets when the holder was sick, provided that a doctor's certificate was produced. He had made this offer in his rebuttal, when he also said that they could use ordinary trains without excess if there had been a rock fall or if they had got wet, on production of a certificate from the quarry manager. He also wrote that 'the directors desire me to say ... they will endeavour to meet the suggestions made in the report'. However, when the board met in August it resolved to inform the Board of Trade that 'the directors cannot see their way to make any allowances especially as the finance state of the company was so bad that the shareholders had to go without any dividends, the line being practically carried on for the convenience of the public and the quarrymen and after keeping up the line to the requirements of the Board of Trade there was nothing left for the shareholder, but that the suggestion of Colonel Yorke as to the ventilation of the carriages and the lighting would be carried out'. Penrhyndeudraeth Parish Council's request, made in August 1907, that the quarrymen's weekly ticket should be reduced from 2s 3d to 1s 6d was refused.

There's an intriguing footnote on the file relating to this issue. Dated 13 February, it reads: 'The president would be glad to see the [papers] relating to a memorial which he understands the Festiniog quarrymen have submitted regarding workmen's trains (?) on a local railway.' Another note was added two days later: 'The president was seen. He would be glad to follow the case.' The president of the Board of Trade in 1906 was David Lloyd George. When he practised as a solicitor in Portmadoc he recorded in his diary that he used the train to visit clients in Blaenau Festiniog.

A special meeting was held to consider 'the position of the railway in respect to receipts and expenditure and the falling off in the traffic', in January 1906. Three directors, Hughes and R. M. Greaves, a shareholder, were present. Declaring that 'the great depression in the slate trade which has adversely affected every kind of traffic on the line being accountable for the present state of things', they examined the pay sheet but could find no way of making savings. They also inspected Boston Lodge.

A reduction in wages was imposed on the workforce in September 1906. No figures were given in the minutes but Hughes probably suffered most because his £600 salary was cut to £450! To encourage him he was to be paid £50 for each 1% of dividend declared on the ordinary stock. At the end of the year revenue was £1,200 down on 1905, but expenditure had been reduced by £1,000 so net receipts were only £226 down. Expenditure as a percentage of receipts, which had ranged between 59% and 69% in the 1880s and had fallen to 53% in 1894, was 73% for 1906. No dividend was paid.

Correspondence and a series of meetings between the FR and the Cambrian took place over several months in 1905/6. The FR had decided that there was scope for increasing slate shipments via Minffordd if the facilities were improved. There was a depression in the slate trade, wharves near the quarries were well-stocked and the owners and merchants were looking for additional storage. Putting this to Cambrian representatives at a meeting held at the Euston Hotel in London on 23 November 1905, the Cambrian immediately responded by offering to contribute to the cost. Some Minffordd traders shipped a small amount of slate to stations in the Chester area and felt aggrieved by the higher shipping costs. The Cambrian agreed to adjust its rates for a two-year trial period, each party standing half of the reduction; it is difficult to understand what was preventing the FR from shipping its slate from Minffordd back to Blaenau Festiniog and then via the LNWR.

The board agreed to build the wharves in February 1906 but

Tan-y-bwlch station house was built in the first years of the 20th century; the precise date has not been established. In this photograph *Prince* is facing downhill, having been turned at Glan y Pwll.
Author's collection

the Cambrian, which had agreed to do the work, estimated it at £400. Hughes took the initiative over them and built the first one using ships' ballast, billing the Cambrian £17 15s 9d. On 19 June, the invoice was rejected for want of a legal agreement. Hughes thought that the urgency with which the wharves were discussed and a site meeting that he had with Cambrian officers was sufficient, but the Cambrian would not budge over the bill until it had been approved by its board. Hughes obtained legal advice that the 1871 agreement between the two railways was still effective and that a fresh agreement was not required. The Cambrian's Traffic & Works Committee met on 7/8 November 1906 and resolved to defer any further consideration of expansion at Minffordd. Votty & Bowydd had taken the new wharf by August 1906.

Still at Minffordd, the Maenofferen Slate Quarry Co agreed a new lease of their slate wharf there for a term of 21 years from 1 January 1906, an annual rent of £1 payable provided they covered the wharf with a substantial shed suitable for stacking slabs in within one year of the lease being signed. In February 1906, the board resolved that Oakeley Slate Quarries Ltd's new incline from their upper and middle quarries, which connected with the railway at Dinas instead of at Rhiwbryfdir, would not affect its charges. When Oakeley queried the cost of the new point that the railway had installed to connect the new incline it was resolved to say that 'it was actual cost and that the board could not see their way to allow anything off the account'. Oakeley was to be asked £10 per annum for a new wharf at Minffordd in February 1907.

Expansion at Minffordd continued during 1908. Maenofferen required turntables and sidings on its new wharf and terms were agreed to lease space to Rhiwbach. The annual rent of two wharves for the latter at £7 10s was to be charged from 1 May. Rhiwbach also requested a supply of marked wagons. An application for space from Bwlch y Slater Quarry Co Ltd was approved in June. By August the Cambrian had agreed to pay half the cost of the new wharves.

At Blaenau Festiniog, a seven-year lease on part of the Duffws station building was agreed with Festiniog Urban District Council in November 1908. The rent was to be £10 per annum, the council making the necessary alterations and the company agreeing to refund some of the council's capital expenditure if the lease was not renewed.

Perhaps it was an indication that the harbour was also in decline, when the board decided to complain to the Tremadoc Estate, in June 1906, about the nuisance caused by 'the two old hulks now standing before the Portmadoc station'.

The Catherine & Jane lead mine's application for a rail connection near Cei Mawr was discussed in June 1906. A figure of £40 was to be charged for signals and £50 per annum for the signalman, while traffic to Portmadoc was to be charged at 1s 6d per ton.

Little progress was made on implementing the 1893 Railway Regulation Act concerning working hours despite making a regular return to the Board of Trade. When the board considered the Board's circular in July 1906 it resolved that 'it be arranged if possible that a reduction be made in the hours of those drivers and stokers who were working over ten hours per day'. It seems, though, that the signalmen worked more hours, more often, than loco crew. In February 1906, there had been 36 occasions on which signalmen worked 12 hours, although it was noted that six hours of these days were occupied in cleaning stations and helping to weigh slate trains. In July 1906, a 12-hour day had been exceeded by signalmen on seven occasions, loco crew twice and passenger guards once, and there had been two occasions when signalmen had worked more than 16 hours.

Ten tons of bullhead rail was ordered from the Barrow Haematite Co in February 1907, required for patch repairs. No other manufacturers had any of the same section in stock. A further 50 tons, including fishplates, chairs and sleepers was ordered from Guest, Keen & Co in November. A further 13 tons was acquired from an unspecified source in May 1909. Approval was given for the tunnel to be relaid in 1913, Bolckow, Vaughan & Co's tender being accepted in April.

The company took the opportunity to buy 1,000 sleepers at a good price in January 1909, when the PBSSR sold some of the stock that it had in hand for its failed expansion around Beddgelert in 1905/6. These cost 1s 2d each, 6¾d cheaper than those offered by Burt, Boulton & Haywood of Newport. Another 1,000 were purchased at 1s 2d in February 1910 and then at the end of that year 2,000 more at 1s each.

The 1892 Railway Rates & Charges No 6 (Festiniog Railway &c) Order Confirmation Act changed the rules over charging for fractions of a ton, but the company had continued to charge according to its 1869 act, which meant that customers shipping fractions of a ton had been overcharged. No one noticed until Rank Ltd, 'a firm of flour merchants', raised it in September 1907, the board resolving to bring its rates into line with the 1892 act. Presumably Rank was a big enough company to have an auditor double-checking its invoices.

When Bruce Peebles & Co, electrical engineers of Edinburgh, was working on the PBSSR project to build an electric railway from Portmadoc to Nant Gwynant some plans had been borrowed from the FR. When it became clear, in October 1907, that they were not likely to be returned, the board decided to charge ten guineas for their loan and to seek a categorical assurance that Peebles was unable to return them. In February 1908, faced with non-committal answers the board decided to treat the plans as lost and charge £100 for them. Peebles, faced with losses arising from its involvement with the PBSSR, was in liquidation very shortly afterwards.

Alfred Crick was appointed secretary on 15 October 1907, to take effect from the previous day at a salary of £100. No explanation was given for the change despite Hughes's presence at the meeting. Sydney Crick became traffic manager on the same date. By the time of the next meeting, on 26 November, Hughes had submitted his resignation as manager and engineer, the board agreeing to accept it, to take effect from 31 December. An agreement between Vaughan and the company concerning the management of the company from 1 January 1908 was considered at the same meeting. Vaughan became managing director on that date.

Just as Hughes's departure so soon after Vaughan's arrival cannot be unconnected, it is likely that Elliott's decision to stand down from the board, submitted on 20 February 1908, arose from the same event. Hughes died in Nevin on 26 January 1915.

Vaughan certainly made an impression on the board, and many agenda items were marked: 'Left for Mr Vaughan'. Not in full-time employment by the company, he made many journeys that may not have been on company business but for which he claimed expenses. In 1909 the company paid him £50 towards the cost of moving his household from Dublin.

Vaughan quickly made an impact on the company's operations, too, in March calling for all invoices to be passed through him for payment and declaring that, except for shunters and brakesmen, staff wearing company uniforms should pay half of the cost. In September 1908, he had ten men at Boston Lodge sacked to save £143 per annum; appeals from four of the men for reconsideration were rejected. Loco department wages were reduced in October.

Frederick P. Robjent, from Newport, Monmouthshire, joined the board in June 1908. A stockbroker, it became apparent that he was concerned about the company's share performance and in November he proposed that a consultant should be recruited to assess the position at Boston Lodge, for which a fee of 20 guineas was agreed in January 1909. C. D. Phillips, also from Newport, submitted his report on 10 March, together with supplementary documents on locomotive and wagon repairs. The report, which has not survived, was considered in May 1909, but merely 'noted'.

The chairman, G. A. W. Huddart, died between the September and October 1908 board meetings and Richard Methuen Greaves was elected in his stead. George William Otter Huddart was elected a director on 24 February 1909.

Since 1907, board meetings had been held most months, although there had been several cancellations because insufficient directors had been able to attend. In November 1911 it was resolved to hold meetings quarterly, with additional meetings called if required. The directors also resolved to pay themselves 20 guineas per annum, the chairman already receiving 50 guineas, which was to continue, plus out-of-pocket expenses.

A decision taken in August 1908 to 'abolish 2nd class carriages and reduce 1st class fares' was amended in September to 'the abolition of 2nd class fares and the reduction of 1st class fares to the existing 2nd class rates, the change to take effect from 1 October'.

Locomotive superintendent William Williams, employed by the company since 1851, was dismissed in June 1909; he was to be paid £1 per week 'terminable at the discretion of the board', in view of his long service. In 1869, he had made *Topsy*, a 3⅛ in gauge model of an England loco, for Charles Easton Spooner's garden railway at Bron y Garth and had been locomotive superintendent since 1881. Living at Boston Lodge, he asked the board to reconsider, he had a crop in the garden and had made improvements, renewed window frames and installed a new range, but it would not change its mind. He died in 1915, when his widow's application for the £1 payment to be paid to her was refused.

In December 1909, Williams's successor, Robert Williams, who was paid £2 per week, suggested that Boston Lodge personnel be put on short time during the winter, a proposal that was accepted; full-time working was resumed at the end of April 1910.

Despite having a large wagon fleet that consisted of four basic types, 2 ton braked and unbraked and 3 ton braked and unbraked, the FR worked a system of allocating particular wagons to particular quarries by painting coloured stripes on the sidebar. On the face of it, this can only have had any significance where a quarry or wharf had limited clearances that restricted access for the larger 3 ton wagons. On 15 November 1909, Davies Brothers, slate merchants, asked about a wagon allocation, leading to Vaughan suggesting that the allocations be abolished. A census carried out in January 1910 showed that wagons were allocated to Votty & Bowydd, Maenofferen, Wrysgan, Diphwys Casson, Rhiwbach, Oakeley and Bwlch y Slater, with a few unallocated. Following a meeting with the quarry companies, the wagons were put into a common pool from 1911.

The FR had discovered that it had been carrying parcel traffic originating from the LNWR and GWR for some time and was not being paid for it. Vaughan pursued a claim for payment and secured £150 from those companies in January 1912.

The hire of a locomotive to the Vale of Rheidol Railway was considered in 1912 for when the VoR was expecting heavy traffic from military camps along the line. A charge of 25s per day, including driver, was decided upon. Once again, *Palmerston* was selected and it was away from 31 July until 21 August. Another loan was agreed for 1913, if required.

Votty & Bowydd Slate Quarries Co's Vulcan Foundry 0-4-0T *Taffy* was the subject of discussion in February 1913, when approval was given for it to be repaired at Boston Lodge. In May, the board agreed to charge tools £20 8s, labour £53 3s 11d, materials £23 1s 6d, total £96 13s 5d, and to repair another loco on the same basis if required. In January 1914 Votty queried the account for £91 6s 2d in respect of their Manning, Wardle 0-4-0ST *Meirion*.

The possibility of extending the FR to Borth y Gest was under consideration in 1912/3, seemingly at the instigation of the Portmadoc Improvement Association. When the board met on 22 November 1912, £21 had been paid for engineer's estimates, the board resolving '...that if an application is made ... to sanction extension to Borth-y-gest this company will be prepared to subscribe one third of the cost of construction as per the estimate ... and to work the line ... subject to the consent of the shareholders'. On 26 September 1913, the board resolved to inform Ynyscynhaiarn Urban District Council that it would be better if the council applied for a Light Railway Order because the council would get a better Ministry of Transport grant. The

FESTINIOG RAILWAY
TIME TABLE
For JULY, AUGUST and SEPTEMBER, 1902.

RECEIVED 15 NOV 1902 No. 14163 BOARD OF TRADE

CAM. RYS.			A.M.	A.M.	A.M.	A.M.	P.M.	P.M.	P.M.	P.M.
Aberystwyth ... depart	..	..	7 15	..	10 5	12 15	1 10	3 0	3 ..	
Barmouth ...	..	..	9 16	..	12 20	2 50	..	..	6 15	
Minffordd ... arrive	..	..	9 58	..	1 6	3 23	4 33	5 26	6 56	
Pwllheli ... depart	..	7 25	..	9 50	11 15	1 40	4 0	..	4 46	
Criccieth ... "	..	7 50	..	10 23	11 32	2 5	4 30	..	5 15	
Minffordd ... arrive	..	8 9	..	10 44	E	2 25	4 50	..	E	

UP TRAINS.

	1 A.M.	Ply. 2 A.M.	3 A.M.	4 A.M.	5 A.M.	6 P.M.	7 P.M.	8 P.M.	9 P.M.
Portmadoc ... depart	B5 35	6 30	8 20	9 50	10 50	..	3 30	..	6 50
Minffordd (Cam. R.) "	5 45	6 40	8 30	10 0	11 0	1 15	3 40	4 55	6 58
Penrhyn ... "	5 50	6 45	8 35	..	11 5	1 18	3 45	5 0	7 3
Tan-y-bwlch .. "	6 10	7 5	8 55	10 18	11 25	1 35	4 5	5 20	7 21
Dduallt ... "	6 20	A	A	10 28	A	A	A	A	A
Tan-y-grisiau "	6 28	7 23	9 13	10 38	11 43	1 53	4 23	5 38	7 41
§ **Bl. Festiniog** (L.N.W.R.) "	6 33	7 28	9 18	10 43	11 48	1 58	4 28	5 43	7 46
* **Bl. Festiniog** (G.W.R.) "	..	..	9 19	10 44	11 49	1 59	..	5 44	..
Duffws ... arrive	6 35	7 30	9 20	10 45	11 50	2 0	4 30	5 45	7 48

L. & N. W. R.						P.M.			
Blaenau Festiniog .. depart	..	8 5	9 55	..	12 15	2 15	4 45	..	7 55
Bettwscoed .. arrive	..	8 40	10 30	..	12 51	2 50	5 20	..	8 30
Llandudno Junction "	..	9 19	11 11	..	1 32	3 35	5 57	..	9 10
Chester .. "	..	11 32	1 5	..	3 30	5 24	7 25	..	10 52

G. W. R.									
Blaenau Festiniog .. depart	..	..	9 35	..	12 10	2 45	..	7 5	..
Festiniog .. arrive	..	..	9 49	..	12 25	2 58	..	7 19	..
Bala .. "	..	..	10 44	..	1 10	3 50	..	8 12	..
Llangollen .. "	..	..	11 58	..	..	4 44	..	9 23	..
Chester .. "	..	..	1 2	..	3 35	5 53	..	10 30	..

DOWN TRAINS.

G. & N. W. R.	A.M.		A.M.	A.M.		A.M.	P.M.			P.M.
Chester .. depart	2 46	..	6 0	9 0	..	10 5	12 10	..	..	3 52
Llandudno Junction "	4 25	..	8 20	10 20	..	11 30	2 5	..	..	5 20
Bettwscoed "	5 25	..	8 59	10 64	..	12 2	2 46	..	..	6 5
Blaenau Festiniog arrive	6 12	..	9 41	11 37	..	12 52	3 27	..	..	6 47

G. W. R.										P.M.
Chester .. depart	..	..	..	6 48	..	8 55	..	..	..	3 5
Llangollen .. "	..	..	..	8 15	..	9 58	..	..	..	3 34
Bala .. "	..	..	7 45	9 30	..	11 34	..	..	..	5 15
Festiniog .. "	..	..	8 41	10 23	..	12 26	..	..	3 40	6 5
Blaenau Festiniog arrive	..	..	8 57	10 40	..	12 40	..	..	4 0	6 20

	Ply. 1 A.M.	2 A.M.	3 A.M.	4 A.M.	5 A.M.	6 P.M.	7 P.M.	8 P.M.	9 P.M.	10 P.M.
Duffws ... depart	6 40	8 30	9 50	11 55	C12 25	1 10	3 40	4 55	D5 50	6 55
Bl. Festiniog (G.W.R.) "	..	..	9 51	11 56	..	1 11	..	4 56	..	6 56
Bl. Festiniog (L.N.W.R.) "	6 42	8 32	9 53	11 57	12 29	1 12	3 42	4 58	5 52	6 57
Tan-y-Grisiau "	6 47	8 37	9 58	12 2	12 38	1 17	3 47	5 2	5 57	7 2
Dduallt "	A	A	A	12 10	12 45	1 25	3 55	5 10	6 5	7 9
Tan-y-bwlch "	7 5	8 55	10 18	12 20	12 58	1 35	4 5	5 20	6 15	7 21
Penrhyn "	7 25	9 15	10 36	12 40	1 18	1 55	4 23	5 38	6 35	7 38
† **Minffordd** (Cam. Rys.) "	7 30	9 20	10 40	12 45	1 23	2 0	4 27	5 45	6 40	7 42
Portmadoc .. arrive	7 40	9 30	10 50	12 55	1 33	2 10	4 35	5 55	6 50	7 52

CAM. RYS.				P.M.						
Minffordd .. depart	..	10 0	..	1 8	..	3 25	4 35	6 58	..	8 22
Criccieth .. arrive	..	10 18	..	1 27	..	3 45	4 55	7 15	..	8 45
Pwllheli .. "	..	10 50	..	2 0	..	4 20	5 20	7 40	..	9 10
Minffordd .. depart	8 9	..	10 44	..	1 30	2 25	4 50	..	..	7 41
Barmouth .. arrive	8 47	..	11 30	..	Harlech Sat only	3 15	5 40	..	..	8 32
Aberystwyth .. "	10 55	..	1 30	..	..	5 40	7 55	..	..	..

§ Change for L. & N. W. Railway.
* Change for G. W. Railway.
† Change for Cambrian Railway.

A Stops by Signal to take Up and set Down when required. Notice to be given to the Guard at the preceding Station.
B (Quarrymen's Train) on Mondays will leave Portmadoc at 5-45 a.m.
C (Quarrymen's Train) Saturdays only.
D (Quarrymen's Train) Saturdays excepted.
E Change at Portmadoc.

Return Tickets are available to return on the following day. The Company cannot guarantee the times being kept under any circumstances, nor will they be responsible for delay.

Portmadoc July 1st, 1902. J. S. HUGHES, General Manager.

W. O. Jones, Printer, 27, High Street, Portmadoc.

FESTINIOG RAILWAY TIME TABLE FOR

RECEIVED 15 NOV 1902 No. 14163 BOARD OF TRADE

UP and DOWN SLATE TRAINS,
FOR JULY, AUGUST & SEPTEMBER, 1902.

UP EMPTY TRAINS.	1 A.M.	2 A.M.	3 A.M.	4	5 P.M.	6 P.M.	7
Portmadoc leave	6 30	8 20	10 50	...	1 0	3 30	...
Minffordd "	6 40	8 30	11 0	...	1 15	3 40	...
Tan-y wlch "	7 5	8 55	11 25	...	1 35	4 5	...
Dinas Junc. arrive	7 25	9 15	11 45	...	1 55	4 25	...

DOWN LOADED TRAINS.	A.M.	A.M.			P.M.	Except Saturdays. P.M.	
Dinas Junc. leave	7 40	9 20	...	...	2 10	6 15	...
Tan-y-grisiau "	7 43	9 23	...	...	2 13	6 18	...
Tan-y-bwlch "	8 0	9 40	...	...	2 30	6 35	...
Penrhyn "	8 17	9 55	...	...	2 47	6 52	...
Minffordd "	×8 20	×9 58	...	...	×*2 50	×†6 55	...
Portmadoc arrive	9 30	11 30	...	...	4 0	...	...

* Stops at Minffordd on Saturdays, arrives at Portmadoc 7-30 Monday morning.
× Cross Passenger Train.   † Arriving at Portmadoc following morning at 7-0.

PORTMADOC,
July 1st, 1902.

J. S. HUGHES,
GENERAL MANAGER.

Printed by W. O. Jones, 27, High Street, Portmadoc.

---

council consulted the Urban District Councils Association on this point and on 8 December 1913 was informed that although several grants had been made to companies, none had been made to councils. Nothing more was heard of the proposal.

In an apparently prescient moment, the Improvement Association's Jonathan Davies, who had attended the 22 November board meeting to discuss the Borth y Gest proposal, 'raised the question as to the completion of the Portmadoc & Beddgelert Railway and then on to Carnarvon'. In a little more than ten years the FR was to be very closely linked with what became the Welsh Highland Railway.

Another WHR-related link came about in December 1912, when the board dealt with Thomas Parry & Co's request to purchase or hire 'timber trucks', 'three pairs' of which could be sold for £27 per pair or let at 2s per pair per day. Parry, of Mold, who had supplied the FR's coal for many years, had just, on 12 November, contracted to take over part of the incomplete PBSSR to haul timber out of the Beddgelert forest to Rhyd Ddu.

Two items of legislation, both enacted in 1911, came to the company's attention in 1912. The National Health Insurance Act introduced a contributory health insurance scheme, whereby the employee paid 4d per week, the employer 3d and the state 2d, the employee benefiting from free medical attention and medicine and 7s a week unemployment pay for 15 weeks a year. To try to mitigate its effect on the wages bill, which Vaughan estimated at £58 per annum, the company sought to find ways of having some work undertaken by indirect labour.

On 13 August 1914, Vaughan found it necessary to inform staff that 'a workman cannot claim unemployment benefit by working every other week'!

The other 1911 act, Railway Companies (Accounts & Returns), specified the format for accounts and annual returns and required that they be returned to both the Board of Trade and the Registrar of Companies. It also removed the requirement to prepare half-yearly accounts.

It may just have been coincidental, or maybe the new legislation encouraged Robjent to read up on what had gone before, leading him to query Vaughan's position as managing director, writing four letters about it in February 1913. He appeared to think that as managing director Vaughan was holding an 'office for profit' as defined in the 1832 act and that it followed that his directorship was vacant, so he (Robjent) proposed John Macaulay to fill the vacancy in September 1913.

The company's local solicitors, Breese, Jones & Casson, thought the appointment was satisfactory but counsel's opinion declared it *ultra vires*. The article in the 1832 act was one of those repealed by the 1869 act, but a similar article was included in the 1845 Companies Clauses Act, where the relevant phrase was 'no director shall be capable of accepting any other office or place of trust or profit under the company', which was incorporated into the 1869 act in its entirety. The September meeting must have been quite heated, the board being split, and Vaughan saying that he would not vote but he was satisfied that his position was valid!

Festiniog Granite Co, developing a quarry between Blaenau Festiniog and Tanygrisiau, commenced discussions with the company over rates for setts and macadam in April 1909. Its opening offer was rejected by the board, but 10d per ton for macadam, subject to a minimum of 20,000 tons, was agreed in May and a pass was granted for use while loading in 1910. The FR was asked to make a rail connection to the quarry but refused, but it was made during 1913 and connected in 1914; the point,

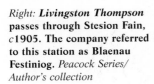

Right: **Livingston Thompson** **passes through Stesion Fain,** *c*1905. **The company referred to this station as Blaenau Festiniog.** *Peacock Series/ Author's collection*

Below: **Welsh Pony at Duffws water tower on 8 September 1906. A rake of five Ashbury four-wheeled carriages is stabled in the headshunt; the quarrymen's train was stabled under the shelter on the right.** *FR Archives*

supplied by the FR, was locked by a key on the train staff. In 1913, the board had agreed to sell the company 25 wagons 'made suitable for tipping purposes', at £25 each, or to rent them for £7 10s each per annum, half payable in advance. By January 1914 the number of wagons had been reduced to 20 and the granite company was to pay £2 10s on account as each was altered. In July, the board gave instructions for the company's outstanding account to be placed with the solicitors for recovery.

Over the years from 1900 to 1913 net receipts had declined from £6,570 to £2,974. The lowest point was the three years from 1907, when the operating ratio, expenditure/receipts, reached or exceeded 80%, giving little to spare for dividends; the 4½% preference share holders had nothing, while the 5% holders received only 1¼% in 1907 and 1909, and nothing in 1908. Apart from 1900, when it was 3½%, the highest paid on the ordinary stock was 1¾%, in 1903. The ordinary stock holders might only have received ¼% in 1910 but in 1906-09 they had nothing at all. In 1914, there was nothing for them and only 2¼% for the 4½% preference share holders with only the 5% preference share holders being paid that year, taking a cut to 2½%.

The board took the situation seriously, although its reaction after hearing the departmental reports for the last quarter of 1913 was to instruct the locomotive superintendent 'to do only light repairs'. Behind the scenes, it had another strategy, as revealed in this letter addressed to Vaughan, dated 16 February 1914 and carefully transcribed into the minutes: 'With reference to the conversation which we had recently at the Trefeddiau Hotel, Aberdovey, my directors have had under consideration the suggestion made by Mr Greaves to Lord Kenyon and I am directed to state that two of their number, with myself, would be prepared to meet a small committee of your directors with a view to further consideration of the matter.' The letter, signed by S. Williamson, the Cambrian's secretary, was code for 'we are prepared to discuss terms for taking over your railway'. The board agreed to a further meeting, with Greaves and Robjent delegated to attend, but nothing more has come to light about the proposal and its obvious failure.

The state of the company's finances did not discourage the directors from taking their own fees. Possibly as a result of Robjent's interest in legal issues, the board commenced, in 1914, an annual ritual of seeking shareholder approval for their proposed fees, followed by a ritual shareout. Article 69 of the Companies (Consolidation) Act, 1908: 'the remuneration of the directors shall from time to time be determined by the company in general meeting' appears to be appropriate. For 1914, the apportionment was: Greaves (chairman), £50; Bowton, £21; Robjent, £21; Huddart, £21; and Vaughan (managing director), £200. Robjent and Huddart voted against. Huddart's resignation was accepted on 22 October 1914, John Macaulay being elected in his place.

Audit clerk Robert Evans was awarded a 2s 6d increase in pay, making £1 12s 6d per week. Joining the company from school in 1883, his first appearance in the minutes had been in 1900, when he was paid 14s per week.

The declaration of war with Germany, made on 28 July 1914, was followed by the Railway Executive Committee's notification to the company that it was exercising the powers of an Order in Council under section 16 of the Regulation of Forces Act of 1871 and taking over the railway. The notice was actually issued by the War Office at midnight on 4/5 August, but the FR received it with a letter from the Railway Executive Committee dated 8 August, which suggests that possibly it had been overlooked initially. The company was instructed to '... carry on as usual, subject to the instructions ...'

MINFFORDD TO DDUALLT

Right: **Prince** shunting empty wagons past the Minffordd goods shed, *c*1905. *FR Archives*

Below: **A busy scene at Minffordd, *c*1900. For a wayside station the building was quite ornate.** *Author's collection*

Bottom: **An unusual scene at Minffordd in the 1930s, as the train has only two carriages and no brake van; the photograph was published, unattributed, in *The Railway Magazine* in 1936 so could have been taken in connection with the accompanying article.** *Photochrom/Author's collection*

Top: **Prince** with two goods brake vans in the Minffordd mineral line.
Author's collection

Above: **Passengers board a down train standing in the former mineral line; the loco is *Welsh Pony*, c1925.**
Author's collection

Left: Exchanging the token at Minffordd, c1900. *Author's collection*

Above left: **A view along the embankment between Minffordd and Penrhyn; Gwyndy farm is on the left, the Moelwyns in the background.** *Author's collection*

Left: **Cei Mawr, at 62ft and on a curve, the highest and most imposing of the FR's dry stone wall embankments.**
R. H. Bleasdale/
Author's collection

Below: **Prince shunts goods stock on the wrong line at Tan-y-bwlch. One would like to think that the gunpowder van next to the loco is empty! The covered meat van has ventilation panels in the side.**
Author's collection

Above: **Taliesin** stands alongside the waiting shelter at Tan-y-bwlch, early 1870s. There is only a small amount of back traffic in the slate wagons, some of which are timber framed. *Author's collection*

Right: **Merddin Emrys** leaves Tan-y-bwlch for Portmadoc. The coal yard/goods shed siding that replaced the 1873 centre road is visible by the end of the train. *F. U. Sergeant/Frith*

Below right: Tan-y-bwlch station house was quite new when this colourful scene with **Livingston Thompson**, was created, *c*1904. *R. Hughes/Author's collection*

Tan-y-Bwlch. Harrow Gate Station.

Above: **Palmerston** arrives at Tan-y-bwlch with a loaded slate train in 1934. The churns transported milk from Creuau farm to the dairy at Blaenau Festiniog. *R. W. Kidner/Author's collection*

Right: A long passenger train, still with wagons attached, at Tan-y-bwlch in the 1920s. The nearest brake van is one of the 1880 vehicles, that in the middle of the train is No 2, the converted 'curly roof' van. *E. M. Jones/Author's collection*

Below: The fireman prepares to jump off as an England locomotive arrives at Tan-y-bwlch light engine in the 1930s. *Author's collection*

Above: **Bessie Jones poses with *Taliesin's* fireman in May 1937, while Will Jones stands behind and the guard locks the carriage door. The picture clearly demonstrates the appalling visual state of the locomotives at the time. As recently as 1926 a man had been employed to clean engines at night; it seems likely that when the company ceased to employ cleaners, engines did not get cleaned.** *Stuart Marsh/Author's collection*

Right: **Bessie watches the train depart as Will climbs on the loco. The carriages are rebuilt brake No 5 and No 20.** *Stuart Marsh/Author's collection*

Below right: **An uncommon pre-war view of a locomotive on Tan-y-bwlch water tower, 1926.** *C. L. Mowat/Author's collection*

Above: **Little Wonder** with a long demonstration train posed for the photographer on the Creuau embankment, the point where construction was started in 1833. The far end of the train is on the later site of Tan-y-bwlch station. *Author's collection*

Left: During the course of shunting, **Prince** and its short train run on the Creuau embankment; a comparison can be made with the photograph of **Little Wonder**. *J. Valentine/Author's collection*

Below: **Prince** and a four-wheeled van approaching Garnedd Tunnel. The Oakeleys' artificial lake, Llyn Mair, forms the backdrop; from this vantage point it would have been possible to see an up train climbing to Tan-y-bwlch on the far side of the lake. *J. Valentine/ Author's collection*

Top: *Taliesin* leaving Garnedd Tunnel with a down train in 1934. *R. W. Kidner*

Above: A view from the train, seen from near Dduallt manor house in 1934. The goods portion comprises three vans, the Cleminson wagon, about 40 slate wagons and a brake van, the latter just passing a permanent way ganger's hut. A water tank that was used before the opening of Tan-y-bwlch station in 1873 is visible just above the carriages, right. *R. W. Kidner/Author's collection*

Right: **Dduallt**, *c*1950. *Brian Hilton/Author's collection*

9

From government control to the Welsh Highland takeover

1915-1921

The takeover by the Railway Executive Committee had little immediate effect on the day-to-day running of the railway. It set the scenario for undermining the company's stability during the war, however. The legislation provided for compensation for 'any loss or injury' without defining the basis for it. Agreement was reached with the railway companies collectively that the net receipts of 1913 would be protected, which in the FR's case meant that there would be enough to pay the debenture interest and most of the interest on the 5% preference shares. From February 1915, the government paid a war bonus of 3s per week on wages of less than £1 10s, otherwise 2s, rising to £1 13s per week in 1918 and £2 6s in 1921. Responding to trades union pressure the government also promised that the enginemen's working day would be reduced to eight hours on the cessation of hostilities, a promise that was put into effect on 1 February 1919. Despite the inflation that accompanied the war, and the provisions of the 1913 Railway & Canal Traffic Act that established that increased wages costs could be countered by increased charges, the government did not increase rates until 1920. Taken together, these actions were to cause significant problems for the company when control was handed back in 1921.

The first decision of substance that the board took in 1915 was the amount of remuneration to request from the shareholders, which was the same as in 1914. An increase, to reflect the extra time that Macaulay was spending on company business, was obtained in 1916, the apportionment being: Vaughan, £200; Macaulay, £100; Greaves, £50; and Robjent and Bowton, £21 each, totalling £392. Robjent had objected to the 1914 apportionment.

An application for a Light Railway Order came to the board's attention in February 1915. It had been made in

November 1914 by the Portmadoc, Beddgelert & Carnarvon Light Railway Committee, a joint committee of local authorities, to acquire the assets and rights of the North Wales Narrow Gauge Railways and the Portmadoc, Beddgelert & South Snowdon Railway and to complete the railway between Portmadoc and Carnarvon. Although it was left to Vaughan and Macaulay to deal with, nothing came of the application for several years, it going into limbo because of the war.

The only operational matter dealt with by the board during 1915 related to *Merddin Emrys*. In August it was resolved to get two estimates, one for a complete rebuild, including a new boiler, the other for 'ordinary repairs to enable the engine to work for another three to four years'. The estimate was considered in November, but no action was taken.

The railway became more closely involved with the war when Boston Lodge was designated a National Shell Factory in the autumn of 1915. This followed the failure of the battle of Neuve Chappelle and Artois in March 1915 when the government had collapsed after being blamed for a shell shortage. Under the coalition government that followed, David Lloyd George was appointed Minister of Munitions, charged with the task of improving the shell supply. It is speculation to suggest that he might have played a direct part in the designation of Boston Lodge, but it cannot be ruled out.

An annual rent of £35 was agreed for a part of Boston Lodge to be used for the factory, and locomotive superintendent Robert Williams was released to manage it, provided that he remained available to advise the company on locomotive matters for which a £10 annual payment was approved. The shed foreman, Hugh Hughes, was appointed locomotive superintendent. A part of the erecting shop was taken over and a machine shop established. The enterprise was noteworthy for bringing women into the works to operate the machines. (See photographs on p51.)

The ladies pose for a photograph while *Merddin Emrys* runs round its train at Portmadoc. *Author's collection*

Above: **A Sunday scene at Duffws, pre-1920. The rake of carriages includes one of the 1896 Ashburys, an 1880 van and Nos 15 and 16, as well as three four-wheelers. On the right wagons are loaded with fabrications, possibly to be taken to one of the quarries.** *FR Archives*

Right: **A layout plan submitted to the Board of Trade concerning the Brookes Quarry connection in 1918.** *National Archives*

There were occasional reports of misbehaviour that came to the board's attention. On 26 August 1915 Thomas E. Roberts, John Evans and Hugh Williams were convicted at Penrhyndeudraeth magistrates' court of throwing stones at passenger trains; the penalty was not reported. In another incident, in 1919, three boys caught damaging a bench at Minffordd station were called before the board and 'severely cautioned by Mr Greaves'. They agreed to pay £1 each for the damage and the solicitors' charges. Arthur Lloyd Sturgess wrote on 28 August 1919, apologising for trespassing on the railway, for which he was cautioned.

Other instances of employees' activities coming to the board's attention were more serious than that recorded on p84. David Jones, a brakesman, was hauled before the board in November 1915, held responsible for an accident that had happened to a down slate train on 21 October. He was reprimanded and warned to be more careful. Two more employees who appeared before the board were Ellis Jones and E. J. Griffiths, who were held responsible for 'irregularity in working [the] staff between Minffordd and Portmadoc' on 6 January 1920. They received a 'severe reprimand' and caution from Greaves.

Following the derailment of a shunting engine at Duffws on 11 October 1920, W. Humphreys was not called to the board but he was to be 'severely cautioned and if a similar occurrence takes place through his inattention the matter would not be overlooked'.

When Festiniog Granite Quarries Ltd, successors to the unincorporated Festiniog Granite Co, applied for a monthly ledger account in November 1915 the board refused. In March 1917, when Ripon Urban District Council's borough surveyor enquired about the rates for macadam from the quarry he was given an account. The quarry was taken over by Leicestershire-based Groby Granite Co *c*1921. The branch line is reputed to have been closed in 1930, a victim of the depression, although quarrying probably lasted longer.

Another enterprise to make a rail connection to the FR was the Zinc Mines of Great Britain Ltd. The zinc mine was close to the north end of the tunnel and its branch included a short incline on a 1 in 3 gradient, the gradient requiring a runaway siding to

protect the FR. In 1919 Vaughan told the Board of Trade that there would also be a loop siding capable of holding 16 wagons, a platform for the miners and a connecting point locked by a key on the train staff, as approved at the Festiniog Granite siding in 1914.

A small reorganisation had been put in place in February 1916. Macaulay had undertaken a review of the company's position and recommended that F. G. Crick, traffic manager and accountant, should be asked to retire on 31 March on £50 per annum. A. G. Crick was to be superintendent in addition to being secretary and R. Evans to be audit clerk and accountant, both receiving an increase of £20 per annum, making £130 and £104 10s per annum respectively. These changes were to be effective from 31 March, with Evans's increase backdated to 12 November 1915, the date of the last board meeting. Despite being 'asked', F. G. Crick had no choice about his retirement, and when he asked for it to be postponed his request was refused.

Further staffing changes took place in March 1917, following the departure of W. Parkins, Minffordd stationmaster, apparently accused of causing delay to passenger trains. O. S. Williams, a clerk at Portmadoc, was transferred to Minffordd, his old work being shared between the other Portmadoc clerks, T. Rees and O. C. Davies, who were given a small increase in pay; J. Piercy, the Penrhyn stationmaster also received a small rise. The rearrangement saved 10s per week.

Changes in conditions were agreed by the board in September 1918, after employees, members of the National Union of Railwaymen, sought parity with the Cambrian Railways for holidays and overtime.

The death of Rowland Jones, the permanent way inspector, on 10 May 1921, was recorded on 29 May, the board passing a vote of sympathy with the relatives. Although brief, this entry is the most fulsome memorial to be minuted, of either employees or directors, and the only one to include the date of death.

An attempt to obtain 33 tons of bullhead rail had come to nothing in February 1916, when five companies had said that they were unable to supply. The board resolved to reserve £500 in the accounts for 50 tons until it could be obtained, but changed its mind at the end of the year. Bolckow, Vaughan & Co offered to supply in February 1918 and an order was placed; a month later, when overproduction was reported, the board agreed to take the excess of 20/30 tons.

There had been good news on the relationship with the Cambrian in August 1916, when Vaughan informed the board that that company had agreed to contribute to the cost of more wharf space at Minffordd. The work, which involved realigning a standard gauge siding, was completed by December; Greaves had agreed to take the new space created.

Both Williams and Hughes submitted reports on locomotives and rolling stock in August 1916; the former was authorised to obtain 24 cast steel wheels for the quarrymen's carriages. Arising from Hughes's report, new tanks were to be made for *Livingston Thompson*, and *Taliesin* was to be retubed;

the estimates for the tanks were subsequently judged to be too high. The 1st class compartments in carriages Nos 19 and 20 were to be upholstered. Hadfield's tender for tyres for *Prince*, £12 10s each, was accepted in November 1917. New wheels were to be obtained for No 19 in January 1918.

Hadfield supplied the steel for new bogie frames for *James Spooner* in March 1918. Adamson's £595 tender for a new boiler for *Prince* was accepted in July 1918, Vulcan Foundry having tendered £769. Adamson's request for an additional payment of £71, due to 'advance in wages and materials during construction' was refused in March 1920. Unusually, Vulcan submitted the cheapest tender when a boiler for *Merddin Emrys* was considered in September 1919, £1,905 compared with Adamson's £2,175, although the board decided that further tenders should be obtained. In October, Vulcan was informed that if it could deliver in six months it could have the order. The boiler was delivered in December 1920, the last for a Fairlie obtained by the pre-preservation administration.

In October 1920, tenders were obtained for a new boiler for *Princess* from Hawthorne, Leslie & Co, Newcastle upon Tyne, delivery 8/9 months after receipt of order (iron £1,080, steel £960); Vulcan Foundry Ltd, Newton-le-Willows, delivery 52 weeks (steel £997); and Joseph Adamson & Co Ltd, delivery 12 months (iron £1,015). Adamson was asked to quote for supplying in mild steel, the revised tender of £949 being accepted in November.

Despite the war, appearances were still important and in August 1916 Tanygrisiau station was ordered to be repainted. Approval was given to painting Tan-y-bwlch roadbridge in September. The roof of the Boston Lodge paint shop was repaired at a cost of ten guineas, while, in December, Penrhyn station was to be painted 'as soon as possible'.

The zinc mine connection was agreed in September 1916; the mine company had contributed £60 towards the £116 cost. In July 1919, Sir Osmond Williams was to contribute £40 towards the £75 cost of putting a siding into his sandpit at Boston Lodge.

On 5 February 1917, the chancellor of the exchequer, A. Bonar Law, wrote appealing for a 'liberal subscription' to the war loan appeal, to which the board agreed to subscribe £2,000 at 5%. Not having the funds, it borrowed the money from the bank!

An ongoing correspondence with government inspectors concerning the accounts commenced in November 1917. In August 1918 comments were made about the arrears of maintenance statements submitted in 1914 and '15. The details were not minuted.

The abandoned granite quarry at the north end of the long tunnel was reopened in 1917. The developer, Brookes Ltd, of Halifax, asked about reinstating the siding and rates for setts and macadam on 27 November.

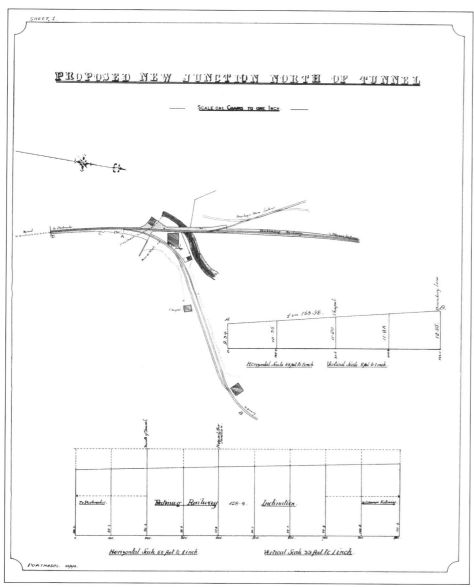

The board quoted rates for transporting to Blaenau Festiniog and Minffordd in existing FR wagons. In October 1918, Vaughan's proposal that Brookes be allowed to supply their own wagons was approved.

Macaulay resigned from the board in October 1918; he had not attended for two years due to illness. He was not replaced.

The lease on Coed y Bleiddiau cottage was transferred to A. W. Wellings in June 1918. Wellings's application to purchase the property was refused in August. At Penrhyn, a lease was agreed at £5 per year for 10 years, with Llanfrothen Co-operative Society for a store shed in July 1918.

When the shell factory was being run down at the end of 1918, the company was given the opportunity to buy the stock of steam coal for £1 12s 6d per ton, a saving of 1s per ton on the year's contract price. On 27 February 1919 Robert Williams asked to be reinstated as locomotive superintendent, and the board agreed that this should be effective from 1 April and that he should be paid £2 10s plus war bonus. Hugh Hughes was reinstated as shed foreman for £1 14s plus bonus. The shell factory equipment was auctioned off on 28 March 1919.

The works were in arrears with the wagon repairs in August 1919 and Williams was called to explain this to the board; he was told to give special attention to them. He was allowed to employ a fitter temporarily.

The electric token system was extended in 1919, tenders from J. B. Saunders & Co being accepted to install it between Glan y Pwll and Tanygrisiau (£132 18s) and Tanygrisiau and Tan-y-bwlch (£150 13s).

Having run the country's railways with minimal maintenance since 1914, the government was faced with the problem of handing back control without having the resources to compensate the railway companies properly. The situation was aggravated by rates and fares being maintained at pre-war levels and by not having kept any records of the traffic handled. On 15 August 1919 the Ministry of Transport Act transferred control of the railways from the Board of Trade to the newly created Ministry of Transport for a period of two years. The ministry had a brief to determine transport policy, so the two-year control period gave it, and the government, time to decide what to do, although it soon became clear that some measure of railway company reorganisation was likely to be put into effect. By June 1920 the government had decided to unify the railways, either completely or partially, in such a way that it would restore their dividend-earning power.

To protect the interests of the independent railways, two pressure groups, the Association of Minor Railways and the Association of Smaller Railways, had been established. Robjent had attended what was probably the latter's inaugural meeting in London on 13 March 1919 and recommended that the FR should join. Notwithstanding Vaughan's objection, in July 1919 the board had decided that the company should enrol and approved a cheque being drawn up for £17 14s, 1% of the gross receipts in 1918, although it was not issued until June 1920. The founder of the AMR was a certain Colonel Holman Fred Stephens.

The quarrymen negotiated revised working hours with their employers, where they would finish at 4pm all the year round, effective from 2 June 1919. Vaughan submitted a revised timetable for the quarrymen's train to Major Charles E. Breese, the local MP, for approval on 26 May, writing again on 29 May when he had received no reply. On 30 May the North Wales Quarrymen's Union asked the three railway companies concerned to change the times of their trains from 5.50pm to 4.20pm. The LNWR replied that it would have to wait until 1 July, when the summer timetable started, and the GWR that it could not arrange an earlier train but would look into it. Vaughan,

on the other hand, wrote that he could not make any alterations: 'as you are probably aware ours is a single line and there is only one passing place'. The proposed timetable that he had submitted to Breese had the afternoon train leaving at 4.45pm which, on the face of it, ought to have been quite adequate.

Nationally, there were tensions with railwaymen over the interpretation and implementation of a pay deal, men were likely to have their wages reduced because of reduced inflation, which led to a national strike that lasted for 14 days at the end of September 1919. Although the strike was considered a success, it provided an opening for the introduction of cheap, war surplus, motor lorries to be used for the transport of goods.

In October the Railway Executive awarded a bonus to those who continued working, the FR board agreeing the following payments: H. G. Griffiths, Duffws, £3 9s 6d; H. D. Jones, Tan-y-bwlch, £3; W. O. Williams, Portmadoc, £2 10s; E. A. Griffiths, Boston Lodge, £3 12 4d; Percy Roberts, Boston Lodge, £1 9s; J. O. Evans, Boston Lodge, £2 9s 7d; T.F. Jones, Boston Lodge, £2 7s 3d; W. Pugh, Minffordd, £1 12s 8d; R. Williams, Boston Lodge, £5; A. G. Crick, £1; R. Evans, £1; T. Pearce, £1 – a total of £31 6s 4d.

With the war ended it was necessary to do something to encourage tourism. The Cambrian Resort Association hosted a five-day visit for 12 members of the press in December 1919, including a journey over the FR in the itinerary. It is unlikely that the journalists would have appreciated a journey in the quarrymen's train, which on 15 December 1920, was the subject of a parliamentary written answer. James Wignall, MP for Gloucester (Forest of Dean), had asked the Minister of Transport, Arthur Neal MP 'if he is aware that the Festiniog Railway Company, Portmadoc, has added 2s to the cost of workmen's weekly tickets; that the carriages on this railway are very old and dilapidated, unclean, not waterproof, and that the only light in them is supplied by an occasional candle; that the increase of 2s is for any distance travelled, the men concerned only having to travel a few miles ...' The minister replied that the fares were very low and the 2s increase was the maximum allowed by the Rates Advisory Committee. There is no explanation for Wignall's interest in the quarrymen's wellbeing.

The FR made the *Liverpool Daily Post* in April 1921, when it was reported that services had been curtailed due to a shortage of coal. Vaughan sent a telegram complaining that the report was untrue.

Votty & Bowydd Slate Co's request for a telephone in its Portmadoc office in June 1920 prompted a comparison of telephone revenue between 1913 and 1918; a loss of £13 6s in 1913 had become £131 13s five years later, mostly due to increased costs, revenue being only slightly down: £114 4s, against £122 10s. Votty was allowed its line provided it paid for the instrument.

Wagons were a particular concern in 1921. In January several were damaged while on Maenofferen property and some had been at Craig Ddu for longer than necessary. Ellis Lewis was instructed to investigate and it was subsequently decided to bring a claim for compensation against Maenofferen. In May, Diphwys Casson accepted responsibility for wagons damaged there and their offer of £10 in settlement was accepted.

Several events in 1921 were to have a serious effect on the FR's future. Before examining them, it is fitting to look at the railway's performance since 1915.

Gross receipts had risen from £12,049 to £30,351 (1920), expenditure from £9,164 to £27,431 and net receipts had crept along at about £2,600, pretty much in line with the government's guarantee. The debenture interest had been paid in full, and most of the interest on the 5% preference shares had been paid.

No interest had been paid on the 4½% preference shares and no dividends on the ordinary stock. They did not know it, but there was no joy in sight for the owners of FR shares and stock.

On 3 March, the Portmadoc branch manager of the National Provincial Bank wrote to express concern about the overdraft. It had risen from £400 in 1915 to £2,611; probably neither party realised that the company had no powers to borrow by overdraft!

There were problems, too, with the rebates due from the government. The precise nature of these is not made clear in the minutes and might have been simply due to bureaucracy, but the news which arrived in March that the Ministry of Transport was withholding £2,000 from the January payment certainly had more than bureaucratic impact, especially when a further £200 was withheld two months later. On 29 May, the board agreed to give a guarantee to the bank for £7,000, including the £2,000 war loan. On the ordinary account interest was payable at ½% above base rate, with a minimum of 5%.

The key event of the year was that the company was the subject of a takeover by outsiders, the promoters of what became the Welsh Highland Railway, Evan R. Davies, Henry Joseph Jack and Sir John Henderson Stewart Bt.

The 1914 Light Railway Order application to take over the PBSSR and the NWNGR and to complete the route between Portmadoc and Carnarvon had been reactivated early in 1921. In 1918, the Aluminium Corporation at Dolgarrog had taken over the North Wales Power & Traction Co, which had been in financial difficulties, and found amongst that company's assets the PBSSR. Jack, the corporation's managing director, was no stranger to the NWPT, having worked for it in 1908, when he was the contact for the disposal of the Ganz-built locomotives supplied to the PBSSR.

Davies had been acting as solicitor on Portmadoc–Carnarvon railway schemes since 1901 and had submitted the 1914 application. Both Jack and Davies were elected members of Carnarvonshire County Council, Jack was chairman, and Davies would have been able to brief him on the background of the railway schemes. Davies was a friend of David Lloyd George and Jack might well have met him when he visited Llanrwst in 1920. In April 1920, the corporation acquired control of the NWNGR and in 1921 Jack became its receiver. How Stewart became involved is unknown; his function will become clear shortly.

Probably realising that trying to get public money to support the revival of a moribund railway and a horse tramway and to complete the construction of a railway abandoned over ten years previously was hardly credible, the promoters decided to take over the FR. When a deputation of local MPs and other supporters of the WHR met the Minister of Transport, Arthur Neal MP, in Parliament on 8 November 1921 Jack was to say: 'It [the WHR] could not be brought forward as a complete and unified scheme until the control in the Festiniog Railway could be acquired'.

From the FR perspective, the first hint of the prospective takeover came on 30 March 1921, when a decision was left 'as there will be a considerable change in the directorate shortly'.

The day before, Robjent had agreed to sell his holding in the FR of £8,203 8s 2d ordinary stock, 571 £10 5% preference shares and 145 £10 4½% preference shares. He might have got 15% for his ordinary stock, and more for his preference shares, the record is unclear; 5% preference shares had been selling for 80% earlier in the year. Davies and Jack had £500 ordinary stock each, Stewart the remainder. By 15 July, Stewart had acquired £42,999 18s 1d ordinary stock, £23,420 5% preference shares and £3,660 4½% preference shares in 43 transactions. Jack was to tell the meeting with the Minister of Transport, already referred to, that £40,000 had been spent to acquire control of the FR.

Apart from Robjent, others who sold substantial holdings were Bowton, the slate merchant, £7,755 in three classes, and Macaulay's widow and sister, a joint holding of £7,064 9s 10d in two classes. The most surprising holding, from the point of view of this story, was that of Vaughan, with a total of £13,171 0s 11d in three classes – no wonder he had been so confident about his position as managing director!

Also on 15 July, Stewart's holding was effectively divided into three and transferred to Davies (£14,000 ordinary stock, £9,000 preference shares) and Jack (£28,000 ordinary stock and £18,000 preference shares, in two tranches). In September, Davies and Jack transferred their preference shares, and Jack £12,000 ordinary stock, to the National Bank (Branch Office Nominees) Ltd, a move which suggests that they were being used as security, the whole arrangement being devised to avoid

FESTINIOG "TOY RAILWAY"

having Stewart's name on the certificates. On 29 November, the bank transferred them all back to Stewart who immediately transferred £20,000 preference shares to two men in Dundee! In June 1922, Stewart transferred £12,000 ordinary stock and £7,000 preference shares to two other men in Dundee. They were all transferred back to him on 19 December 1923. Security for loans probably also explains the Scottish transfers.

Before leaving the subject of share transfers, two others of note took place on 16 May 1922, when Davies and Jack transferred their ordinary stock of £24,875 to the North Wales Power & Traction Company, and on 18 June 1924, when that holding was transferred to the Aluminium Corporation.

The change of control came on 16 July 1921, when there were two meetings, the first attended by Bowton, Robjent and Vaughan, when most decisions were 'deferred to new board'; after agreeing to cheques being issued for their expenses, they went through the motions of electing Davies and Jack as directors. At the second meeting the outgoing directors remained with Davies and Jack; Robjent and Bowton resigned and Davies proposed Stewart as a director. Dividing the election of the new directors over the two meetings kept the FR compliant over the number of directors it was permitted. It must be assumed that Greaves had resigned, although his resignation was not recorded; his holdings being transferred to Robjent on 30 July. Greaves was to speak against the WHR when Carnarvonshire County Council met to vote on its £15,000 loan to the railway.

Vaughan's resignation as a director was accepted and he was appointed general manager on a salary of £225, subject to three months' notice on either side. It was only in June that Vaughan discovered that he would have qualified for a war bonus of £197 8s 4d if he had been general manager instead of managing director! The only deferred decision to receive Davies's and Jack's attention was to agree to the hire of a locomotive to the Vale of Rheidol Railway. Jack was appointed chairman on 30 July.

The Railways Act, which led to the grouping of main line railway companies, came into effect on 19 August 1921. When the Ministry of Transport's light railways investigation committee had requested particulars of the FR in 1920 the board had always refused to respond because the FR was not, in the legal sense, a

Above: **A busy scene at Penrhyn as everyone tries to get into the photograph with** *Merddin Emrys*. **The station building, or parts of it, might have been part of the original Portmadoc station. The leading bogie carriage in the train is one of the 1896 Ashbury vehicles.** *E. M. Jones' series/Author's collection*

Below right: **A gravity train passing Tunnel Cottage,** *c*1920s. **The line to Brookes Quarry passes through the rather fancy gate on the right. The zinc mine and its 1-in-3 incline is behind the train.** *FR Archives*

light railway. Beyond its membership of the Association of Smaller Railways, the grouping and its effects was not discussed by the board. The FR was first allocated to the North Western and Midland group but fear of traffic being lost from Portmadoc had caused it to be transferred to the Great Western Group; even in the 1920s, the FR still held a strategic position. However, when the bill returned to the House of Commons for its third reading on 17 August it arrived with a Lords amendment calling for the FR to be excluded altogether, apparently as the result of a last-minute intervention by Portmadoc Urban District Council submitted by telegram. There would, in consequence, be a non-statutory grouping of North Wales narrow gauge railways; in addition to the FR, NWNGR and the PBSSR the promoters took control of the Snowdon Mountain Tramroad during 1922.

Not noted in the minutes was the report on the NWNGR, the PBSSR and the FR commissioned for the promoters from a consultant, Major G. C. Spring, and submitted later in 1921. His conclusion, 'It is fairly obvious that before further extensions are considered the Festiniog Railway itself must be first placed in a paying condition', turned out to be quite perceptive.

When comparing the years 1913 and 1920 he noted that locomotive mileage had increased despite a decline in traffic, attributing the difference to a reduction in the number of gravity trains run. Working expenses, 74% of receipts in 1913, had risen to 160%. Staff employed on the track and in Boston Lodge did not seem excessive, except for 'the large number [five] of apprentices employed'. There were too many clerks at Minffordd. Any savings made by replacing the gates at Minffordd and Penrhyn crossings with cattle guards would be minimal as one of the keepers was a pensioner, the other a woman.

The mileage of the two shunting engines was largely unproductive, especially as the top shunter was based at Boston Lodge during the winter, but its cost had to be borne by the business.

Concerning the slate wagons, Spring noted that the railway had given up trying to charge demurrage on wagons that overstayed in the quarries or wharves. On the basis that there was a fleet of about 1,200 wagons he allowed 12½% to be unavailable for maintenance, giving 1,050 available for traffic. Calculating that there was a daily demand for 425 wagons, and knowing that the quarry managers complained about shortages, he concluded that they were either kept under load for disproportionate periods, that they remained in the quarries, or that they were blocked in sidings by new arrivals. He had noticed that two loaded wagons descending an incline required four empties to balance them.

The maintenance of the works was 'an expenditure out of all proportion to the mileage and stock of the railway'; either the workshops must do more outside work or be run as a separate undertaking. Time was wasted because there was no crane capable of lifting carriages off their bogies, there was no hand crane to lift wheels into the wheel lathe, there was no planing machine for the carpenters, and with heavy loco repairs done in the loco shed and machining in the works there was too much 'unnecessary walking to and fro'.

Amongst Spring's recommendations were proposals reducing the number of loco turns of more than eight hours, working on a one-engine-in-steam basis at the expense of dislocating the service, and closing the station booking offices, the guards selling tickets. He also recommended terminating passenger trains at the GW station instead of at Duffws. Whilst the FR met the criteria regarding speed and axle weight for being treated as a light railway, he thought 'it would appear that an order to treat the Festiniog Railway as a light railway would not have the effect of cheapening operation'.

The new board met four times before the end of 1921.

Personnel issues included C. E. Hemmings being designated assistant secretary; he was secretary of the Aluminium Corporation from 1922 to 1923. James Williamson, of the Cambrian Railways, was appointed engineer on a salary of £130 from 1 October. No allowance was to be paid for working at Boston Lodge on Christmas Day. The GWR's offer of the services of S. C. Tyrwhitt 'for a short time to tide over a period during which the proposals for reorganisation of the Festiniog and neighbouring railways are under consideration' was accepted, Tyrwhitt being appointed assistant general manager. The GWR's motives for making this offer are not apparent; perhaps it still thought that there was a chance that it might take over the FR despite the promoters making it clear that the FR and WHR would only be available as a package.

Operationally, 500 slate wagons were ordered to be withdrawn, preferably the wooden ones, in August; this seems to pre-empt Spring, who was still seeking information to complete his report in September.

Administratively, any legal work was to be passed to Evan R. Davies & Davies, solicitors, Town Hall, Pwllheli; the registered office was to be transferred to 4 Broad Street Place, London EC, also the Aluminium Corporation's registered office. Taking note of Spring's report, Tyrwhitt was instructed to 'negotiate with the GWR for utilising the GWR station as terminus of this railway at Blaenau Festiniog same as joint station'.

Financially, the FR ended 1921 with an operating loss for the first time since 1842. It owed £6,445, on which it had paid £298 interest to the bank. It had still paid the debenture interest and 4½% on the 5% preference shares. On 31 December it received £1,543 from the government as the first instalment of compensation due for the control period, but that was not enough to cover the loss and there was still money owing from the state.

As the FR had become, once again, the master of its own destiny, it faced an uncertain future in a changing world, and with new owners having big plans for expansion but very little money.

THE LONG TUNNEL TO DUFFWS

Above: **Merddin Emrys** passes Clogwyn Daniel, near Tanygrisiau, 1930s. *Fox/Author's collection*

Right: **Two abandoned formations near Clogwyn Daniel, 1950s. The 1836 route is on the right, while the 1850s improvement cuts through it.** *Author's collection*

Below right: **Tanygrisiau station was not as substantial as it looks in this 1949 photograph. Only the goods shed survives.** *R. K. Cope/FR Archives*

Top: **Dinas junction, 1887.** The train, standing on the line to Duffws, looks as though it was set up for the photographer, with an assortment of wagons and a few empty slates for good measure. To the left is the Nith y Gigfran incline, Dinas is straight ahead; the 1881 loop line is behind the train. *R. H. Bleasdale/Author's collection*

Above: **Dinas station,** the railway's original terminus, and its 1863 loco shed, were derelict by 1954, when photographed. *FR Archives*

Left: **Welsh Pony near Glan y Pwll on 3 June 1932.** The tank across the road is part of the LMS terminal infrastructure. *H. C. Casserley/Ian Allan Library*

*Left: **Taliesin**, c1890, with an 1880 van and carriage No 15 or 16. The small door at the right-hand end of the van is the dog compartment which, unlike that in the 'curly roof' vans, was ventilated.* FR Archives

Below left: **The base of the water tower seen in this photograph survived many years of closure; *Merddin Emrys* enters Stesion Fain in July 1939.** *R. W. Butterell/Author's collection*

Bottom left: **Merddin Emrys** *passes the ground frame for the Stesion Fain loop in 1929.* *Author's collection*

Right: **With Glan y Pwll school as a backdrop, *Palmerston* shunts on the mineral line in 1933. The battery-powered headlamp must have been an advantage in the winter months.** *H. W. Comber/FR Archives*

Above: **Merddin Emrys** *with a slate train, probably in the 1940s.* FR Archives

Left: **In 1937, a group of camera-wielding lads watch as *Merddin Emrys* arrives with a train for Portmadoc. To the left of the locomotive is the North Western Hotel, part of the LNWR's investment in the town.** *E. P. Olney/FR Archives*

Above: **Apart from the track layout, Stesion Fain showed no sign of change in 1950, only deterioration, over the 70 years since it was opened.** *Author's collection*

Right: **One of Maenofferen's Ruston & Hornsby diesel locomotives at work on the leased section in March 1955.** *G. E. Baddeley/ Author's collection*

Below: **Taliesin's locomotive crew chat with the guard, and would-be train crew possibly, at the GW exchange platform on a wet day in the later 1930s.** *Ian C. Allen/FR Archives*

Above: **Taliesin** between the GW platform, to the right, and **Duffws.** *Author's collection*

Left: **A rake of GWR slate wagons in the GWR yard, 1952.** *R. Jones/Author's collection*

Below: **Duffws is lower centre of this 'aerial' view; the standard gauge viaduct is visible in the top right-hand corner. Quarrymen's carriages await their next duty.** *Photochrom/Author's collection*

Left: **A typical view of Duffws seen from the road overbridge;** *Livingston Thompson* **is prepared for its return journey to Portmadoc on 10 June 1920; the ash pile to the right of the locomotive indicates that fire cleaning is a regular practice here.** *Author's collection*

Below left: **A guard looks on as** *Merddin Emrys* **and four quarrymen's carriages receive the photographer's attention in July 1928.** *W.H. Wright/FR Archives*

Bottom left: **A busy scene at Duffws,** *c*1910 **with** *Little Giant,* **the top shunter, and** *Taliesin* **by the water tower, right.** *Author's collection*

Above right: **A nice portrait of** *Little Giant* **during a break in shunting operations at Duffws.** *Author's collection*

Right: **The guard unloads the milk from Creuau farm from a recently arrived passenger train hauled by** *Palmerston,* **August 1927.** *Author's collection*

Below: **The way to the quarries; Duffws on 13 May 1949.** *Denis P. N. Callender*

10

Managing decline –
the end of the passenger service

1922-1934

It appears that in planning the Welsh Highland Railway the promoters had been unaware that the PBSSR had no station in Portmadoc and that it had no connection with the FR that would facilitate through working. By the time they had taken control of the FR they had realised that they were not going to get any more funding from the Ministry of Transport or the local authorities for the WHR. Therefore, on 8 February 1922, they resolved to apply for a Light Railway Order to authorise the working of the FR as a light railway and to effect a physical junction with the 'Portmadoc, Beddgelert & South Snowdon Light Railway'.

Spring had said (p105) that he did not think the FR could make savings by being worked as a light railway. The board, though, had determined that as a light railway it would become exempt from paying government duty on fares, just over £150 per annum during the 20th century. As an order was needed to make the WHR connection, then it was probably best to get the most out of it.

The debt situation was eased slightly in February, when the £2,000 war loan was sold for £1920, an undeserved loss for responding to the chancellor's personal appeal!

The new engineer made an impression later in February, when the board considered a siding required by the Moelwyn Granite Co. Williamson had prepared the plans and said that his fee would be 5%, which he then increased to 10%. The board declared that it would be the former and that the amount should be written into the contract. Was the board expecting that he would invoice for fees in addition to the salary it was paying him?

Tyrwhitt reported good progress over the facilities at the GW station, and negotiations concerning the modifications to accommodate the FR there were said to be nearly complete in February 1922. The estimated cost of the alterations was £300, while annual savings could be £600. Approval was given to the work being done.

Vaughan resigned unexpectedly; he certainly gave less than three months' notice and his employment ended on 31 March 1922. He had attended a board meeting on 6 February but not that held three weeks later. The board proposed that Jack should write a letter of appreciation to him, particularly noting the 'cordial support he had given to the board of directors as at present constituted'. The *Liverpool Daily Post* recorded his retirement on 5 April. He died before the meeting held on 19 April and when his widow asked for privilege tickets in January 1924, Stephens instructed Evans not to issue them, saying: 'I doubt that she is entitled to them.' Tyrwhitt was appointed general manager of both lines with effect from 1 April 1921.

The company commenced negotiations with the National Union of Railwaymen to secure a reduction in the wages of enginemen. On 6 May 1922 Tyrwhitt was instructed to inform the union that he needed a reply to the company's proposals within seven days and that if it was unfavourable 'the board would have to consider the immediate closing down of the railway'!

Compensation due from the government, because the company had been able to show that it had 'suffered abnormally by the standardisation of rates of pay, hours of duty, and other conditions of service', had been determined at £3,324. Payable in two instalments, the first was received in May 1922, the second in December.

A. G. Crick submitted his resignation as secretary on 13 June 1922, but continued in company employment. On 24 June, the board appointed W. R. Huson as Crick's replacement. Huson worked at 7 Victoria Street, which became the company's registered office on the same date. He was secretary of the WHR and was also to hold the same post with the Snowdon Mountain Railway.

The draft notice of application for a Light Railway Order was also approved on 24 June 1922. The order was to constitute the FR as a light railway, authorise the construction of a junction railway across the Britannia bridge to connect with the WHR, sanction the acquisition of land for a new station at Portmadoc, and for other purposes. The application was submitted in July; Freeman, Fox's estimate (Table 10) was dated 26 July. At a meeting on 10 August the shareholders were told that the new station was in substitution of the present station and that the order would amend the borrowing powers and sanction the sale or lease of the company to any existing railway company.

Table 10

Estimate for 1923 Light Railway Order

Preliminary expenses (legal and engineering)				£1,500
Lines Nos 1 and 2	Length of lines	10 chains		
	Gauge	1ft 11½in		
Construction of line				
Buildings to be constructed			£3,000	
Alterations of bridge			£1,500	
Permanent way, including metalling of public roads			£500	
Contingencies 10%			£1,000	
				£6,000
Land and buildings to be acquired for lines Nos 1 and 2				£1,000
Rolling stock				£5,000
				£13,500

When the board met after the shareholders' meeting Davies reported that Gaumont had filmed the railway the previous week; the WHR had been filmed on the same day. Tyrwhitt was asked to report on the refreshment rooms at Tan-y-bwlch and the possibility of obtaining additional land for them. Unfortunately, it was December 1934 before Mrs Inge, the Oakeley beneficiary, finally agreed to rent a field next to the

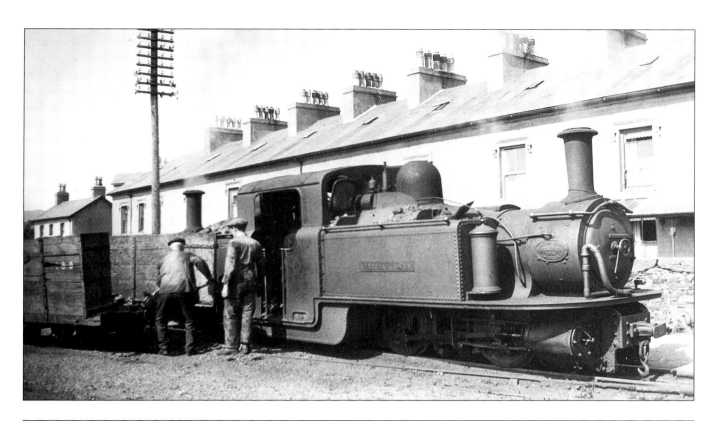

station at £25 per annum and even then it proved impossible to complete an agreement. There was actually only one refreshment room, the front parlour of the station cottage.

Tyrwhitt appears to have been too liberal with his expenses for the board's taste. He was asked to resubmit them, allocating them to the relevant railway, and was also instructed to keep the costs of his hire car down; 'the present charges are too high'. He was probably behaving as he thought a railway manager should behave, and as a former employee of a much grander concern, the GWR.

The LRO public inquiry was held in Portmadoc on

Top: **When the WHR opened, trains ran through, bypassing the FR's old Portmadoc station. A temporary coaling stage, seen here, and water supply were set up by the goods shed. When complaints were received from the residents of Britannia Terrace, behind, instructions were given for locomotive servicing to be returned to the original site adjacent to the water tank. The locomotive in this 1925 view is *Merddin Emrys*.** *R. W. Kidner/Author's collection*

Above: **An early 1920s view of Tan-y-bwlch. Outside the cottage the table is laid for tea.**
Commercial postcard/Author's collection

8 September. As a solicitor, Davies led for the FR. He explained that whilst receipts since 1914 had increased by 105%, wages had increased by 135%. If the railway could not make economies it would have to curtail public services until expenditure was brought down to match the receipts. Having the works at Boston Lodge was expensive and inconvenient; the railway would be better served by having the facilities in Portmadoc. The new Portmadoc station would be more convenient for passengers changing to or from the GWR station. In justification for the £20,000 additional capital required, he said that it comprised £13,500 for the new works, £5,000 for losses incurred during the war and £1,500 for working capital. Regarding the losses, he explained that £3,529 had been spent during the period of control, some of which had not been recognised by the Ministry of Transport for reimbursement and which the company might have to fund by other means. Jack said that the purpose of the WHR was to enable the FR to be of greater use to the district. 'A railway of 12¾ miles could not possibly hope to prosper, but if 25 miles of railway were added to it, it would give such an average per passenger as to cover the expenditure, and one might therefore hope to make it a success.'

There was a misconception amongst the local authorities concerning the purpose of the order, with William George, David Lloyd George's brother, representing Portmadoc Urban District Council, asking for the embankment tolls to be abolished. Festiniog Urban District Council's representative hoped that the rates would be reduced when the FR was a light railway and clearly thought that the railway would be remade of a lighter construction, while Penrhyndeudraeth Parish Council's representative thought it meant that the trains would be slower! The National Union of Railwaymen representative thought the track would be re-layed with lighter materials.

At a pre-inquiry meeting held with Portmadoc Urban District Council on 4 April Davies had said that the reasons for the order were largely economic: 'it [the FR] could for one thing be run more on the lines of a tramway ...'! Tyrwhitt had said that ten or 12 jobs would be lost but those affected would be offered jobs on the WHR.

The order was made on 30 January 1923. The connection with the WHR was specified as two railways. Railway No 1, five chains long, was in substitution for the 1836 line across the Britannia bridge and located on new spans mounted on existing piers; the 1836 line across the bridge was formally abandoned. Railway No 2, also 5 chains long, crossed the High Street and entered Madoc Street to make a junction with the WHR opposite the corner of Madoc Street with Smith Street. The new station was authorised, giving it the unusual status of being owned by a different company from the railway it served. The FR had power to enter into agreements with the WHR and was permitted to make use of the WHR as far as the point where the latter crossed the GWR. It could also be leased to the WHR after the junction railways had been completed, provided the consent of the Minister of Transport was obtained.

Publicity for the WHR brought publicity for the FR, too. A supplement of *The Times* included a two-page feature headed 'Welsh Highland Railway – new transport facilities' on 22 November 1922. It had an Edwardian photograph of Tan-y-bwlch station prominent amongst the illustrations, the unnamed writer describing the WHR as an extension of the FR.

A problem that the 1921 board had inherited from its predecessors related to a claim made by Sir John Eldon Bankes for tolls in respect of goods carried over his land that were not specified in the 1832 act, as confirmed by the 1869 act. In April 1920 he had asked for tolls to be paid for granite; the old board had asked him to reconsider but, when he persisted, consulted the company's solicitors and then obtained counsel's opinion. At a special meeting held on 23 November 1922, the solicitors, Evan Davies & Davies by this time, reported that agreement had been reached confirming that the company's obligation extended only to slate, goods and heavy objects passing over Bankes's property but agreeing that the company would pay him two-thirds of 1d per ton on granite until 31 December 1927!

A Ministry of Agriculture inspector visited the line later in 1922 and submitted a comprehensive report of recommendations for planting to improve the appearance of the stations. The board approved expenditure of £37 to have the planting carried out under the supervision of the Snowdon Mountain Tramroad's gardener.

Despite apparent progress over the use of the GWR station at Blaenau Festiniog earlier in the year, a draft agreement had only just been submitted when the board met on 1 December 1922. The board decided it needed closer examination and Davies was deputed to deal with it. During December, Tyrwhitt placed advertisements in local newspapers promoting the revised arrangements that were brought into effect from 1 January 1923.

The details of the disallowed Ministry of Transport claim came to the board on 22 December 1922. The £2,600 concerned related to the new boilers obtained in 1919, 1920 and 1921 as the ministry felt that their cost was disproportionate to their pre-war cost, and that the government had received little benefit from them. The ministry was prepared to settle on the basis of allowing the proportion of cost that would have been allowed on the 1913 prices. The same applied to some unspecified improvements carried out on unidentified wagons and a van. The company could therefore look forward to receiving about £1,000, but only when the remainder of the transactions had been audited. The ministry's investigators visited Portmadoc on 9 and 10 January 1923 and agreement was finally reached; the company would receive £1,555 6s 4d in total settlement of all claims.

Freeman, Fox & Co was instructed to prepare plans and specifications for the new works but to restrict the station to a siding, platform and shed, estimated cost £75, and to include re-laying the long tunnel and provision of two observation cars in the scheme(!), total cost, including land, not to exceed £5,000. Sir Robert McAlpine & Sons tendered £3,640 to undertake the works required in connection with widening the Britannia bridge, constructing the junction railway and providing the new station building. Work was in progress by 14 April and was expected to be completed by 12 May.

Davies made the arrangements for a £10,000 bank loan secured on 5% debenture stock issued on 14 April 1923. A long-established link was broken when Saunders & Co's contract expired on 31 March. A new telephone maintenance contract was completed with the North Wales Power Company at an annual charge of £400, £100 less than paid to Saunders.

Williamson's service as engineer ended on 31 March 1923. Clearly dissatisfied with his performance, the board had decided, on 1 December 1922, to give him notice. Nothing came of a proposal to replace him with Freeman, Fox & Co as the railway's consulting engineers but Davies and Jack found an alternative, Colonel Holman Fred Stephens, well known for his management of a collection of mostly impecunious light railways. Although he was based in Tonbridge, Kent, Davies and Jack would have known of him from the publicity relating to the 1921 Railways Act; they went to see him. He visited the railways on 16 April and was appointed engineer and locomotive superintendent of both the FR and the WHR from 1 May 1923. His salary was £100 plus expenses.

Despite its enthusiasm for making cuts on the railway, the 1921 board was no different from its predecessors when it came to expenses. Not only sharing £400 per annum as fees, on 14 April 1923 it voted 'each director ... the sum of three guineas towards his expenses for each visit ... to or on the business of the railway'.

A trial run over the junction railways was made on 12 May 1923. Jack, Davies and Stephens accompanied Ralph Freeman, the consulting engineer, and Alfred McAlpine, the contractor. Colonel Alan H. L. Mount made his inspection on 24 May and submitted his report on 1 June. The board was obviously quite taken with this, and the correspondence that accompanied it, because it was all copied into the minutes. He was accompanied by representatives from the railway, the engineers, the contractors and the local authority.

Of the station, he said that it had a loop 150ft long and ground level platforms, and the corrugated iron station building, 40ft x 12ft, was approaching completion. A footpath had been made to the GWR station. On the Britannia bridge, the road was now 28ft wide between the parapets, it was previously 21ft 6in

wide; the track centreline was 5ft 6in from the parapet. The highways engineer was unhappy with the track because it was higher than the old and was already causing drainage problems despite holes being made through the parapet. Mount did not like the angle-iron check rails and the inadequate road surface. At the highway engineer's suggestion, Mount agreed to require a kerb with a gulley, to separate the railway from the road on the bridge. Railway No 2, the connection to the WHR, was properly check-railed in the road but was lower than the existing surface in Snowdon Street, so again there was concern about drainage. Mount was also unhappy with the standard points and levers used in the street, which he said were unsuitable for the purpose.

He approved the station, but although he thought the junction railways were fit for passenger traffic, he felt that they should not be finally approved until the local authority was happy with the road. On 5 June, the company was notified that both station and junction railways should be re-inspected after six months. The junction railways had been formally opened on 2 June and a through train was run over the FR and WHR from Blaenau Festiniog to Dinas. The date is that given in the minutes, the WHR had opened the day before. Mount had second thoughts about the wisdom of installing the kerb on the bridge, and the railway was instructed, by letter, not to build it.

Despite the completion of the works, for which McAlpine was paid £3,000 on 10 July, there were ongoing problems with several land purchases that remained outstanding until 1924. The issue of a £966 12s debenture certificate to William Hepburn McAlpine, not recorded in the minutes, indicates that the company had insufficient funds to fulfil its obligations.

The FR provided an array of services to the WHR, ranging from loco repairs to the supply of stores and cast-iron wheels for a brake van, and charged a proportion of both its overheads and the wages of those whose work involved both railways.

The board had intended that the administration of all three of its railways should be transferred to the Aluminium Corporation's office at Dolgarrog. Robert Evans had been travelling there several days a week, an experience not to his liking. A. G. Crick, however, took to Dolgarrog and offered to move, a proposal that was accepted on 27 August 1923, the company agreeing to pay his hotel bill until he found a house.

Tyrwhitt gave notice to terminate his contract with the company on 30 September 1923 and John May was appointed superintendent of the line at £5 per week until a successor was found. It was when writing to May on 20 October that Davies said, *inter alia*, there is 'little use curtailing the service unless there is a corresponding reduction in the staff we employ ...', one of the FR's underlying problems.

The 1907 claim against Bruce Peebles for the lost drawings had been settled by Peebles's liquidator allocating 18 7½% preference shares to the company in 1911. These were sold in August 1923 for £26 2s, not the best return for a £100 claim but better than nothing.

Davies reported that the LMSR and GWR had been very co-operative in his efforts to promote joint excursions to the three railways. A 16-page brochure had been produced and the main line companies had contributed half of the cost. In connection with them he had arranged a four-day visit by journalists from London and provincial newspapers in June.

Additions to the rolling stock and motive power fleet made during the summer of 1923 were reported to the board on 27 August. Kent Construction & Engineering Co had supplied an ex-War Department 40hp Motor Rail 'Simplex' petrol locomotive, or 'tractor' as it was often referred to, in July. Normally used for shunting at Portmadoc and Minffordd, it was photographed at the former with two carriages about to depart on a trial run over the WHR. In August, Robert Hudson Ltd of Leeds, supplied six 32-seat 'observation cars' at £165 each, complete with vacuum brakes. These also had military origins, being designed as troop carriers during the war. Tests with the tractor, carried out in Minffordd yard under Stephens's supervision, were reported as satisfactory in February 1924; the superintendent was 'requested to make use of the tractor to the exclusion of ordinary engines'.

Stewart's resignation was submitted on 29 December 1923 and accepted. As has already been stated, the circumstances surrounding his involvement with the WHR and the FR are a mystery. He was the owner of a family distillery in Dundee and his baronetcy, of Fingask, had been created in 1920, 'for public services'. The £40,000 Jack referred to in 1921, that it cost to acquire control of the FR, must have come from Stewart, who bought the shares. By 1923 he was seriously in debt, owing over £600,000 when he committed suicide on 6 February 1924. Newspaper reports made knowing remarks about 'the Welsh railway shares' and were outspoken on the subject of a £50,000 gift to an unidentified political party that had been returned in

1922 because he was being pursued by his creditors. There was no hesitation in calling him 'a con man and a friend of David Lloyd George'; the latter's office released a statement denying any connection. His FR shares had been transferred to Jack on 31 January 1924 and George Westall replaced him as a director on 18 March.

Davies got the GWR to undertake an engineering survey of the railways, the report dated 7 December 1923 being considered in February 1924. Copies were passed to the superintendent and engineer, but no indication was given about what any recommendations might have been or whether they were implemented. No copy has come to light.

Crosville, the bus company, started a service between Portmadoc and Blaenau Festiniog on 7 February 1924. As the bus fare was cheaper than the equivalent rail fare, Jack was to talk to May about reductions on the FR. Davies met the bus company's managing director in Chester and suggested that tickets be issued that were valid by train one way and bus the other.

Eric Nicholls became managing director with effect from 17 May. His salary of £500 included his fees as a director of the FR company and his services as general manager of the WHR. Arising from his first report to the board, on 18 June 1924, were the dismissal of May, not later than 30 September; the acceptance of Stephens's resignation, Nicholls to make arrangements with the GWR for oversight of both FR and WHR engineering activities; the abolition of signalling at Blaenau Festiniog, including the signalbox at Glan y Pwll; cancelling the employee uniform issue; and developing a sand trade at Blaenau Festiniog using the sand at Boston Lodge. It is not clear from the minutes if Stephens's resignation was voluntary or the consequence of persuasion/pressure.

The board agreed that the FR should manage the WHR for a fixed fee of £10 per week to cover overheads, the arrangement taking effect from 12 May 1924.

Nicholls and Davies had a meeting with GWR officers at Paddington on 5 August, when the GWR said that its personnel could act as consultants if they did not have to take responsibility for their actions or recommendations. This was obviously unacceptable, so no agreement was made. Jack returned to Stephens and 'secured his consent to continue to act until satisfactory permanent arrangements are made to conduct the work'.

In Nicholls's second report, submitted on 5 September, he sought approval for sacking F. G. Crick, as well as May; for the secretary to inform Williams, at Boston Lodge, that all officers were under the control of the managing director, who had the powers of appointment and dismissal; to terminate agreements with the National Union of Railwaymen and the Railway Clerks' Association unless he could make satisfactory arrangement to revise them to reduce running costs; and to reduce the winter train service from six trains each way, plus quarrymen's, to four plus quarrymen's; and 'to make a small weekly allowance during the winter months to any old servants ... whose services have to be dispensed with in order to secure an alert and efficient staff to run the company's service'. Obviously he was not a man to be trifled with. Crick complained to the Portmadoc UDC, which in turn complained to the Ministry of Transport.

A debenture certificate for £533 was issued to Sir Douglas Fox & Partners on 5 September 1924, another indication that the company was unable to pay its bills. At some stage another £250 debenture was issued to Fox that, like the McAlpine debenture already referred to, appears to have been overlooked for recording in the minutes.

Stephens rejoined the company on 20 October 1924, when he became a director. Jack had been to see him with a view to strengthening the board. The motion was written into the

The company transferred its rights and obligations in the Duffws road bridge to the Merionethshire County Council in 1931. The structure had probably been severely damaged by the corrosive effects of locomotive exhaust. An admiring crowd looks on as *Prince* passes the site with loaded slate wagons while the bridge was being rebuilt. *Paul Molyneux-Berry collection*

minutes to be signed by all directors 'in consequence of it being difficult for them to arrange a meeting' but only Davies signed it.

The 20 November 1924 meeting was quite busy with Jack submitting his resignation as chairman and Nicholls submitting his resignation, to take effect from 22 April 1925. Jack wrote, he was not present, that he was acting on medical advice to limit his workload. Whilst both notices were deferred to a future meeting, they were accepted without further comment.

On 16 December, Stephens found himself in the position of being chairman, engineer and locomotive superintendent! He was to be managing director when Nicholls left and was also responsible for the WHR. Wearing all these hats, he was paid a further £200 a year. In October 1925, Stephens issued a set of working instructions that was applied to both railways.

One benefit of being a light railway came through in December, when a refund of £431 8s 9d was received in respect of passenger duty.

Negotiations with the unions reached a sticking point when they offered to accept reductions worth £25 per week when the company needed £50 a week. An agreement made between the company and the unions on 3 May 1922 had established that supervisory, clerical and operating personnel were paid 25% less than the equivalent national agreement rates. The unions had offered that Boston Lodge staff should get 10% less and were prepared for WHR staff to be brought into line with the FR, even if it meant a reduction. The board decided that as no progress was being made with the unions it would put its case direct to the men, a move that would be beneficial if the men decided to strike or seek public sympathy. On 21 July 1925 Stephens reported that the unions had settled for a 25% reduction for all staff and that overtime would be paid at ordinary rates until ten hours had been worked. 'The men had agreed these proposals and were working satisfactorily.'

Granville Bantock, the composer, became the new tenant of Coed y Bleiddiau from 15 February 1925; the lease was for five years, with an annual rent of £10. He used it as a holiday home.

The company had twice appealed against the level of rates payable, the amount having increased considerably since 1913. An appeal in March 1925 won a 50% reduction for the future, provided the current year was paid in full. A second appeal was lodged at the Merionethshire & Carnarvonshire Quarter Sessions, when it was proposed to retain the services of the Southern Railway's rating surveyor, but was returned to the assessment committee. The latter made a further reduction of 30%, reducing the original assessment from £1,399 10s to £455, the settlement applying to all of 1924 and 1925. As a result, the company received a refund of £177 in 1925 and was not to pay more than £257 in the future; after 1930 it never paid more than £50.

In November, the bank had asked the company to sell its £1,000 New South Wales stock; it had raised £812 8s which had been applied to the loan account, reducing the loan to £10,687 12s. At the same time the Inland Revenue had been pressing for £864 arrears of income tax due since 1923. Davies had worked his magic and persuaded it to suspend proceedings. In November 1926 the board resolved to offer £50 on account but it remained outstanding until December 1933. With the arrears standing at £1,135 19s 1d, the Revenue offered to accept £568 in full settlement, payable over 12 months – Davies, or his staff, had visited at least three times a year, and written many letters, in the interim!

Jack submitted his resignation as a director on 9 November 1925, once more citing medical advice. The date was seven days after the Dolgarrog dam collapse, for which Jack accepted responsibility on behalf of the Aluminium Corporation. 16 people died; the dam had been badly built by a previous incarnation of the Corporation. However, he remained a director of the

119

corporation for another two years, when he resigned because he was close to a nervous breakdown. Therefore Jack's resignation from the FR, and the WHR, must be viewed as an indirect consequence of the dam failure, rather than a direct one. His impact on the FR is difficult to assess. He was probably the key figure in the WHR and saw control of the FR as a means to bring the WHR to fruition. Surviving correspondence shows that he was particularly concerned about reducing expenditure.

The nine-day General Strike in May 1926 appears to have had little impact on the FR, although some of the men did strike. Evans was instructed, by Stephens, to try to run a passenger service if the buses ran. In July, Stephens reported that steps had been taken to protect the company's interests and to maintain adequate coal supplies, but it was November before he complained about its poor quality and high price!

The re-inspection of the junction railways, which should have taken place in 1923, had been overlooked; Mount returned on 8 October 1926.

A 'great storm' hit the area on 28 October 1926, inflicting little damage to the railway but some to the wall that separated it from the embankment road. The 1869 act, which imposed the wall's construction on the FR, was quiet on the subject of its maintenance. Stephens agreed that the company should, without prejudice, take any action necessary to safeguard the public while he made contact with the Tremadoc Estate.

The company's administration was not really facilitated by Stephens being based in Kent. He kept in touch by letter and telegram and he, or his assistants Austen and Iggulden would visit from time to time. In May 1927 Stephens instructed Evans to explain the £990 difference between the expenditure for 1926 as shown in the accounts and the directors' reports. Apart from an underestimation in the stores stockholding of £330, it was accounted for by items dealt with at Tonbridge, including office expenses, of which Evans had no knowledge.

Passenger revenues caused concern in the later part of 1927. During the six weeks prior to the 25 November board meeting average passenger revenue had been £58 per week: £38 from quarrymen, the remainder from school children and the public. Following a long discussion it was decided to dismiss the works foreman, but allow him to stay on at his company-owned house free of rent with an honorarium of one guinea per week until he found another job; to sack the permanent way inspector; and 'to pay one of the workmen an extra 5s per week to act as ganger'; and to cancel the 2.25pm and the 5.8pm trains from Portmadoc and return for the remainder of the winter period; and to make any cuts possible arising from the cancellation. The service cuts would be reviewed in the spring with a view to devising an effective timetable that would attract holiday traffic.

Huson resigned as secretary in 1929 and Cynon Evan Davies was appointed in his stead, effective from 25 April. C. E. Davies was the elder of Evan R. Davies's sons, also a solicitor. A change in the directors occurred the following year when George Westall died. He was replaced by his son, Hubert Lander Westall on 4 March 1930. Stephens resigned as chairman in 1931, citing continued ill health; his signature had become progressively weaker since 1928, possibly an outward manifestation of his decline. Davies senior became chairman on 30 April and on the same day reported 'a considerable saving had been effected' by the suspension of passenger services; henceforth the FR would be dependent on the slate trade and tourists for its income.

A fire in the Boston Lodge loco shed damaged the roof in the early hours of 9 July 1930. Evans informed Stephens that the cleaner, G. H. Jones, had dropped his lamp in the pit and started a fire which spread to a loaded wooden coal wagon above and to the shed's wooden chimney. Failing to extinguish the fire, he fetched the drivers, Tom Davies and Morris Davies, who lived at Boston Lodge, to assist. The fire had spread to the roof when they arrived so they called for the fire brigade. In the meantime, Evan Thomas, a butcher in Portmadoc, noticed the fire and turned out with a fire extinguisher from his shop, and ran to Boston Lodge, according to Evans. The extinguisher dampened the fire while the fire brigade could do little due to the lack of mains water.

Part of the roof and the chimney sustained damage, and the wagon was badly burned. There were four steam locos and the Baldwin petrol loco in the shed, the latter under repair, but none was damaged. The falling lamp had ignited petrol that had leaked into the pit from the Baldwin. An insurance claim was submitted and settled for £18 3s 5d plus two guineas for Evans to disburse to those who had helped deal with the fire. Evans admitted to Stephens that the shed roof was already damaged and that the wagon was a cripple, so the company did well out of the claim! The size of the settlement suggests that the repair was not done to a very high standard.

A retrenchment took place at Duffws in September 1931, when the company agreed to surrender its leases on land owned by Lord Newborough. The rents had been in arrears for some time and Newborough had been pressing for settlement. A small plot was retained, as presumably it had an essential length of track on it, at an annual rent of £8, and the arrears were cancelled. At the same time the company agreed to convey the approach to the Duffws overbridge to the Merionethshire County Council in exchange for being released from its obligation to maintain the bridge; the conveyance was sealed on 10 October 1931.

The 1931 tourist service had done well in August, the peak month, and traffic was doing so well in September that the company decided to continue the service into October. The railway had benefited from holiday contract tickets issued by the LMSR that had brought in passengers from all over North Wales. Lack of connections militated against continuing the service in the winter months.

When Davies and Westall met on 2 November 1931 they were faced with finding a way to run the railways following Stephens's death on 24 October. Stephens had been 'unable to attend to his duties for upwards of 18 months' and during that period the work had been carried out by his staff in Tonbridge under Davies's direction. As managing director, engineer and locomotive superintendent, Stephens had been paid £233 6s 8d and charged a £42 contribution for office rent and overheads. For their work for the FR, and possibly the WHR, his assistant, J. A. Iggulden, was paid £175 10s and another £35 for his work as audit accountant. His accountant, J. A. Coggins, was paid £52 10s and H. Nevitt, his permanent way and locomotive assistant, £52 10s.

Davies said that Stephens's deputy, W. H. Austen, had agreed to take on the duties of engineer and locomotive superintendent with immediate effect for which he would be paid £55 for the period until 31 December 1932. Iggulden would continue at his present salary, also until 31 December 1932 and would receive an additional £100 for audit work and assistance given to the board and Robert Evans. Coggins's appointment would be terminated when he had completed the year's accounts and Nevitt would continue at £40 per annum. Davies himself would be managing director at £320 per annum.

These arrangements were calculated to save £263 6s 8d per annum. There was a minor rearrangement within the next two weeks, when Coggins offered to continue as accountant for £30, Iggulden's salary being reduced by that amount. C. E. Davies was elected a director to replace Stephens.

Above: **Bessie Jones at Tan-y-bwlch became an attraction in her own right during the 1930s. Living in the station house with her platelaying husband Will, she turned out to meet the tourist trains in Welsh dress and served refreshments. She was the subject of many picture postcards, some of which were produced for her to sell to passengers. This photograph, dated 24 June 1933, clearly shows that *Prince* has not been cleaned for some time.** *Fox Photos/FR Archives*

Left: **In the 1930s, FR and WHR stock was painted in different colours to raise its impact. *Welsh Pony*, seen here with a train approaching Stesion Fain in August 1933, was notoriously painted blue.** *R. S. Carpenter collection*

Surviving correspondence shows that Stephens took a close interest in the FR's day-to-day running but the minutes suggest that he made little impact at board level or on strategy. The railway would undoubtedly have benefited from having someone of his capability working for it full time and based in Portmadoc.

The debt situation was serious, with £189 8s 1d due from the GWR since before 1925 of not being recognised by that company and written off in May 1932. The £81 19s 1d due from the WHR was cancelled after notification from that company's receiver but there was still another £1,036 2s 5d outstanding from that source. By 31 December 1932, Sir John Bankes was owed £236 4s 11d and he had agreed to accept payment in three instalments by February 1934.

The Tremadoc Estate was owed £1,331 9s 3d by January 1933; Evan R. Davies had agreed a settlement of £540 payable

in three instalments. Evan Davies & Davies's account for 50 guineas for this work, and the Inland Revenue settlement (p119), was approved in December 1933. On the plus side, in May 1933 the accountant had identified £900 that had been in a capital reserve account since 1895/6 and recommended that it be transferred to the general reserve account.

Davies also succeeded in renegotiating the tolls due to Sir John Bankes with effect from 1 January 1933, although the agreement did not come into effect until after Davies died in December 1934. The arrears, at the revised rate, were £75 7s 6d up to 3 September 1934.

The condition of the railway generally had been deteriorating for some time and in January 1933, Davies and Austen decided to reorganise the permanent way staff to improve efficiency. Roberts, the man in charge of the telegraphs, was made foreman

Until the 1920s, the Minffordd loop line was used only by goods trains. *Merddin Emrys* was photographed in August 1928.
E. A. Gurney Smith/Author's collection

on a three-month trial, for 6s extra per week. William Williams, who had been foreman, was demoted; two others, who were over 65, were put on part time and a younger man was to be employed; 'it is anticipated that by this arrangement the permanent way should very soon be put into better condition'.

Davies was still confident about attracting tourists if the connections were good. For the benefit of passengers from the North Wales coast, he persuaded the LMSR to run a new train from Carnarvon to Afon Wen and the GWR to provide a connection to Minffordd. The FR would run a new train to Blaenau to connect with the LMSR there. He also proposed running a train late in the afternoon. Evans had estimated the extra costs at £12 per week, for which the FR would run a service of two trains each way from Whitsuntide to mid-July and four trains each way from mid-July to September, including Saturdays.

The idea of converting an unoccupied house at Boston Lodge into a hostel was one of Davies's. He thought that Miss Lanes, who lived next door, could be responsible for catering, take the revenue, and any profit from that, and not charge the company for housekeeping. The conversion, and a promotional leaflet, was approved in May 1933.

No fees were voted for the directors at the general meeting held on 26 May 1933.

During 1933, Davies came up with a scheme to lessen the debt by wiping out the arrears of debenture interest and making all debentures bear interest at 4%. Proposing to issue 50% of the arrears in script, effectively capitalising it, and to pay the remainder in cash, he thought that such a move would make the debentures marketable, enabling the company to sell those held by the bank as security and thus cancel the overdraft. The scheme, put into effect on 19 July 1934, saw £27,799 12s of old debentures cancelled and replaced with new 4% certificates; the 37 holders agreed to forgo 60% of the arrears and were promised the remainder over five years. These included at least eight members of the Huddart family, Robjent, the Elliott family and Vaughan's widow. The debenture interest arrears was reduced from £4,281 in 1933 to £1,778. The bulk of Jack's

shareholding was transferred to Davies on 12 March 1934, leaving him with just £33,000 5% preference shares.

Davies's efforts at marketing the railway and making it more attractive to tourists paid off in 1933, with passenger revenue increased by £1,000, although the net receipts increased only by £300. It had carried 39,285 tourists and 26,589 quarrymen; the 1931 figures had been 11,805 tourists and 46,171 quarrymen; the best post-war year was 1925, when 70,240 ordinary passengers and 137,766 quarrymen were carried for revenue of £4,688. Buoyed by the success of 1933, the board decided to have *Merddin Emrys* put into working order for 1934. Davies wanted to put another train out in the summer and was trying to persuade the GWR to sell a 10s contract ticket that covered its lines between Pwllheli, Dolgellau and Aberystwyth, extending the FR's range.

It was surely the success of the 1933 season that caused Davies to consider that the FR should take a lease on the WHR. That railway had failed to live up to the promoters' expectations, it had paid interest on its debentures only once, and had been in receivership since 1927. Its best year had been 1923 and since then it had been scraping along with a limited goods service and a seasonal passenger service. It had also done well in 1933, doubling its passenger numbers, to 6,445, (the FR had carried 39,285 ordinary passengers plus 26,589 quarrymen!) and making an operating profit of £30 but its closure from 1 January 1934 had been announced. In May Davies started discussions with the investing authorities and the Ministry of Transport and, anxious not to miss the tourist season, signed a lease effective from 1 July.

Considering that Davies was a solicitor, the lease did not serve the FR well. The 42-year lease allowed the FR to withdraw after six months. It would pay £1 for that period, while for the following 13 years it would pay 10% of the gross receipts, so if the WHR made a loss the FR would still have to pay. For the next 7½ years the FR would pay 10% of the gross receipts plus 5% of gross income over £2,000. After 21 years the rent would be reviewed. The 'introductory' rent reflected the effort the FR would have to put in to spruce up the WHR.

Why Davies accepted this lease cannot be imagined as he knew that both railways were struggling to pay their way. He cannot have been under pressure from the investing authorities as they had already signalled their willingness to abandon the

WHR. There was no need for it to be for such a long period; at the very least the rent should have been based on net income. As it was the WHR made a loss of £600 in 1934.

To put the board in a better position to deal with two railways, Davies proposed the election of D. H. Roberts, the Snowdon Mountain Railway's general manager, as a director on 8 June. Salary increases, in recognition of the increased workload, were paid to C. E. Davies (£50), Austen (£50), Evans (£50 bonus, presumably described as such to avoid income tax), Coggins (£25) and Iggulden (£2 per month to 30 September). The additional salaries were to be debited to the WHR account, with staff expenses divided between the two railways.

The rent on the 1865 station site at Portmadoc had not been paid since September 1932. In May 1934, Davies had negotiated with the Tremadoc Estate to cancel the existing lease in favour of a new one at half the £62 10s of the previous rent and a reduced tonnage of 1d instead of 1½d. The new lease was to be backdated to September 1932 and the arrears paid at the new rate.

The lease of Coed y Bleiddiau was assigned from Granville Bantock to Harry St John Philby for five years on 29 September 1933, backdated to 1 March 1930; the rent was £10 annually. On 29 September 1937 Philby renewed the lease for ten years at £15. Philby was the well-known spy's father and it is rumoured that William Joyce, 'Lord Haw Haw', was one of those who stayed at the cottage.

Evan R. Davies died on 2 December 1934 and his brother, Walter Cradoc Davies, was elected to the board and appointed chairman. Ninian Rhys Davies, Evan R. Davies's younger son, was appointed assistant secretary. He and his brother, Cynon Evan Davies, the secretary, inherited their father's shares. They were all solicitors. On 15 December 1934, Evans was authorised to 'pay the same [Christmas] gratuities to the staff as were paid last year'. There had been no previous reference to this practice.

Evan R. Davies was the last of the WHR triumvirate that had taken over the FR to pursue the dream of completing the railway link between Portmadoc and Carnarvon. The declining business that they had taken on continued to dwindle at a steady, even rate. Just as they, the Ministry of Transport and the local authorities had obviously chosen to ignore the realities of the weakness in the WHR business plan, they then ignored the FR's weak post-war position. If the FR could barely make profits as an established business then the WHR, with twice the route and half the rolling stock, was never going to outperform it, never mind pay nearly £4,000 a year in debenture interest.

The FR had made an operating loss of £1,606 in 1921, as the effects of the release from government control and exposure to inflation began to bite, while a profit of £70 in 1922 had been followed by losses totalling £5,056 in the two years 1923 and 1924. These returns gave no scope for paying rent and other overheads, let alone interest and dividends on debentures and shares. In fact, in 1921 and then every year from 1923, the FR had a negative balance to carry forward. The 65,827 tons of slate carried in 1921 had fallen to 54,558 tons in 1934 and 130,612 passengers had fallen to 71,400 over the same period. These figures are slightly misleading for there were increases in the latter 1920s but the underlying trend was down.

Davies, Jack and Stewart were three men with good contacts who knew how to work the system to get what they wanted. Davies was certainly the key link to Downing Street and Whitehall. He and David Lloyd George were friends; Davies could even write letters giving Downing Street as the address. Jack was seen as a bully; he was unquestionably influential in getting the local authorities to sign up to the WHR. Stewart probably had connections; he was certainly the money man, even if it was someone else's! Without Stewart or someone like him there probably would have been no WHR.

When it came to the FR, the key player was certainly Evan R. Davies. He worked tirelessly for it; in London during the week he kept in contact with the Tonbridge office, and at home at Pwllheli he kept in touch with the railway. He realised that promotion, a good service and good links were essential and that with them good returns from the summer season were assured. He also tried to do something positive about the debt situation, although the effect of rescheduling the debentures would have been marginal. He failed miserably with the WHR lease contract.

After ten years out of service *Livingston Thompson* returned to traffic in 1932 with an overhauled boiler and a new name – the single Fairlie *Taliesin* having been withdrawn, its name was transferred to the double engine. It was photographed at Minffordd in 1934. *FR Archives*

11

Fading towards extinction

1935-1954

The first issue on the agenda when the board met on 7 May 1935 was the directors' fees; £400 voted in 1925 had not been spent and had been placed in reserve. Coggins suggested that as no fees had been paid 'for some years' the £400 should be transferred to the general reserve.

A nine-week strike at most of the Blaenau Festiniog quarries started on 14 March 1936; one unidentified quarry continued working. As the only FR traffic at this time of year emanated from the quarries the company had to take action to minimise its expenses and warned traffic, locomotive and works staff, some 44 people, that lay-offs were likely. However, the quarries wanted to continue transporting dressed slate from stock using foremen and clerical staff as loaders. The company found it expedient to accommodate this strike breaking as, Davies reported: 'veiled suggestions had been made ... to the effect that some of the quarries might be removing their depots from Portmadoc and Minffordd to Blaenau Festiniog with resulting loss to the company'. A skeleton service was run on three days a week and 1,500 tons of slate carried to Minffordd. The affected staff worked part-time except for the works foreman, the apprentices and 'one or two other hands' who attended to running maintenance. This incident of industrial goodwill cost the company £348 against revenue of £276!

'The position here is far from satisfactory' was Davies's introduction to a report on the WHR on 25 May 1936. A year previously the quarries at Rhos Tryfan, which had shipped slate via the WHR's Bryngwyn branch, had changed over to road transport, depriving the WHR of anticipated income. The passenger service had operated from 8 July to 30 September, making a loss of £496 plus £10% of the gross receipts, £100, due as rent from the FR. When sending the WHR's accounts to the county council on 23 April Davies had asked for the rent to be waived and indicated that 'unless there was a considerable improvement in the passenger traffic and receipts for 1936 the company would have to consider seriously whether it was justified in continuing to run the railway'.

The Boston Lodge hostel, one of Evan R. Davies's initiatives of 1934 had not been a success and had been closed. On 22 June 1936, a ten-year lease on the property in favour of L. De Thierry at a rent of £26 was approved. A lease for the adjoining cottage was sanctioned on 8 December; Rev J. T. Phillips was to be the tenant for 10 years at £19 10s! Both of them saw out their lives there.

The quarrymen's strike had, of course, deprived the company of funds with which it could pay the debenture interest and the proportion of the arrears due on 15 July; the debenture holders had been circulated to that effect. A further circular, to inform them that the weather in July, August and September had been so poor that revenue was seriously reduced and that the railway was threatened with the loss of traffic from its largest customer, was approved on 26 September. Net receipts were £490 at the year end, less than half those of 1935.

The threat had come from Greaves's Llechwedd quarry, demanding a 6d per ton reduction on the 1s 4d net that it paid to have its slate shipped to Minffordd. The board decided that it

Above: **Photographs were taken to commemorate the FR's centenary in 1936 and this may be one of them. The train crew is looking out for the photographer and there is a loco blowing off in the LMS platform, too.** *Author's collection*

Right: **A view from the back of the train at Cei Mawr. The brake van is a rebuild of a 'curly roof' van carried out in 1921. It gained two 3rd class compartments and a new roof profile.** *Author's collection*

could not afford to lower the price but that it should consult with the GWR as that company stood to lose more if the traffic was lost. At a meeting held at Paddington on 2 December, the GWR offered 3d per ton provided the quarry owners agreed to guarantee that a specified percentage of their output would be sent via Minffordd. If the guarantee was not forthcoming, the FR said, then it would have no option but to close down during the winter months and 'merely run a passenger service during the summer months to meet the demand of the tourist traffic'.

Evans was given permission to put staff on short time over the winter if he thought fit. The services of the boilermaker were to be dispensed with. Later, the foundry moulder asked for a rise of 7s 6d per week, from £2 10s; he refused an offer of 2s 6d and submitted his notice. On 14 May 1937 the board resolved that if he left, any future moulding work should be done at a local foundry.

Morris Davies, who was retiring from the company after 53 years' service on the same day as the board meeting, 26 September, wrote to inform the board of his departure; if he anticipated a reward he was disappointed. The secretary was 'instructed to acknowledge receipt of the letter, to convey to Mr Davies the board's appreciation of his long service and to state that having regard to the financial position and prospects of the company the directors regretted being unable to express their appreciation in any tangible form'.

Austen submitted his resignation as engineer to take effect from 31 October 1936. On 8 December the board agreed to the appointment of S. Alexander, engineer of the Snowdon Mountain Railway, in his stead, his salary to be £30. By 1 April 1937 Davies was unhappy with Alexander's services! In the event, Alexander's appointment was terminated on 30 August, when he also left the SMR.

Davies met representatives of Oakeley, Greaves and Votty & Bowydd to discuss the rates issue on 22 January 1937. The quarries opened by demanding 8d per ton. Davies countered with the GWR's 3d reduction but offered to extend it to Portmadoc and to take back slate from Portmadoc to Minffordd without charge, conditional on a guarantee. Greaves said that if agreement was reached on rates it would cease to use the LMSR and send 80% of its output to Minffordd, reserving the remainder for road transport; Oakeley would guarantee 10,000 tons. They still held out for more than 3d but eventually settled on 4d with the offer of an additional 1d if traffic exceeded 15,000 tons in 12 months. The GWR gave its approval to the reduced rate on 3 March and it was brought into effect on 22 March.

Davies and Evans had attended a meeting of the WHR's investing authorities in Caernarvon on 31 December 1936, when Davies had asked for the FR to be relieved of paying the rent. The committee would not agree to the FR being released from the lease but asked that Davies should provide it with a letter that would be sent to the Treasury and the Ministry of Transport. If those two bodies were agreeable then an application would be made to the court asking the WHR's receiver not to press for the rent.

Reviewing both the report of the meeting and Davies's letter in response on 16 February 1937, the board resolved that 'under all the circumstances this company should take no steps whatsoever to run the Welsh Highland Railway during the coming season neither should any further monies be expended in connection with the line or rolling stock'. A resolution 'that all traffic be suspended as from the 1st June next and that the local manager be instructed to give notice to all merchants hitherto using the Welsh Highland Railway, the station agents concerned and the LMSR Railway' was approved on 1 April. On 9 May, the board resolved that no debenture interest should be paid 'until such time as the position with regard to the surrender of the Welsh Highland Railway lease be clarified'.

Regarding Alexander's replacement as engineer, Davies had been in touch with James Williamson, engineer from 1921 to 1923. On 26 October, the board agreed his appointment from 1 November; he was to be paid £50 per annum plus expenses to examine and report on the permanent way immediately and to inspect it on one day per month thereafter.

Despite the reduction in slate carried, 37,088 tons in 1937, from 99,700 in 1928, wagon shortages continued. On 27 October 1937, C. E. Davies reported that he had informed the quarry owners and merchants that the reason for the shortage was the length of time wagons were kept under load on the wharves; if they were returned to use within four days there would be plenty for everyone. A general 5% increase in railway rates had come into effect; the FR applied a 1d per ton increase on haulage to the LMSR and GWR stations and 2d per ton to Minffordd and Portmadoc, effective from 1 December.

The Boston Lodge chargehand, Morris W. Jones, was appointed acting locomotive superintendent from 1 January 1938. Jones had served his apprenticeship at Boston Lodge and had subsequently gone to sea, where he acquired a Board of Trade certificate as chief engineer.

During 1937 and 1938 the track in the long tunnel was relaid. The rails came from a wharf owned by the Tremadoc Estate which took the old ones in exchange. It is hard to imagine any wharf that would have had enough rail to re-lay the tunnel, never mind that it was fit to be used anywhere on the FR main line. On 9 May 1938, Williamson recommended the recruit-

The Baldwin tractor on the access road to Minffordd yard on
8 July 1936. The presence of passenger stock on the mineral line
suggests that the train has set back to collect empty slate wagons.
S. W. Baker/FR Archives

ment of two more men on the track; if supplied with 200
sleepers per month, and sufficient chairs, useful work could be
done, he thought. Receiving his report that the condition of the
permanent way was suitable for passenger services, the board
resolved to restart services on Wednesday, 1 June. The 5%
increase was applied to all fares.

Agreement of a Merioneth County Council scheme to widen
the road at Penrhyn crossing was finalised on 9 May. The
railway was to sell a plot needed for the work to take place for
£130 and would receive £75 as compensation for the additional
cost of maintaining and operating the enlarged crossing. The
council had also opened negotiations over land needed to widen
the road at Glan y Pwll.

Reviewing the season's operation on 21 October 1938,
Davies said that despite 3,000 fewer passengers being carried,
revenue was slightly up, which was due to the fare increase and
more people booking from Portmadoc. Receipts on slate and
goods were only £30 down despite 1,000 tons less being carried.
The board was reluctant to cancel the quarrymen's train during
the winter because the quarrymen would turn to the buses; the
service was worth £250 revenue annually. The loco that worked
the morning quarrymen's train stayed in Blaenau Festiniog to
assemble the slate train and then took the quarrymen home in
the afternoon. A second loco took the empty wagons during the
morning but had to return to Boston Lodge without a load, the
slate train still being a gravity operation. A tractor worked
between Minffordd and Portmadoc and shunted at Minffordd
and elsewhere. The board wished to find a way of working the
service using only one steam locomotive.

The roof of the Boston Lodge loco shed, and a supporting
wall, was reported to be in poor condition, probably the combina-
tion of poor maintenance and the damage done by the 1930 fire.
Now the repair estimate was £200; a repair using corrugated iron
was put in place, and was completed in January 1939.

T. G. Jack, the Snowdon Mountain Railway's locomotive
superintendent, was invited to inspect the works and assess the

locomotive position. A £200 estimate to repair *Prince* by the
Port Dinorwic Dry Dock Company was accepted on 16
December but the work was not done.

The year 1939 started with a review of outgoings. Starting
from the top, salary reductions were approved: chairman, £100
(from £120); secretary, £200 (£225); accountant, £50 (£78)
and manager, £300 (£334). The audit accountant's salary was
unchanged, while the secretary was to arrange for the auditor's
fee to revert to its pre-WHR lease level.

The services of six personnel were dispensed with on
7 January: O. Owens, porter, Portmadoc (£3 6s 9d); H. G.
Griffith, clerk, Tanygrisiau (£2 10s 6d); Wilson, blacksmith
striker (£2 9s 6d); J. P. Roberts, carpenter (£2 9s 1d); W. H.
Jones, blacksmith (£2 12s 10d), and B. Jones, extra cleaner,
Boston Lodge (£2 0s 1d).

Rents were also reviewed. O. Owens lived in the Portmadoc
station house and paid a nominal 1s annual rent; as he had been
sacked, the board resolved to allow him to continue living in the
house 'as a consideration for cleaning the offices and the
station'. W. Lloyd, Glan y Pwll crossing, increased to 5s a week
(from 2s 1d); William Jones, Station House, Tan-y-bwlch,
increased to 2s 6d per week (was 1s per annum nominal); Miss
Mary Davies (not an employee), 2 Boston Lodge, £10 8s
annually (£6 5s). The board was unable to resolve the position
of D. Ll. Williams who lived in Minffordd crossing house. He
was 74 years old and paid a nominal 1s per annum.

By January 1939, the board had realised that Williamson,
the engineer, had no mechanical engineering knowledge and
that Boston Lodge was therefore lacking someone in 'an author-
itative and supervisory capacity above the foreman fitter, Morris
Jones'. C. E. Davies, the secretary, who was also managing
director of the Snowdon Mountain Railway, reported that he
had found 'his company's locomotive superintendent Mr T. G.
Jack well versed in all work appertaining to locos and also very
able in his direction and supervision of work' and recommended
his appointment as locomotive superintendent. Jack was to
spend two half-days a week at Boston Lodge and be paid £2 14s
6d per month plus £1 per month for travelling expenses.

Evans telephoned Blaenau Festiniog police on 25 January
1939 as the day before a bicycle had been found on the track
near the Tanygrisiau foundry. A gravity slate train went past
without difficulty but the loco that was following caught the

bicycle's handlebar, fortunately without causing any damage. PC 20 E. D. Jones established that the culprit was John Dewi Griffiths, age 19, a shop assistant at the Star Supply Store in Blaenau Festiniog. Griffiths explained that he was visiting Tyn y Pistyll, the white cottage that is now much closer to the railway than it was in 1939, and had gone along the railway to get to it as he didn't know of any other way. Evans reported the incident to the chairman, concerned about the collision that might have happened if Griffiths's timing had been adrift, and concluding 'I shall be glad if you will kindly instruct me in the matter'.

Williamson was also concerned about trespass, reporting seeing children on the line to Evans on 11 November 1939. Evans acknowledged his report saying: 'there is no end of trespass on the Blaenau Festiniog branch and although we have prosecuted from time to time they continue to use the railway.' He said that he had written to his friend, Superintendant Evans, asking him to arrange for the schools to be visited, 'to caution the children and tell them that unless the trespassing stops there will be no alternative but to prosecute and demand a heavy penalty'.

On 10 February 1939 there was another fire at Boston Lodge. Jack's report to C. E. Davies gives no details of the cause or the circumstances, but machinery required reconditioning and shafting replacing. The Norwich Union Fire Insurance Society settled the claim for £705. On 9 June, the board visited Boston Lodge and considered the conversion of buildings 'to ensure more efficient working', and an architect was to be invited to produce plans. 'The directors were glad to note that the premises had been tidied up, and a good deal of scrap had been assembled ready for delivery to the scrap merchant.'

Of the railway's other buildings, the exterior woodwork and ironwork of Portmadoc station and goods shed were to be repainted in June. Penrhyn waiting room had been let to the Llanfrothen Co-operative Society for £4 annually in April; the station was dilapidated and the board agreed that, except for the waiting room and booking office, it should be demolished, including the urinal! The council's roadworks had been carried out but Williamson had withheld his certificate because the new crossing gates were unsatisfactory and the paintwork was poor.

On the track, partial re-laying on the embankment had started by April 1939 and Williamson said the line was ready for the resumption of passenger services at any time. In June, board visited the site of the Capel Nazareth underbridge. A complaint about its width had been sent to the Ministry of Transport which had referred it to the county surveyor. There was evidence that motor vehicles had been scraping the walls. As the width of the bridge was sufficient to meet traffic requirements when built, the directors did not consider that there was any liability on the company to widen it.

The outbreak of war on 3 September 1939 discouraged holidaymakers from travelling and the company immediately suspended the passenger service. It also established that the railway was not going to be taken over by the government as had happened in 1914.

The directors met on 15 September 1939 to consider the railway's options. Evans submitted a report comparing the year to date with 1938. Although he presented the information in an inconsistent manner, making exact comparisons impossible, he did make it clear that the tourist service had been subsidising the goods service. Between 1 January and 9 July 1938, he said, there had been an operating loss of £1,002 which had been reduced to £110 by 24 September, because of the seasonal passenger traffic, and increased to £758 by the end of the year; the average weekly loss for the 12 weeks to 31 December 1938 had been £50. The operating loss of £807 incurred between 1 January and 8 July 1939 had been reduced to £28 by 2 September. He forecast a considerable loss on the following two weeks because the traffic had been so low; 50 wagons a day during the first week of September had reduced to 35 wagons during the second week. To enable the railway to work without

Photographs of Fairlies alongside the goods shed at Portmadoc invariably show them with water running over the tanks, the reason being that the track was elevated for high speed! *Taliesin* **(formerly** *Livingston Thompson***) was photographed in 1938.** *FR Archives*

incurring a loss, assuming the slate traffic stayed constant, he thought that the wages and coal bills should be halved.

Average weekly slate tonnage had fallen to 546 tons which yielded £70; costs were £115. He thought that traffic might fall further and that there might not be any passenger traffic to make good the loss on slate traffic in 1940. As some of the quarries were closing for one or more weeks per month and Oakeley had ceased working on Saturdays, he recommended terminating the quarrymen's train, particularly as it earned only £4 per week. This would allow the railway to operate a shorter working day and to work with only one steam locomotive.

Faced with this information, the board decided to operate the railway, and open the works, on just three days per week and to discontinue the quarrymen's train. These decisions set the pattern for the railway's operations until 1946. When Jack left to join the forces, Morris Jones became locomotive superintendent once again, his appointment being backdated to 1 January 1940. In December 1940, W. C. Davies reported that he had not taken his chairman's salary for the past 12 months. C. E. Davies took up a commission in the RAF and in May 1941 N. R. Davies became acting secretary.

When reconstruction of bomb-damaged areas started during 1941 demand for slate increased. Due to a shortage of labour, the quarries had difficulty in meeting it, but it did lead to some reorganisation in Minffordd yard. New leases were granted to all the tenants: Maenofferen Slate Quarry Co, Davies Brothers, J. W. Greaves & Sons Ltd, M. E. Morris, Oakeley Slate Quarries Co Ltd and R. Bowton & Co. Some good news came from this, for the total rent income was now £176 7s per annum, instead of £75 10s!

Derelict stock at Portmadoc in 1953. Van No 3 was beyond repair, although a few components were kept, including the brass rain strips over the side doors. *M. E. Ware/Ian Allan Library*

The attempts to terminate the WHR lease were handicapped by the lack of an effective board with which to negotiate and, with the WHR being in receivership, by the requirement for every action taken to be approved by the court. A draft agreement had been reached in 1938, that the FR would pay £600, in two instalments, in settlement of all claims, and be allowed to keep *Moel Tryfan*. C. E. Davies had explained that the loco had never run during the lease period, having been dismantled at Boston Lodge since it failed a boiler examination in 1934, that there was therefore no obligation for the FR to return it to working order and that it would take more effort than it was worth to return it to Dinas. Davies also laid claim to the junction railways and, erroneously, to the WHR as far as the standard gauge crossing.

In a move to circumvent the impasse, the county council, representing the investing authorities, agreed to the Ministry of Supply issuing a requisition order for the WHR's removable assets. Thus, in April 1941, the FR could no longer be compelled to comply with the lease and operate the WHR. Whilst a court-approved winding-up order was issued against the WHR in 1941, it was 12 August 1943 before the surrender document was issued, and 31 March 1945 before C. E. Davies reported that the surrender had been completed. The first, and probably only, payment under the terms of the surrender, £100, was made on 30 August 1943.

Although the FR was not taken over by the government, it did contribute to the war effort with the War Department renting buildings on occasion. Transactions recorded were: Boston Lodge, £6 10s, 2 September 1941; Festiniog Railway station, Portmadoc, £83 4s, 10 April to 30 June 1942 and Festiniog Railway station, Portmadoc, £120, 10 July 1942. In November 1942, the Boston Lodge machine shop was taken over by the Glaslyn Foundry under the terms of an agreement made under the Location of Industry (Restriction) Order 1942. The foundry

was to use the facilities to manufacture components for the Ministry of Supply, and when the machines were not in use both the FR and the Britannia Foundry were allowed the use of them. It is not known when this arrangement ended. Around 1940 *Palmerston* had been set up as a stationary boiler to power a steam hammer, apparently for the benefit of a tenant.

The Ministry of Supply and the War Department both requisitioned wagons c1943, 14 by the former and 20, in two batches, by the latter, the company receiving £1,080 for them. Evans managed to get £33 each from the War Department but only £30 each from the Ministry of Supply! The 6 ton hand crane that Stephens had been responsible for acquiring in 1926 was sold to the Broughton Moor Green Slate Quarries Ltd for £142 10s. Coggins was quick to point out that these were all capital assets and the money could only be applied to the capital account, not against current expenses.

In 1942/3 No 2 Dutch Commando was based in Portmadoc and a photograph shows them drilling on Oakeley's wharf behind the station. It is said that the unit was billeted at the FR station but this is unlikely given that the building was full of the detritus of over 100 years of operation when nothing was ever thrown away. It is more likely that, if the unit was billeted in a station, it was the 1923 station which was both empty and out of use. A first-floor office in the FR building was let out to Major S. L. Richards, a consulting engineer, for most of the 1940s. The only other spaces that could have been available were the booking hall and the ladies' waiting room.

The railway took on a very run-down air. Sidings at Portmadoc were littered with wagons and one of the iconic 'curly roof' vans was left in the platform. The track was long past its Victorian heyday; the only place the weeds failed to establish was where it was used as an unofficial footpath.

In January 1941, Evans had written to Coggins: 'Jerry is getting nearer each week, he has been dropping bombs in the district during the last few nights, and we have had few warnings ... there are no shelters anywhere here and should bombs be dropped we are at his mercy or flee to the hills around us. This town and district are full of evacuees, both children and adults. I do find business difficult in every way, apart from having to do the work myself there is a great deal of worry in connection with all the work both inside and outside ... Glad to say things are getting better in the slate trade and the tonnage of slates carried is increasing, the quarries are now in difficulties, the output is getting small to supply the large orders for slates, they cannot also get men to work at the quarries ...'

Even running at a minimal level, and despite Evans's

optimism in 1941, the FR still ran at a loss, barely paying the wages, let alone the rents, tolls and £632 per annum debenture interest. Between 1939 and 1943 it had lost more than £3,000; the debenture interest arrears had reached £3,747, nearly what they had been when E. R. Davies proposed his rescheduling scheme in 1934. Maintenance was seriously in arrears. In addition to Evans, the railway was employing 14 people in 1945, six in the traffic department, two of whom appeared to be crossing keepers. Two worked on loco operating, four on permanent way, only one full time, and there were two fitters in the works. By 1946 the railway ran on Tuesdays, Wednesdays and Thursdays. There were only two engines steamable, *Princess* and *Merddin Emrys*, the latter usually steamed on Wednesdays.

Amongst all this loss-making activity something quite remarkable happened: in 1945 Adamson's delivered a new boiler for *Prince;* quite how this came about is a mystery. It is alleged to have been ordered in 1943 but that is not recorded in the minutes. Neither is there any explanation as to how the boiler was paid for, no increase in borrowing, for example, or anguished cries from Adamson about lack of payment. It was taken into the works, ready to be placed in *Prince's* frames. In 1946 Evans tried to find a buyer for it, fortunately, as things turned out, without success.

After the war ended, the FR's future was a topic of interest for the local authority and others. Portmadoc Urban District Council wrote twice before it elicited a response from C. E. Davies. Writing on 17 June 1946 he said that only with a considerable increase in slate traffic could the track and rolling stock be reconditioned for passenger services to be resumed. At a meeting of councillors on 15 July Evans said that the Ministry of Transport would make no grant for track repairs unless it was essential for the slate industry. However, the Slate Quarries Association had said that provided slate could be moved around Blaenau Festiniog the remainder of the railway was unnecessary.

On 2 August 1946, Evans wrote to employees and quarry owners to say that the railway was going to close. The staff, except for Morris Jones, were given 24 hours' notice. The quarries were told that when they resumed after their annual closure on 12 August they were to gather up all the FR's wagons and leave them at the foot of their inclines to await collection. It was presumably Jones's task to collect them. All the sidings at Portmadoc, Boston Lodge and Minffordd became choked with rolling stock.

Some correspondence from Greaves has survived. It may not be representative, but Greaves was quite horrified at the prospect of losing its free wagons, writing to the LMS and the Director of Roofing at the Ministry of Works to try to secure others. The railway was, however, still prepared to help the quarry owners and arranged a lease on a 650 yard length of railway between Duffws and the LMS yard. This allowed slate from Votty & Bowydd, now owned by Oakeley, and Maenofferen to be taken to the LMS yard using the quarries' own locomotives. Evans was contradictory about when this arrangement started. In a letter to Iggulden he said it was started 'last Monday', 7 October 1946, but when he wrote to C. E. Davies on 18 October he said that the work to put the track in order was in hand and 'it may be completed next week'; there was one man working on it. The FR earned 1s per ton, minimum of £5 per week, and rental on the wagons used, from this arrangement.

By December 1948, when C.E. Davies mentioned the matter in a letter to Coggins, the company had received two offers to buy the rolling stock and track. One, of £4,000, was from George

Left: **In contrast, 24 July 1946 was a fine day when *Princess* was photographed with empty wagons near Garnedd Tunnel. The railway was closed completely just a few days later.** *B. B. Edmonds*

Below left: **During the war, and afterwards, Glan y Pwll loco shed was leased to a timber merchant. It was photographed in 1947.** *FR Archives*

Right: **While the line was closed Will and Bessie Jones extended their front garden to include the down track; March 1954.** *John B. Snell/Author's collection*

Cohen & Co, the company that had dismantled the WHR, the other, of £7,000, from an unidentified bidder. If this offer was accepted, he said, the company would be left with the premises and land to dispose of – he was not certain of the procedure.

There are no clues to the board's thinking in the minutes; the last board meeting recorded took place on 3 November 1949. In October 1950, W. C. Davies called the shareholders to a special meeting to be held on 9 November when a vote would be taken on the proposal to apply for an abandonment order from the Ministry of Transport, concluding his explanation of the railway's circumstances and the purpose of the meeting. 'The railway has served its day and generation, but modern transport facilities have effectively terminated its usefulness.'

The meeting approved the action, apparently not unanimously. The notice of meeting and the meeting were the last occasions the directors had any contact with the shareholders. Submitted under the terms of the Abandonment of Railways Act, 1850, the next day, the application was flawed, because the act's preamble is quite explicit that it applied to joint stock companies that had been authorised to make railways 'and it has been found that such railways ... cannot be made or carried on with advantage...' It did not apply to statutory companies or railways that had already been made.

On 4 December 1950, the ministry advised that the 1850 act, as amended by the Railway Companys Act, 1867, did not allow it to issue a warrant. The FR's 1869 act, like its repealed 1832 predecessor, made no provision for the railway's closure, leaving the board in a quandary.

While the board was embroiled in this legal quagmire there were others who thought the railway, or part of it, should be reopened. Some were in a better position than others. The first to enquire about acquiring control was, although Evans did not know it, a 16-year-old schoolboy, J. K. A. Firth, writing from Radley College, Oxfordshire, in October 1946. Someone who did have the resources to take on the FR was Captain J. E. P. Howey, proprietor of the 15in gauge Romney, Hythe & Dymchurch Railway, who visited in the same month.

This is not the place to discuss the various proposals for the railway with varying degrees of credibility put forward during the early post-war years; they have been published elsewhere. Whilst the Davieses thought they would get a good price for the scrap, they were not that encouraging of anyone talking about reopening or preservation.

The derelict railway became an attraction for enthusiasts, the idly curious and those who wanted to remove anything of value. Some sought permission to visit, others just turned up. In 1949 some boys were disturbed removing wagon plates at Portmadoc; a policeman tracked them down to a school camp

in Nant Gwynant where their headmaster explained that their interest had been aroused because one of the school's old boys 'had written an interesting book about the Festiniog Railway'.

Boston Lodge was the main attraction, though, with its engines adorned with copper and brass. Evans soon learned that keeping the works secure was a problem, but he had an ally in the resident of 4 Boston Lodge, Rev Timmy Phillips. He had been a Boston Lodge apprentice and took it upon himself to keep the site secure. Evans eventually refused visits, although the persistent circumvented his refusal by writing to the secretary.

The company heard from two sectors of the state later in 1951. In December the British Electricity Authority served notice that it intended to apply for powers to acquire compulsorily certain property needed for a hydro-electric power station it wished to build near Tanygrisiau. So far as the railway was concerned it would take all the land between the long tunnel and Blaenau Festiniog and the Dinas branch.

At the same time, the Ministry of Supply had taken an interest in the 14 miles or so of scrap rail owned by the company. On 1 January 1952 the Ministry of Transport wrote that it had been advised 'that the company is under no legal obligation to operate the railway and knows of no legal objection to the disposal of rolling stock and rails without having the statutory authority to abandon the railway'. When this view was passed to Davies he replied, on 14 January, that he had been advised that 'no one has authority to dispose of the permanent way and rolling stock by way of sale. The directors have no power, neither the receiver if one was appointed.' Had the assets been sold the board still would have been left with the problem of dealing with the liability of numerous dilapidated buildings and other structures.

Perhaps by this time, the Davieses had become more amenable to the idea that they could, or even should, pass control of the railway to someone who was willing to take it on. Earlier, in 1950, Leonard Heath Humphrys started a correspondence with C. E. Davies. It is unlikely that the latter knew that Humphrys was a 17-year-old schoolboy. Humphrys called a meeting of interested persons in Bristol and a committee was formed. By the end of the year the nascent Festiniog Railway Society was the only party interested in the FR. Humphrys was called up for military service in 1951 but his successor, Fred Gilbert, continued negotiations with Davies.

It was to take a while to find a solution but, on 22 June 1954, Cynon Evan Davies and Ninian Rhys Davies met as directors of the Festiniog Railway Company for the last time. Ernest John Routly was in attendance. He had with him a transfer in respect of £25,000 of the company's ordinary stock between the Aluminium Corporation and himself. The Davies

Above: **Part of the track leased to the quarries, seen on 18 May 1957. The GWR station is to the left of the FR.** *F. W. Shuttleworth/Author's collection*

Right: **After the lease of Duffws station was relinquished to the Newborough estate in 1931 a fence was erected to separate the railway from the Newborough property. The roof of the quarrymen's train shelter is visible behind a train hauled by an Oakeley Ruston & Hornsby loco in this March 1955 view.** *G. E. Baddeley/Author's collection*

brothers approved the transfer and sealed it. They then elected Routly, Alan Francis Pegler, Henry Trevor Selborne Bailey and Leslie John Walshaw Smith as directors before submitting their own resignations and that of Walter Cradoc Davies. After the minutes had been typed up they were initialled by the Davies brothers and subsequently signed by John Routly, as the chairman of the next meeting.

Routly was acting as trustee for Pegler, whose father had contributed £3,000 to enable the change of control to take place. Of this, £1,500 went to the National Provincial Bank in settlement of the overdraft and loan, with the remainder to the Davies brothers for their controlling shares. The Aluminium Corporation had donated its shares to the society.

Just what the Davies brothers were thinking is difficult to discern. It is quite likely that they had realised that the FR was, otherwise, going to be a liability to them. They had inherited their shareholding but had little to show for it apart from some

fees for their roles as secretary/assistant secretary, so, perhaps, they saw a chance to get some money in exchange for the effort they had put in. The starting position for their shares was £3,000, but they settled for half that. They might not have shown as much enthusiasm for the FR as their father had, but he had volunteered for it; they had had no choice. When the author met Ninian Davies *c*1987 he said that they thought that concentrating on one railway, the Snowdon Mountain Railway, which they also controlled, was better than dividing their effort between the two. It was C. E. Davies who had handled all the negotiations.

We should be grateful that they didn't receive an offer to sell the scrap in 1946 and go straight to Parliament with an abandonment bill. They could have had an act in the summer of 1947 and the scrap men could have cleared it by the end of the year, putting those who came to talk of preservation in an impossible position.

12

Locomotives and rolling stock

Being built as a gravity railway and with a gauge of a mere 2ft, the FR's translation to a public steam railway would never be easy. Whilst there had been advances in both the techniques used to build standard gauge steam locomotives and their operational reliability, the same could not be said, in the early 1860s, of the narrow gauge. The FR's loading gauge, which had been more than adequate for horse and gravity working, placed severe restrictions on the design of both locomotives and passenger rolling stock, and the continuous gradient, against the load for passenger trains, gave locomotive designers special challenges. That the FR managed to work all its traffic with two basic locomotive designs for more than 80 years is nothing short of remarkable.

The adoption of steam haulage is described in Chapter 2. Within four years of the first locomotives arriving in 1863 the railway had a fleet of six four-coupled tender engines, to the same fundamental design but with some significant differences. Charles Menzies Holland was acknowledged as their designer but George England played a noteworthy part in their design, in addition to being their maker. The first two locomotives were supplied without domes, at Holland's insistence, a feature that was soon rectified. The first four locos had side tanks and no cabs, and as tank engines they were unusual in also having tenders. Later, rounded weights were put on the tanks, bridging the boiler, to improve adhesion but with the effect of making the loco look as though it had a saddle tank. The 1867-built locomotives set the standard for the FR England locomotive, being slightly larger, with a saddle tank and a cab and, except for *Mountaineer*, the first ones were rebuilt to this design.

Nominally, there were six tenders for the six England locos and each was numbered, but in the period from 1875 to 1889, however, No 4 is not recorded as receiving attention. Then, when five tenders received attention in 1908, No 3 was the missing one. In 1877/9 the tenders of *The Prince*, *Welsh Pony* and *Little Giant* were referred to specifically, as was the 'shunting engine tender'. In 1880, Williams recorded 'No 2 a new tender for shunting engine made with brake fitted on'. Tender No 1 was also braked; possibly these braked tenders were used by the designated shunting locos. A 'new No 6 tender [was] made' in 1885, which was attached to *Palmerston* in 1890.

Little Wonder, the first of the Fairlie double locomotives, arrived in 1869, manufactured at George England's old factory by the Fairlie Engine & Steam Carriage Co. The Avonside company supplied *James Spooner* in 1872. Designed by George Percival Spooner, it established the parameters for the classic Festiniog Fairlie outline, apart from also being delivered without a cab. *Taliesin* was a single Fairlie, also designed by G. P. Spooner and effectively half of a *James Spooner*; built by Vulcan Foundry, it entered traffic on 18 September 1876.

Two locomotives were erected at Boston Lodge using components manufactured elsewhere, Charles Spooner having convinced the board that money could be saved. Also designed by G. P. Spooner, *Merddin Emrys* entered service on 21 July 1879. Construction of the last of the Victorian Fairlies, *Livingston Thompson*, was started in 1882; it was put into traffic on 29 June 1886.

The locos were named and numbered but, even in reports to the board and the loco repair records, were always referred to by their names. Nothing has come to light to reveal who chose the names. The numbers were painted on to the front edge of the Englands' running boards; cast number plates were affixed to some of the Fairlies.

The Princess **at Duffws in the 1860s, with original tender and a larger weatherboard.** *Palmerston* **is hiding behind the tender.**
Ian Allan Library

Table 11

Festiniog Railway locomotives

Name	Number	Built	Status	Remarks
The Prince, latterly *Prince*	1	1863	Extant, in traffic	Named after the Prince of Wales, Prince Albert Edward, King Edward VII from 1901.
The Princess, latterly *Princess*	2	1863	Extant, on display in Portmadoc station	Named after the Princess of Wales, Princess Alexandra, wife of Prince Albert Edward; they were married on 10 March 1863.
Mountaineer	3	1863	Withdrawn 1879, probably out of service for up to two years previously, it was last in works for a new lead plug and a new blower on 1 June 1877	The name of a coach that ran between Barmouth and Carnarvon via Tremadoc three days a week.
Palmerston	4	1864	Extant, in traffic	Politician with a major share in the Welsh Slate Company.
Welsh Pony	5	1867	Extant, undergoing cosmetic restoration	
Little Giant	6	1867	Withdrawn 1932	A class of two-masted schooner, built in Portmadoc for the slate trade.
Little Wonder	7	1869	Withdrawn 1882	
James Spooner	8	1872	Out of service c1930, withdrawn 1933	
Taliesin	9	1876	Withdrawn 1932; replica built 1995	A bardic chief, died AD570.
Merddin Emrys	10	1879	Extant, in traffic	A mythical bard or wizard, King Arthur's Merlin.
Livingston Thompson	11	1885	Extant, on display at the National Railway Museum, York	Later No 3.

The details given below are taken from William Williams's repair books and are intended to give an insight into the work carried out at Boston Lodge. It is not always possible to identify damage repairs as other work was usually carried out while the repair was made. The amount of collision damage requiring attention might be a reflection on the efficacy of the handbrakes. Of particular interest is the number and nature of the firebox repairs carried out to *Little Wonder* shortly before its withdrawal. A locomotive could be given a thorough overhaul in three months. The fitting of snow ploughs to several locomotives in December 1888 suggests that that winter was particularly severe.

Princess

● 20 December 1882 Firebox taken out to straighten plates, all new rivets in, 26 new iron roof stays 1in diameter and 88 new copper stays, patches of boiler plate in boiler shell, one new smokebox complete with new door handle. Tanks strengthened with angle-iron uprights and bolts, three cast-iron pieces on top of tank for adhesion, two new cast-iron sand boxes with brass knobs, lids and chains etc. Tried 20 January 1883.

Prince

● 5 October 1877 Damaged – trailing buffer repaired and refixed, footplate straightened, buffer plate of tender repaired, tender buffer repaired.

By the time this photograph was taken at Boston Lodge in 1887 *The Princess* had a braked tender, weights over the boiler and new sandpots. *R. H. Bleasdale/Author's collection*

Above: **The Prince** posed on the embankment in 1887. The locomotive has weights over the boiler, FR-style sandpots and a braked tender. *R. H. Bleasdale/ Author's collection*

Left: **Prince** at Portmadoc in the 1930s, with saddle tank, extra weights on the front running plate, and an enclosed cab. The cap to the sandpot is propped against the handrail. *Author's collection*

Below: **In July 1936 Palmerston** was photographed at Penrhyn station; it has a braked tender in this view. *H. B. Tours/FR Archives*

Right: **Palmerston** at the Portmadoc coaling stage in the 1930s.
Ian Allan Library

Below: **Robert Evans** looks on as the photograph is taken of *Palmerston* rigged up as a stationary boiler, 26 July 1951.
R. C. Riley/ Author's collection

Mountaineer

- 19 October 1876 Damaged and in for repairs; new buffer fitted on, drawbar repaired and brake rods adjusted.
- 17 March 1877 New handle fixed on smokebox door, blower cock ground, tank lid mended, brake blocks fitted on, patch put on front of cylinder, two buffers repaired, one mud hole tapped and new brass plug made.

Palmerston

- 8 May 1876 A new set of brasses, crankpin collar keys refitted, new brake blocks on, new lamp holder fixed on smokebox, two brass handles fitted on ditto, steam chest cover joint made, smokebox door catches repaired, to Llanwanda, 9 May.
- 9 July 1877 After Llanwnda – wheels turned, new driving crank pins, new brasses, crosshead pins turned, piston heads turned, six cast-iron rings fitted (in cylinders), two glands and two bushes made for piston stuffing box, two piston

head cotters made, slide bars closed, axleboxes refitted, eccentric straps let together, link motion overhauled, quadrant closed, reversing lever joint made, four mud holes retapped and four new plugs, new brake blocks, valves set, new gauge glass, tank and boiler washed out; out 30 July.
- 16 December 1879 Old steel tyres taken off and those of the *Mountaineer* put on and turned.
- 15 March 1881 Cylinder burst.

Welsh Pony

- 5 September 1881 Old tyres taken off centres, four new tyres bored to fit and placed hot, three studs in each tyre, wheels turned to gauge, a piece dovetailed in frames to repair crack.

Little Giant

- 10 July 1877 On Llan line 8 days; returned 19 July.
- 15 September 1879 Bottom part of boiler cut out, firebox

Top: **Welsh Pony** at Duffws c1876, with braked tender No 2 and original cabside plates. *John Thomas/FR Archives*

Above: A slightly later view of *Welsh Pony*; it has an unbraked tender, different cabside plates and an extra line of rivets on the lower right-hand side of the saddle tank. *FR Archives*

Left: *Welsh Pony* and personnel in Portmadoc, c1907; extra weights have been placed on the running plate and the saddle tank has been replaced. *FR Archives*

Below left: **Welsh Pony** in light blue livery at the GWR exchange platform in 1934. *R. W. Kidner/Author's collection*

Top: **Little Giant** at Duffws *c*1876; it has an unbraked tender with a patch on its side. All the plates are painted; the works plate reads 'G. England & Co London Engineers No 235 1867'. *John Thomas/ FR Archives*

Above: When photographed in 1887, **Little Giant** had cast plates and a different, or repaired, tender. *R. H. Bleasdale/ Author's collection*

Left: **Little Giant** at Portmadoc, *c*1910, by which time the saddle tank and smokebox had been replaced. *Author's collection*

taken out and new plate riveted on to complete as before. 154 ⅞in copper stays used, fire door refixed, frame fastened to boiler, ash pan repaired, 136 tubeplate holes bored and 136 new steel tubes and 136 cast-iron ferules put in (tubes bursting September 1882).

- 4-20 June 1884 Boiler patched with plate ⁷⁄₁₆in thick at front of firebox in two corners and screwed to fit mud plugs, one patch ¼in thick at the front of firebox shell between frames fastened with 12 ⅜in bolts, all leakages in boiler caulked, five new brass mud plugs, one new fusible plug.
- April 1888 All brasses closed. Spectacle eye repaired after accident at Boston Lodge powder line, fire bars cased, a set of new brake blocks, new pins in collars, one new brake nut.

Little Wonder

- 27 September 1875 Frames cracked and patch put on, whole frame examined, steam pipes examined.
- 4 June 1878 Tank off and patch of copper fixed on side of firebox, 14 ½in holes drilled and tapped, two days.
- 14 December 1878 Copper patch fixed on boiler, 14 ½in holes, ten copper stays fixed, bogies overhauled.

*Top: **Little Wonder** at Duffws, c1876. Charles Easton Spooner is standing on the footplate and George Percival Spooner is on the right-hand end of the locomotive. FR Archives*

*Above: The fireman's side of **James Spooner** at the first Portmadoc station on 29 August 1874, as built and with bells. The reason for the bells is not known; it has been suggested that the tramway nature of the railway over the embankment might be relevant, or the 1870 Tramway Act, but the latter is silent on the subject of bells or other modes of alarm. Frith/Author's collection*

- 28 March 1879 Two copper patches put on firebox.
- 24 November 1879 Four iron patches put on corner of firebox, bogie frames overhauled, eight springs repaired, link motion examined and tightened.
- 18 August 1880 Wheel tyres refastened and three holes drilled and three steel studs put in.
- 30 March 1881 One frame patched, 10 holes drilled and riveted, motion overhauled, two exhaust ball joints turned and two new glands made, four new stays to strengthen frame, crack in centre of bogie repaired; out 25 April 1881.

Left: The driver's side of *James Spooner* at Duffws, *c*1876, with the bells removed. Second-generation quarrymen's stock can be seen in the shelter behind. Lengths of rail like that on the left-hand slate wagon were used as sprags, to scotch the wagon wheels. *FR Archives*

Below left: *James Spooner* at Portmadoc, complete with cab, *c*1900.

Bottom left: *Taliesin* at Duffws, *c*1877. *John Thomas/FR Archive*

Above right: By 1887, when *Taliesin* was photographed at Boston Lodge, it had accrued FR-style sandpots, a toolbox on top of the water tank, and a new smokebox. *R. H. Bleasdale/ Author's collection*

Right: *Taliesin* re-entered service on 12 May 1900 following an overhaul that had started on 30 September 1898. It had an enclosed cab and new, larger, water tanks, a new boiler, a larger smokebox, and a new chimney; photographed *c*1901. *Author's collection*

- 9 January 1882 Motion and bogies overhauled, regulator and whistles repaired, tubes removed to examine boiler, patch on firebox with two ¾in bolts.
- 18 July 1882 Bogies taken out to fasten cylinders on frame, one new wrought-iron plate on the side of bogie.
- 30 August – 6 September 1882 Ash pan at top end taken down to caulk ring in bottom of firebox, new metal in two eccentric straps, and all the motion right side taken down to straighten suspension links and rods.
- 24 October 1882 Brasses in side rods closed, slide bars closed, all bolts tightened, new handle to injector tap.
- 6 December 1882 Condemned.

In the first part of the period covered by this list *Little Wonder* and *James Spooner* alternated in traffic.

James Spooner

- 8 June 1875 Repairs after being damaged at Tanygrisiau.
- 14 August 1875 Four copper patches fitted and bolted to firebox doors; out same day.
- 14 October 1876 Broken frame; out 21 April 1877 thoroughly repaired.

- 25 April 1878 Damaged by running into a sand wagon at Boston Lodge; repaired 16 July 1878, including four new coupling rods and four new connecting rods with new brasses and pins, two new whistles, eight new axleboxes, wheels turned, new crank pins etc.

Taliesin

- 4 November 1876 Six new cast-iron piston rings put in and new steam gauge fixed on.
- 24 November 1876 Hind bogie put right, cab altered after damage at tunnel, new injector spindle and bracket, four brake blocks attended to, catch for holding fire tools, two hooks put on weather board, oil holes drilled in brasses of trailing bogie, new staff holder put on, thumb screw on coal door, new brake blocks put on, two new lamp brackets, new front buffer plate, new front spring box and buffer head, new hind buffer head with springs attached to keep it in centre; out 26 November.
- 1 November 1887 Patch put on firebox shell, five ⅝in studs put in same. Old gauge (*Little Giant's*) taps cleaned and repaired and fixed in *Taliesin*. Finished 16 December.

Merddin Emrys

- 20 October 1879 Connecting rod brasses all closed, eight ⅝in studs fixed into steam pipe ball joint, steam pipes and pistons examined, nine steam joints made, cab apparatus altered, new brake blocks fixed on, connection pipes put on, blow off cock.
- 15 January 1882 Old wheels turned down to fit tyres, steel tyres bored on and fixed and pinned, injectors taken off and overhauled; out 24 February 1882.
- 7 March 1882 In on account of hot axlebox, both bogies taken from under, grooves made in two boxes and filled with Babbit metal [anti-friction metal, 89.28% tin, 8.93% antimony and 1.79% copper, invented by Isaac Babbit in 1839].

Livingston Thompson

- 1-14 December 1886 Brasses in side rods closed, pistons examined, three new rings put in, three pins driven in each piston to prevent rings from turning, valves planed and valve face refaced, two brass markers on telescope joint of steam pipes, new brake blocks, steam gauge pipe altered, clasp ball seats made true and one new ball put in, regulator glands cleaned and packed, piston rods and valve spindles packed, new hinges on ash pan doors, bottom of fireboxes caulked, two sets of fire doors, valves examined.

Top: **Merddin Emrys** in later years, with the harbour as a backdrop. *Author's collection*

Above: **Livingston Thompson** posed at Duffws shortly after it entered service in 1886. The van, No 2, is attached to a train of third-generation quarrymen's carriages. *J. Valentine/ Author's collection*

With the advent of the WHR, Boston Lodge took on the responsibility for the single Fairlie, 0-6-4T *Moel Tryfan*, and the Hunslet 2-6-2T *Russell*. The former had been built by Vulcan Foundry for the North Wales Narrow Gauge Railways in 1875 and incorporated many components from the similar *Snowdon Ranger* since it was rebuilt in 1917. *Russell* was supplied to the NWNGR by the Portmadoc, Beddgelert & South Snowdon Railway in 1906. Both were altered to fit the FR loading gauge, not very sympathetically or successfully in the case of *Russell*. *Moel Tryfan*, however, did work through to Blaenau Festiniog, although, as yet, no photographs record it. C. E. Davies's attempt to acquire *Moel Tryfan* for the FR in 1941 is mentioned in Chapter 11; approval was given for it to be transferred to the FR provided certain payments (arrears of rent) were made – the payments never were made but the FR became the *de facto* owner.

The 1917-built ex-War Department Baldwin 4-6-0T No 590 was bought by the WHR in 1923. No attempt was made to make it fit the FR's loading gauge but it was stabled at Boston Lodge when necessary.

FR running numbers were painted on the buffer beams of *Moel Tryfan*, No 11, and *Russell*, No 12. Superstition might have inhibited the application of the Baldwin's No 13.

The Baldwin was cut up in 1941, *Moel Tryfan* in 1955; *Russell* is extant and belongs to Welsh Highland Railway Ltd.

Two four-wheeled internal combustion locomotives were acquired in the 1920s. A First World War petrol-engined Motor Rail 'Simplex' used as a shunter around Portmadoc was obtained in 1923; it had a 40hp engine and weighed 6 tons. Its return trip over the WHR in 1923 is mentioned in Chapter 10 – the report in *Railway Gazette* makes no comment on the prodigious amount of petrol that must have been consumed. It was never allocated an FR running number. In 1925 the FR purchased a 45hp Baldwin petrol tractor, also with military

Top: **The WHR's Baldwin 4-6-0T No 590 reached Boston Lodge for servicing and maintenance, but its size precluded it from going any further and it is seen there on 9 August 1935.** *H. F. Wheeler/ FR Archives*

Above left: **The Motor Rail 'Simplex' tractor shunting at Portmadoc harbour in 1933.** *H.M. Comber/FR Archives*

Above: **The Baldwin petrol locomotive in the Boston Lodge erecting shop in 1934.** *FR Archives*

Left: **Presumably this is one of the six inspection trolleys bought in 1925/6. It was photographed at Boston Lodge in October 1948.** *J. I. C. Boyd/Author's collection*

origins, that weighed 7½ tons. Numbered 11 in the FR roster, it was apparently equipped with vacuum brake equipment in 1928 to enable it to haul passenger trains; beyond a photograph of it taken at the Portmadoc flour mill, details of its activities have not survived. Both of these locomotives have survived, however: the former named *Mary Ann* and restored to its military condition, complete with petrol engine, and the latter named *Moelwyn* and equipped with a diesel engine and a leading truck. Both are in the FR's heritage collection.

According to the company's annual reports (Appendix 6)

three inspection trolleys were bought in 1925, cost £14, and a further three in 1926, cost £23. No details are known of these but they probably had military origins and may have been used by permanent way gangs on both the FR and WHR.

It is to be regretted that those records concerning the FR's hauled stock are nowhere near as extensive as those relating to its locomotives. Apart from references extracted from the board minutes already mentioned in the main text it has not been possible to add to previously published accounts.

The railway's first passenger carriages were supplied by

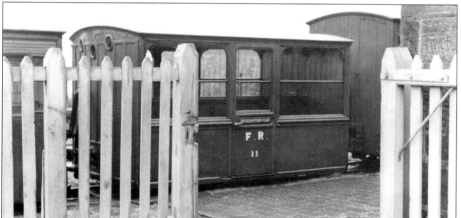

Above: **Three Brown, Marshalls four-wheeled carriages, two of them observation cars, bring up the rear of a train approaching Glan y Pwll in 1934.** *R. W. Kidner/Author's collection*

Left: **The observation cars were turned out in all weathers, even when there were no passengers for them, as illustrated by this photograph of No 11 taken on a wet day in August 1939.** *Evelyn Mary Cain/Author's collection*

Below left: **No 6 had been rebuilt with matchboard sides when photographed on 31 July 1932.** *W. H. Whitworth/ Author's collection*

Brown, Marshalls & Co in 1863/4. The ironwork, wheelsets and buffers, was made at Boston Lodge. There were eight of them. As delivered, there were two 1st class and six 3rd class including two opens, one of each class. Due to concerns about stability these four-wheeled vehicles were made to ride as low as possible, with the wheels tucked away under a knifeboard seat positioned lengthways. The 1st class carriages were later converted into semi-open observation cars. The 1st class open was distinguished from its 3rd class counterpart by the provision of cushions. It also had a primitive roof that might have been a later

addition; leather aprons provided passengers with an element of protection. Both roof and apron would provide shelter from the weather and locomotive emissions. If it were possible, the 3rd class version was even more primitive, with no roof or cushions. Accommodation was for 12 in the 1st class and 14 in the 3rd class. Five of these carriages survived until 1939.

Ashbury supplied six bodies, one 1st class, five 3rd class, to the railway in 1867; once again, Boston Lodge supplied the ironwork. The layout was more traditional, with two compartments in each. They accommodated 12 passengers, regardless

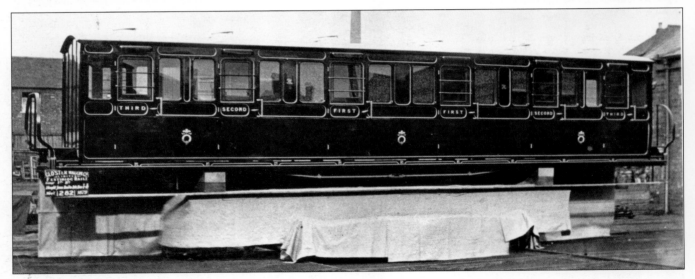

of class. They did not last as well as the Brown, Marshalls stock; none remained in service by 1939. Two bodies were used to make a goods shed at Nantmor on the WHR.

The three four-wheeled vans that operated with these carriages were referred to in Chapter 2.

As noted in Chapter 2, the quarrymen's train service started in 1867 with at least 32 primitive open carriages built for the purpose; they had no suspension and could probably accommodate eight. They were partially enclosed during the 1870s. A semi-enclosed version was put into service in 1875; 14 were built with roofs and only a doorway opening on each side; they had no windows and it was this type that Major Marindin complained

about in 1881. Some of them received glazed doors before they were withdrawn. The bodies of one of them found another use as a waiting shelter and another body was converted to become a hearse van. The latter's existence was not widely known until it turned up in Boston Lodge yard during the closure; it was mainly used at the inland end of the line and was either kept in the quarrymen's train shelter at Duffws or in Dinas or Glan y Pwll loco sheds. The remnants of a vehicle used as a waiting shelter at Llechwedd Coed survive, as does the hearse van.

An 'improved' type of quarrymen's carriage was introduced from 1885; 18 had been built by 1887. They were complete with doors and windows, with seating placed around the periphery.

Above left: **One of the first bogie carriages, No 15 or 16, at the first Portmadoc station in 1874.** *Frith/Author's collection*

Left: **No 18, fresh out of the paint shop when photographed in the 1930s.** *Author's collection*

Below left: **The Gloster Wagon Co photographed No 19 before dispatching it to Wales in 1879. Bogies were provided by Boston Lodge.** *FR Archives*

Above: **No 19's 2nd class compartments had been downgraded to 3rd class for many years when it was photographed at Portmadoc looking very weary. Unusually, No 18 is alongside.** *J. P. Richards/ FR Archives*

Above right: **Built by Ashbury in 1896, No 22 stabled at Duffws for quarrymen's train duty.** *Norman Kerr/Author's collection*

Right: **Ashbury No 22 waits in vain for passengers in August 1939.** *Evelyn Mary Cain/Author's collection*

Below right: **A 'curly roof' van and Ashbury No 22 at Duffws, probably both allocated to the quarrymen's train.** *Norman Kerr/Author's collection*

Over the years five were adapted for other purposes, four as brake vans and one as a goods vehicle for the WHR. Only three survive, two of them as brake van conversions and one as a carriage, No 8.

In the 19th century, the FR bought its bogie carriages in pairs and it usually ran them in matching pairs, too! Brown, Marshalls & Co supplied the first two, Nos 15 and 16, in 1872. Not only did they have a steel underframe but they also had an integral wrought-iron body frame which gave them great strength. By the time the second pair, Nos 17 and 18, were made, also by Brown, Marshalls, in 1876, the integral body frame was deemed unnecessary. In 1879, two more bogie carriages, Nos 19 and 20, were obtained, this time from the Gloster Wagon Company. These last four had their sides shaped inwards to the bottom and have become known as 'bowsiders'. They were also slightly shorter than Nos 15 and 16, having only six compartments instead of seven. All of them had end balconies, the purpose of which has been the cause of much speculation. They have all survived, although No 19 stood outside during the closure period and its body deteriorated as a result. Perhaps significantly, No 19 was the last of the six to undergo a high-quality overhaul/restoration to 19th century condition, completed in late 2006.

Ashbury Carriage & Wagon Co supplied the FR's last 19th century bogie carriages, in 1896. Numbered 21 and 22, they were two 56-seat 3rd class vehicles with matchboard sides, intended for the quarrymen and tourists. Because they were delivered with wagon-grade wheels they did not ride well and were not liked. Both survived until 1939. No 21, in very poor condition after the reopening, was dismantled in the 1960s.

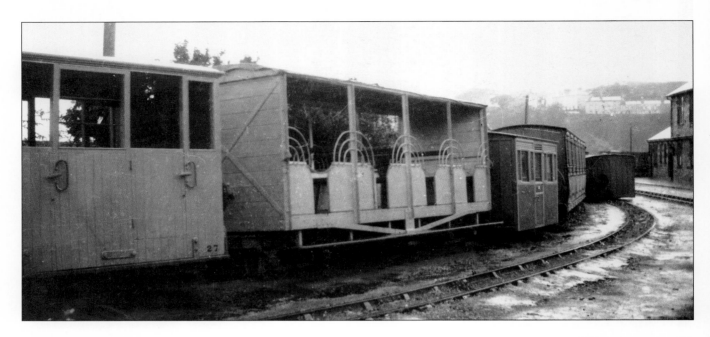

Top left: **The addition of 'decorative features' to the Hudsons, as seen in this 1934 photograph, did little for their appearance and nothing for their comfort. No 27 was an Ashbury tourist car built for the North Wales Narrow Gauge Railways in 1894.** *R. W. Kidner/FR Archives*

Above left: A heavily retouched photograph of 'curly roof' van No 1 when new. The use of a chopper coupling at one end and the wagon coupling at the other can be seen clearly. *FR Archives*

Left: **Brake/3rd No 2, now No 10, was a conversion from 'curly roof' van No 2. The wire hanging from its roof indicates that experiments with some form of electric lighting were in progress; photographed in the 1920s.** *G. F. Parker/Author's collection*

Top: **A 1934 view of No 2 shows that a different paint scheme has been applied.** *R. W. Kidner/Author's collection*

Above: **One of the 1880 vans at the end of a train at Duffws. The milk churns (right) were from Creuau farms at Tan-y-bwlch.** *Norman Kerr/Author's collection*

No 22 was rebuilt with a steel underframe in 1967 and received a new, non-prototypical body in 1991. No 23 was a similar vehicle supplied to the North Wales Narrow Gauge Railways in 1894. It became FR property in 1936 in exchange for three bogie wagons that passed to the WHR. It received a steel underframe in 1962 and was restored to WHR appearance in 1992.

The last new stock bought by the FR before the closure was six bogie observation cars supplied by Robert Hudson Ltd of Leeds in 1923 numbered 37-42. Although they were used on both railways, the suggestion that it was intended to share the purchase with the WHR appears to be unfounded. Despite their newness, only two of them were complete in 1939 and they had spent several years out of service; the others had been converted to flat wagons by 1929. The two that survived the closure were converted to flat wagons after the railway reopened. One of the underframes was used in the construction of semi-open tourist car No 38 in 1971 and another was donated to Welsh Highland Railway Ltd, which organisation has built a replica Hudson 'toastrack' superstructure on it.

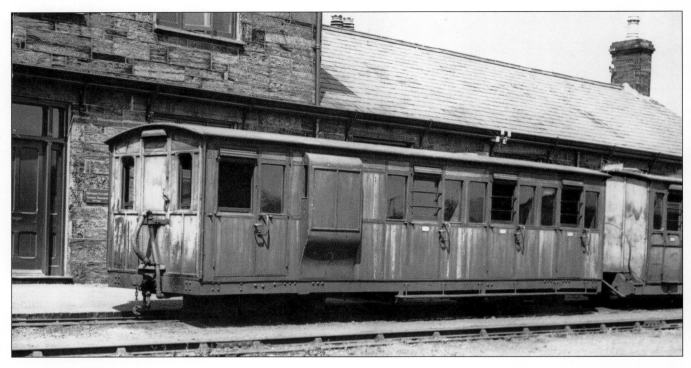

Above left: **Built in 1880, van No 4 was rebuilt with three passenger compartments, two 3rd class and a 1st class, in 1928/9 and is seen in that condition on 3 June 1932.** *H. C. Casserley/Author's collection*

Left: **An unusual formation in the GW platform siding on 7 August 1932.** *FR Archives*

Below left: **The remnants of a second-generation quarrymen's carriage at Llechwedd Coed in March 1954.** *J.B. Snell/Author's collection*

Above: **Quarrymen's carriage No 7. There are detail differences when compared with No 3.** *G. F. Parker/ Author's collection*

Right: **A goods train brake van seen at the back of a train in 1934.** *R. W. Kidner/Author's collection*

The FR had five passenger luggage bogie brake vans of two designs, all built by Brown, Marshalls & Co and numbered in their own series. The first three are now known as the 'curly roof' vans due to the unusual shape of their roofs. Two of them, Nos 1 and 2, entered service in 1873, the third, No 3, in 1876. The earlier four-wheeled vans were withdrawn as the new ones entered service.

Two larger vans, Nos 4 and 5, with ordinary roofs, were ordered in 1879 and delivered in 1880, when the 'curly roof' vans were relegated to secondary services, primarily the quarrymen's train. The adoption of a radical change of design in such a short period might suggest that problems arose in the use of the first three but it was 1921 before any of them were taken out of service or adapted for other purposes.

Van No 1 was out of use by at least 1920 and dismantled in 1921, when its timber frame was found to be rotten. No 2 was rebuilt at Boston Lodge in 1921 and emerged with a brake and two small 3rd class passenger compartments; it was used on track clearance trains in the 1950s and returned to passenger service in 1991. No 3 stood outside at Portmadoc from 1939 and was too badly damaged to repair when the railway reopened. No 4 was rebuilt with a smaller brake compartment, two 3rd class compart-

ments and a 1st class compartment in 1928/9; it was rebuilt as an observation saloon in 1957/8 and its body was mounted on a steel underframe in 1962. No 5 was rebuilt in 1929/30, when it received an observation section and two 3rd class compartments in addition to a smaller brake compartment. Its body was lengthened when it was mounted on a steel underframe in 1962 and it ran as a buffet car from 1957 until 1982.

The bogie stock had Norwegian chopper couplers but because the locomotives had only wagon couplings, a four-wheeled carriage was placed after the loco on up trains. The downhill end of the bogie brake vans also had a wagon coupler for coupling to empty slate or goods wagons.

According to the Board of Trade returns, the FR's 'merchandise and mineral vehicles' fleet increased from 977 vehicles in 1872 to 1,254 in 1897. Over 1,000 of the latter number were slate wagons, one-fifth of them with brakes. The oldest ones had timber frames. After the slate stock the largest wagon group was a fleet of nearly 60 timber opens of 2, 3 and 4 ton capacity used for a variety of goods and coal. There were several bolsters for carrying large timber and a number of one-offs for specialist purposes, a carriage truck, a water wagon, a breakdown van and a rail-bending trolley amongst them.

Above: **The origins of this vehicle are obscure; the Oakeley family's private gravity car, it was probably built at Boston Lodge and was photographed there in 1923.** *FR Archives*

Right: **The FR had many hundreds of wagons of many different types and varieties. A few photographs must serve to represent them. This 2-ton braked slate wagon has disc wheels.** *R. H. Bleasdale/Author's collection*

Below: **A 3-ton braked slate wagon with spoked wheels; neither treads nor flanges appear to have much body in them.** *R. H. Bleasdale/Author's collection*

Above: **A gravity slate train at Minffordd; seven wooden-bodied wagons are visible.** *Author's collection*

Left: **Only one iron horse dandy wagon survives.** *Author's collection*

Below: **Seen in the GWR yard at Blaenau Festiniog in August 1945 is a pair of bolster wagons, a four-wheeled goods van and the six-wheeled Cleminson patent wagon. The last appears to have been an experimental vehicle, the only one of its type the FR had.** *FR Archives*

Top: **The Cleminson appears in this Boston Lodge view with a four-wheel flat and a wooden-bodied slate wagon and 2-ton and 1-ton capacity goods wagons. Both of the 2-ton wagons visible have cast-iron number plates. Notice that the coal, behind the slate wagon, has been very carefully stacked.** *FR Archives*

Above: **An assortment of junk at the back of the Boston Lodge loco shed on 9 August 1935. The much-maligned crane is stabled in front of a WHR (ex-NWNGR) carriage. In front of them are a goods van, a tank wagon, lettered 'FR', and** *Welsh Pony's* **collision-damaged tender. The stone building visible was the Boston Lodge weigh house, the railway then being routed to its right.** *H. F. Wheeler/FR Archives*

Right: **An iron-bodied gunpowder van seen at Duffws on 1 November 1947. The only private-owner wagons used on the FR, they had a timber lining in the cause of spark prevention.** *FR Archives*

Appendix 1
Expenditure from revenue 1836-1869

Amount paid towards construction of Messrs Holland's incline £642 1s 3d
Amount paid towards Rhiwbryfdir Company's incline and sidings £151 4s 1d

	£ s d
	£793 5 6
Cost of main tunnel and approaches exclusive of permanent way	£7,600 0 0
Rock cuttings (widening line)	£256 19 4
New road at Boston Lodge for Penrhyn Isa farm	£200 0 0
Garnedd Tunnel and short deviation	£221 18 9
Deviation of line at Tanygrisiau	£731 14 8
Re-laying new permanent way for entire length of line and sidings, railway bars of 30,361lb [sic] to the yard, timber sleepers substituted for stone blocks, chairs, pins, wedges, turnout points and crossings. Cost of removal of old permanent way and platelayers' wages for renewing not included	£9,377 0 0
Extension of branch line at Duffws	£807 6 5
New works on line for conversion of same into a locomotive railway (including cost of rolling stock for passenger and goods traffic)	£12,844 8 5
The company's workshop, Boston Lodge, buildings and stock 30 June 1868	
Foundry and stock valued at £1,479 7 4	
Engine house and stock valued at £3,355 10 10	
Carpenters' shop and stock valued at £920 7 6	
Smithy and stock valued at £1,038 19 7	
Saw mill and stock valued at £1,088 9 10	
Yard and stock valued at £49 7 6	£7,932 2 7
Wagon stock valued at	£15,421 7 6
Road account £2,941 12 2 less £1,769 14 10	£1,171 19 4
Weighing machine house and new offices	£512 14 9
New permanent way now being laid will cost, less value of old materials £9,774 17 2.	£3,126 0 4
Materials for five miles are being laid at a cost of £5,715 7 0 which is less value of old materials £2,589 6 8	
Fully £10,000 must have been expended in various ways on contingent works – improving the line in many parts the cost of which has been passed through the pays in wages and bills but such expenses have not been separately kept in accounts of the general cost sheets. The greater part of the line had to be fenced in masonry subsequent to opening of the railway for traffic in 1836 with the exception of the walls built for the Bishop of Clogher through his property. A deviation of the line was made at Rhiwgoch at a cost of £570. In 1851 an expensive diversion of the Tan-y-bwlch and Beddgelert TP road was made together with an iron bridge over the same under the Festiniog Railway. Also parliamentary expenses on two occasions subsequent to obtaining the two bills before referred to.	£10,000 0 0
	£78,077 2 10

Submitted to the House of Commons select committee on private bills, 6 July 1869

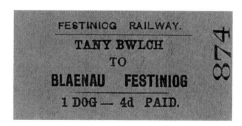

Appendix 2
Estimate for 1869 act

Estimate of the works proposed to be authorised by the Festiniog Railway Company's bill

Widening, enlarging, deviating and altering the existing railway of the Festiniog Railway Company
Length of widening &c 13 miles 7 furlongs 9.70 chains
The railway is at present a single line and it is proposed to make it a double line

	Cubic yards	price per yard	£ s d	£ s d
Earthworks				
Cuttings –				
Rock	97,000	2s 6d	12,125 0 0	
Soft soil	32,000	1s	1,600 0 0	
Roads	2,160	2s 6d	270 0 0	
	131,160		13,995 0 0	13,995 0 0
Tunnels				11,466 0 0
Embankments, including roads, 88,000 cu yd				3,300 0 0
Bridges, public roads, number 3				505 0 0
Accommodation bridges and works				1,455 0 0
Viaducts				450 0 0
Culverts and drains				1,780 0 0
Metallings of roads and level crossings				360 0 0
Gatekeepers' houses at level crossings				350 0 0
Permanent way, including fencing				
13 miles 7 furlongs 9 chains 70 links Cost per mile £1,332 0 0				18,643 0 0
Permanent way for sidings and cost of junctions				3,515 0 0
Stations				2,800 0 0
				58,619 0 0
Contingencies 5%				2,930 0 0
				61,549 0 0
Land and buildings 47a 0r 0p				3,500 0 0
		Total		65,049 0 0

Branch railway in parish of Llanfihangel y Traethau
Length of line 0 miles 2 furlongs 0 chains 75 links
Double line

	Cubic yards	price per yard	£ s d	£ s d
Earthworks				
Cuttings –				
Rock	2,800	2s	280 0 0	
Soft soil	620	1s	31 0 0	
Roads	2,160	2s 6d	270 0 0	
Embankments, including roads, 88,000 cu yd		3,580 cu yd	89 0 0	
Bridges, public roads, number				
Accommodation bridges and works				25 0 0
Viaducts				
Culverts and drains				40 0 0
Metallings of roads and level crossings				
Gatekeepers' houses at level crossings				
Permanent way, including fencing				
0 miles 2 furlongs 0 chains 75 links Cost per mile £2,644 0 0				691 0 0
Permanent way for sidings and cost of junctions				120 0 0
Stations				1,276 0 0
Contingencies 5%				64 0 0
				1,340 0 0
Land and buildings 1a 0r 0p				100 0 0
		Total		1,440 0 0

Branch railway in parish of Festiniog
Length of line 0 miles 0 furlongs 7 chains 70 links
Double line

	Cubic yards	price per yard	£ s d	£ s d
Earthworks				
Cuttings –				
Rock				
Soft soil				
Roads				
Embankments, including roads, 1,250 cu yd 1				87 0 0
Bridges, public roads, number				
Accommodation bridges and works				40 0 0
Viaducts				
Culverts and drains				80 0 0

Metallings of roads and level crossings			
Gatekeepers' houses at level crossings			
Permanent way, including fencing			
0 miles 0 furlongs 7 chains 70 links	Cost per mile £1,960 0 0	189 0 0	
Permanent way for sidings and cost of junctions		36 0 0	
Stations		532 0 0	
Contingencies 5%		27 0 0	
		559 0 0	
Land and buildings 0a 1r 0p		40 0 0	
	Total	599 0 0	
Aqueducts, conduits or lines of pipes		334 0 0	
(including lands, houses and contingencies)			

General summary of total cost		
Total cost of widening etc	65,049 0 0	
Total cost of branch railway	1,440 0 0	
Total cost of short junction railway	599 0 0	
Total cost of aqueducts, conduits or lines of pipes	334 0 0	
	Grand total	67,422 0 0

In accordance with the foregoing details, I estimate the whole expense of the undertaking under the Festiniog Railway Company's bill (so far as it is a bill of the second class specified in the standing orders) at sixty-seven thousand, four hundred and twenty-two pounds.

26 December 1868
C. E. Spooner
Engineer

Appendix 4

Selected transactions between the Festiniog Railway Company and the Festiniog & Blaenau Railway Company 1877-1883

Appendix 3

Employees in 1874 and 1884

	1874	1884
General manager	1	1
Assistant manager	1	1
Traffic Department		
Stationmasters	7	7
Clerks	5	8
Inspectors	1	
Guards	6	2
Signalmen	5	12
Shunters	1	
Porters and messengers	17	9
Goods Manager's Department		
Inspectors		3
Guards and brakesmen		6
Others		5
Locomotive Department		
Locomotive engineers		1
Locomotive foremen	1	1
Mechanics	33	6
Artisans		37
Drivers	4	4
Firemen	4	4
Labourers	16	

	1874	1884
Engineer's Department		
Draughtsmen		2
Foremen	1	
Gangers	2	2
Artisans		2
Mechanics		6
Platelayers	6	
Labourers	7	8
Gatekeepers	4	
Storekeeper's Department		
Storekeeper	1	1
Assistant storekeeper	1	
Clerks		2
Workmen		1
Police		
Police	1	1
Accountant's Department		
Accountant	2	1
Assistant accountant	1	1
Clerks	1	
	129	**134**

Date		Amount
25 July 1877	To locomotive hire including driver's wages from 10th July to 18th July inclusive, being 8 days	£9 12s 0d
11 August 1877	To cost of damage done to our iron slate wagon No 635	£1 4s 0d
9 July 1878	To cost of damage done to our locomotive engine *Little Wonder* by a collision at the Festiniog & Blaenau Railway Junction	£4 13s 9d
11 November 1878	To cost of damage done to points leading from our siding to your main line at Duffws	5s 6d
12 December 1878	To cost of damage done to our coal wagons Nos 98 and 113	£3 5s 0d
24 April 1879	To cost of damage done to brake of our large iron wagon No 967 at Tyddyngwyn station	12s 2d
19 February 1880	To cost of damage done to our iron slate wagons Nos 542 and 581 and to a pair of timber trucks	£2 2s 6d
20 September 1881	20th December 1880 To cost of damage done to brake of our coal wagon No 123	5s 6d
26 January 1881	To cost of damage done to our timber truck No 65: one axle, one bush and two cross-tieing blocks broken, floor damaged &c	£1 15s 4d
24 November 1881	For use of engine to take the 5pm quarrymen train Dyphwys to Festiniog 24 November 1881	10s
31 December 1881	To cost of damage done to our wooden slate wagon No 312 at Tanymanod station	7s 6d
6 June 1882	To cost of damage done to our coal wagon No 28, stone trucks No 60 and 32 and iron slab truck No 21	10s 6d
25 August 1882	Cost of damage done to gate close to our signal cabin at F&B Railway junction	13s 6d
6 June 1883	To cost of damage to brake of our coal wagon No 126	3s 6d
6 June 1883	To cost of damage done to our coal truck No 31 – two bushes broken and two axles bent, including removing and refixing	£1 3s 6d

Appendix 5

Employees in 1911 and 1912

	1911	1912
Way and works	12	10
Locomotive maintenance	7	7
Carriage & wagon	20	19
Locomotive superintendent	1	1

	1911	1912
Traffic		
Superintendence	1	1
Stationmasters and clerks	14	14
Locomotive	7	11
Signalmen and gatemen	8	7
Ticket collectors, porters	14	16
Guards	4	3
Collection and delivery	1	1
Secretary	1	1
	90	**91**

Extracted from Board of Trade returns; these are not absolute figures

Appendix 6

Capital expenditure 1923-1939

	1923	1925	1926	1927	1928	1929	1932	1933	1934	1935	1939
Land, building and compensation	537									144	40
Construction of way and stations, engineering etc	3,120	227	90	9	59	229	-1,404		175		100
Law charges and Parliamentary expenses	400										
Rolling stock											
Locomotives				166		12		-2,500	1,800		
Petrol tractor for shunting	377										
Baldwin petrol locomotive (spares in 1926)		249	3								
Carriages				24	3	150		-910			
Six coaching vehicles	1,016										
Electric lighting			38								
Wagons						74		-2,190	70		
Four 5 ton double-bogie goods wagons		140									
Three inspection trolleys (each year)		14	23								
Two wagon bodies		35									
Repairing works and plant		330		125	25						
Special item transferred								910			
Total £	5,450	995	154	324	87	465	-1,404	-4,690	2,045	144	140

Extracted from annual reports, years omitted had no capital expenditure recorded

Bibliography

Anon; Illustrated Interviews No 34 Mr John Sylvester Hughes; *The Railway Magazine*, August 1900

Beazley, Elisabeth; *Madocks and the Wonder of Wales*; Faber & Faber, 1967

Bigg's General Railway Acts, Public Acts for the Regulation of Railways 1830-1898; Waterlow & Sons, 1898

Bishop, William H.; 'Over the Narrowest Narrow Gauge'; *Scribners'*, Vol XVIII, 1879

Boyd, J. I. C.; *The Festiniog Railway*; Oakwood Press, 1975 (two vols)

Boyd, J. I. C.; *Narrow Gauge Railways in South Caernarvonshire*; Oakwood Press, 1988/9 (two vols)

Bradley, V. J.; *Industrial Locomotives of North Wales*; Industrial Railway Society, 1992

Christiansen, R. & Miller, R. W.; *The Cambrian Railways*; David & Charles, Vol 1 1971; Vol 2 1968

Davies, Edward; *Hanes Porthmadog ei chrefydd a'i henwogion*; Cwmni y Cyhoeddwyr Cymreig, 1913

Ellis, C. Hamilton & Lee, Charles E.; 'The Festiniog Railway'; *The Railway Magazine*, April 1936, July 1936, October 1936

Fairlie, R. F.; *Second Series of Experiments with the Fairlie Engines on the Festiniog, Brecon & Merthyr and Burry Port & Gwendreath Valley Railways*; F. C. Mathieson, 1870

Fairlie, R. F.; *Railways or No Railways – the battle of the gauges renewed*; Effingham Wilson, 1871

Foster, C. Le Neve; *Report of the departmental committee upon Merionethshire Slate Mines*; HMSO, 1895

Gairns, J. F.; 'The Festiniog Railway of Today'; *The Railway Magazine*, August 1924

Gray, Adrian (Ed); *The Spooner Album*; Festiniog Railway Heritage Group/RCL Publications, 2003

Holland, Samuel; *The memoirs of Samuel Holland, one of the pioneers of the North Wales Slate Industry*; Merioneth Historical & Record Society, 1952

Hughes, Henry; *Immortal Sails*; T. Stephenson & Sons, 2nd edition 1969

Isherwood, J. G.; *Slate – from Blaenau Ffestiniog*; AB Publishing, 1988

Janes, Brian; 'The Grouping and the Festiniog'; *Festiniog Railway Heritage Group Journal*, No 83 Autumn 2005

Johnson, Peter; 'Ffestiniog Steam 125'; *Railway World*, April 1988

Johnson, Peter; *An Illustrated History of the Welsh Highland Railway*; Ian Allan, 2002; revised 2004

Johnson, Peter; *Festiniog 150 The History of the Ffestiniog Railway*; Ian Allan, 1986

Johnson, Peter (Ed); *Festiniog Railway Gravity Trains*; Festiniog Railway Heritage Group, 1986

Johnson, Peter; *Festiniog Railway – a view from the past*; Ian Allan, 1997

Johnson, Peter; *Immortal Rails – The story of the closure and revival of the Ffestiniog Railway 1939-1983* (two vols); Rail Romances, Vol 1 2004; Vol 2 2005

Johnson, Peter; *Portrait of the Festiniog*; Ian Allan, 1992

Jones, Griff R.; *Rhiw Bach Slate Quarry – its history and development*; author, 2005

Jones, Ivor Wynne; *The Eagles of Llechwedd*; J. W. Greaves & Sons Ltd, 2004

Lewis, M. J. T.; 'Archery & Spoonerisms: the creators of the Festiniog Railway'; *[Festiniog Railway] Heritage Group Journal*, Nos 50-52, 1997/8

Lewis, M. J. T.; *How Festiniog Got Its Railway*; Railway & Canal Historical Society, 2nd edition 1968

Lewis, M. J. T.; *Sails on the Dwyryd*; Snowdonia National Park Study Centre, 1989

Lewis, M. J. T. & Williams, M. C.; *Pioneers of Ffestiniog Slate*; Snowdonia National Park Study Centre, 1987

Mitchell, Vic & Smith, Keith; *Branch lines around Portmadoc – the Welsh Highland and Festiniog Railways 1923-46*; Middleton Press, 1993

Neale, Andrew; 'The Festiniog Mineral Extension'; *[Festiniog Railway] Heritage Group Journal*, No 50, 1997

Pole, Felix J. C.; 'The administrative reorganisation of the railways following the war'; *Modern Railway Administration*; Gresham Publishing Co, 1927

Ramsey, D. A.; *Groby and its Railways*; TEE publishing, 1982

Rhydderch, Ann; *Blaenau Ffestiniog*; Gwynedd Archives, 1979

Richards, Alun John; *A Gazetteer of the Welsh Slate Industry*; Gwasg Carreg Gwalch, 1991

Spooner, C. E.; *Narrow Gauge Railways*; Spon, 1871

Vignes, Edouard (English translation by D. A. Boreham); *A Technical Study of the Festiniog & Other Narrow-Gauge Railways 1878*; P. E. Waters & Associates, 1986

Williams, G. J.; *Hanes Plwyf Ffestiniog o'r Cyfnod Boreuaf*; Hughes & Son, 1882

Winton, John; *The Little Wonder – The Story of the Festiniog Railway*; Michael Joseph, revised edition, 1986

Index

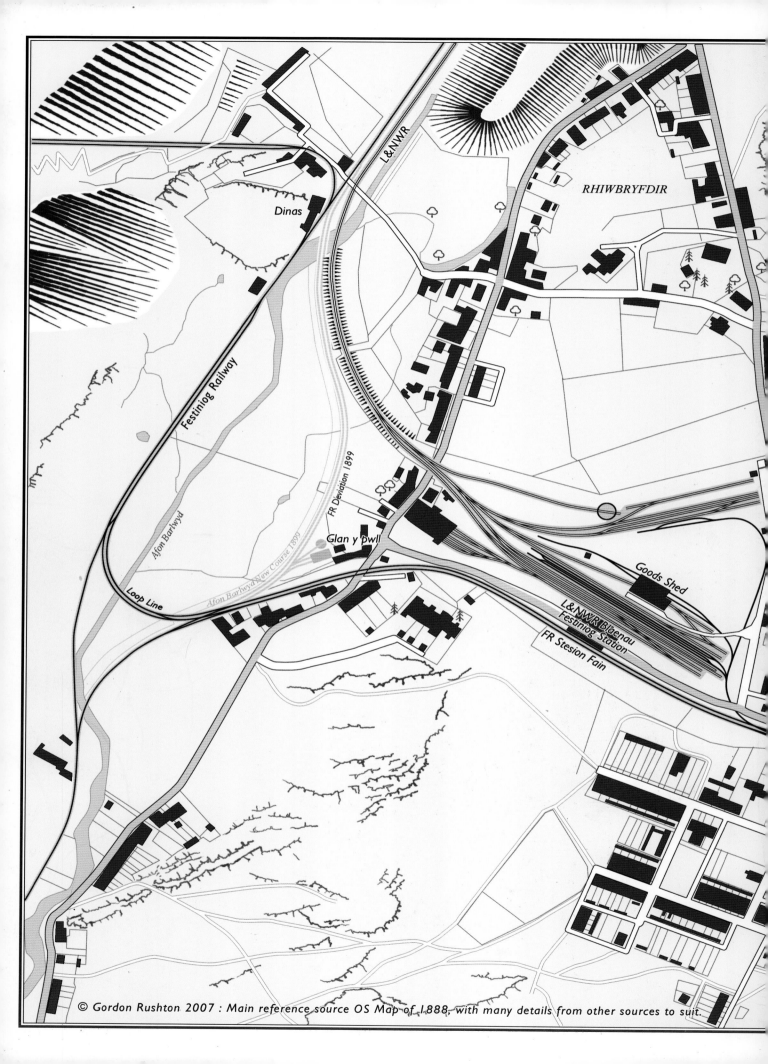

RHIWBRYFDIR

Dinas

L&NWR

Festiniog Railway

Afon Barlwyd

FR Deviation 1899

Afon Barlwyd New Course 1899

Glan y pwll

Loop Line

Goods Shed

L&NWR Blaenau
Festiniog Station

FR Stesion Fain

© Gordon Rushton 2007 : Main reference source OS Map of 1888, with many details from other sources to suit.